The Spanish Civil War

The Spanish Civil War

A History and Reference Guide

JAMES M. ANDERSON

Greenwood Press
Westport, Connecticut • London

Library of Congress Cataloging-in-Publication Data

Anderson, James Maxwell, 1933–
    The Spanish Civil War : a history and reference guide / James M. Anderson.
221 p. cm.
    Includes bibliographical references and index.
    ISBN 0–313–32274–0 (alk. paper)
    1. Spain—History—Civil War, 1936–1939. I. Title.
DP269.A7335   2003
  946.081—dc21   2003045524

British Library Cataloguing in Publication Data is available.

Library of Congress Catalog Card Number: 2003045524
ISBN: 0–313–32274–0

First published in 2003   **03-04**

Greenwood Press, 88 Post Road West, Westport, CT 06881
An imprint of Greenwood Publishing Group, Inc.
www.greenwood.com

Printed in the United States of America

The paper used in this book complies with the
Permanent Paper Standard issued by the National
Information Standards Organization (Z39.48–1984).

10 9 8 7 6 5 4 3 2 1

Copyright Acknowledgment

For Maribel and Fernando

CONTENTS

Note: Photo essay follows Chapter 5.

Preface and Acknowledgments

On the morning of 18 July 1936, the Western world awoke to a new and threatening development in European affairs. A cabal of generals in Spain had rebelled against the legitimate and democratically elected left-wing Republican government. While the conflict had its own unique Spanish causes, that it was not just another military uprising, so familiar to Spanish history, soon became obvious when the insurgents received immediate military aid from Hitler's Nazi Germany and from Fascist Italy in the grip of Mussolini. Other governments and organizations soon began to take sides: Soviet Russia under Stalin, the Communist International, and Mexico supported the Republic, but the democratic countries of Europe such as England and France, fearing an escalation of arms and a general European war, opted for neutrality, denying military aid to either side. Spain was soon engulfed in a complex web of political intrigue, deceit and hypocrisy. The war also engaged the passionate interest of individuals, becoming the focal point of the mid-1930s. Ordinary people in all walks of life took sides in the highly charged, emotional atmosphere.

In the Republican zone, extreme left-wing antagonists tried to assert their ideologies at the expense of each other and of the war effort. United in their campaign, forces of the Right, under General Francisco Franco, inexorably whittled down Republican territory and resistance, achieving total victory at the end of March 1939.

The following nine chapters present the causes, military confrontations, political stratagems and the effects of the war, followed by short biographies of major participants, a glossary of terms and a bibliography.

The author gratefully acknowledges the contributions of Sheridan Anderson, who stood steadfast before the ravings of a bad-tempered author whenever she found errors in the manuscript, and Dr. Joel Prager, who read and commented on the manuscript in scrupulous detail.

Thanks go to Dr. Rodney Roche; to Howard Greaves, always on the lookout for new material; to Paul and Jill Killinger of Cranborne, Dorset, and John and Lucrezia Paxson in London, for generous hospitality during periods of research; to Francine Lahaie-Schreiner of the National Archives of Canada; to Susan Pyzynski, Brandeis University Libraries; to Cary Nelson, University of Illinois at Urbana–Champaign; and to Peter Carroll, Curator, Abraham Lincoln Brigade Archives. Thanks also to Kevin Ohi of Greenwood Publishing Group, and to John Donohue of Westchester Book Services for editing.

CHRONOLOGY OF EVENTS

1812	Cortes of Cádiz approves liberal Constitution.
1814	Fernando VII restored to the throne.
1833	Death of Fernando VII. Isabella II becomes queen. Carlist War begins.
1839	Carlists defeated. Generals become active in politics.
1844	Creation of the Civil Guard.
1868	Isabella II deposed by the army. Clandestine Anarchist organization begins in Spain.
1870	Amadeus I becomes king.
1871	Pablo Iglesias advocates socialism.
1873	Amadeus I abdicates. First Republic initiated. Cantonist insurrections.
1874	General Pavía closes the Cortes. Alfonso XII, son of Isabella II, proclaimed king.
1876	Carlists defeated. Basque privileges abolished. New Constitution.
1879	Socialist Party (PSOE) formed.
1881	Political parties agree to rotate power. Trade unions legalized.

Regions and provinces, 1936.

1885	Death of Alfonso XII. Regency of María Cristina.
1886	Birth of Alfonso XIII. Socialist newspaper founded.
1888	Socialist trade union, the UGT, founded.
1895	Cuban War of Independence begins.
1898	Spanish-American War begins.
1902	María Cristina regency ends. Alfonso XIII comes of age.
1904	Spain and France divide Morocco between them.
1906	Law of Jurisdictions.
1909	"Tragic Week" in Barcelona.
1910	Formation of the Anarchist trade union CNT.
1914	World War I begins.

1917	Russian Revolution. General strike of UGT and CNT. Anarchist strikes in Andalucía and the Levant.
1918	World War I ends.
1921	Spanish military defeat at Annoual in Morocco.
1923	Miguel Primo de Rivera assumes dictatorship.
1925	Moroccan war concludes.
1927	FAI constituted.
1929	World economic depression.
1930	Primo de Rivera resigns. Berenguer heads interim government. Insurrection at Jaca. Pact of San Sebastián.

1931

February	Admiral Aznar replaces General Berenguer.
April	Monarchists defeated in municipal elections. Alfonso XIII abdicates. Second Republic proclaimed. Azaña's army reform decrees.
May	Obligatory religious instruction abolished in schools. Archbishop Segura attacks Republic in pastoral letter. Land reform introduced. Monarchists and workers clash in Madrid. Churches burned. Women receive the vote.
June	Elections for the Cortes.
July	CNT strike in Sevilla crushed by Republican government.
October	Antichurch legislation. Alcalá Zamora resigns and Azaña becomes prime minister. Law for the Defense of the Republic. Assault Guards created.
December	Constitution approved. Alcalá Zamora becomes president.

1932

January	Rebellion at Castilblanco. Civil Guards shoot peasants at Arnedo. Jesuits dissolved. Divorce law introduced.

August	Monarchist General Sanjurjo attempts coup.
September	Agrarian reform and Cataluña autonomy legislation.
November	Aborted railroad strike.

1933

January	Massacre of peasants at Casas Viejas.
February	Gil Robles forms the Catholic party CEDA.
April	Rightist parties gain majority in municipal elections.
September	Azaña dismissed as prime minister. Cortes dissolved.
October	Falange founded.
November	Basque vote on self-government. Right wins general elections. Lerroux becomes prime minister and begins repeal of leftist reforms.
December	Anarchist uprising in Cataluña and Aragón.

1934

February	Falange and JONS merge.
March	Mussolini promises aid to Falange.
April	Sanjurjo granted amnesty.
June	Anarchists rural strikes in Andalucía and Extremadura. Macía dies. Companys takes over Catalan Generalitat.
October	Lerroux forms government with members of CEDA. Asturias miners' revolt crushed by the army.

1935

April	Gil Robles enters Lerroux government.
September	Founding of the POUM.
October	Alcalá Zamora refuses premiership to Gill Robles *Straperlo* scandal. Conservative government falls.
December	Portela Valladares forms government.

1936

| 4 January | Cortes dissolved pending elections. |
| February | Elections bring Popular Front to power. Azaña becomes prime minister. Military plots. |

March	Falange banned. Jose Antonio arrested. Army warns government about disorders.
April	Socialist and Communist youth groups form JSU. Alcalá Zamora deposed.
May	Azaña elected president. Casares Quiroga appointed prime minister. Catholic schools closed.
12 July	Murder of Monarchist Calvo Sotelo.
17 July	Military uprising begins in Morocco. Civil war begins.
18 July	General Queipo de Llano takes Sevilla by *coup de main*. Casares Quiroga resigns.
19 July	Uprising crushed in Madrid and Barcelona. New government formed by Martínez Barrio, followed soon after by José Giral, who arms the workers.
20 July	Giral appeals to French Prime Minister Blum for arms. Franco sends emissaries to Hitler. General Sanjurjo killed in air crash.
21 July	Rebel forces converge on the Guadarrama mountains.
27 July	German and Italian planes begin airlift from Morocco.
August	Aragón front established by Anarchists and POUM.
8 August	French close borders. Beginning of NIC policy.
14 August	Nationalist troops under Yagüe take Badajoz.
15 August	British ban arms sales to Spain.
16 August	Mallorca invaded by loyalists. Mission failed.
19 August	Federico García Lorca murdered by Nationalists.
24 August	Germany, Italy and Portugal accept NIC in principal.
27 August	Rosenberg and other Russian officials arrive in Madrid.
3 September	Talavera de la Reina taken by Nationalists.
4 September	Largo Caballero forms government. Prieto becomes minister of navy and air; Negrín, minister of finance.
5 September	Irun falls to Nationalists.
6 September	Italian air force units arrive in Mallorca.

7 September	Aguirre forms Basque government.
9 September	First NIC meetings in London.
13 September	San Sebastián falls to Nationalists.
25 September	Alvarez del Vayo pleads Republican cause at League of Nations.
27 September	Nationalists take Toledo and relieve Alcázar.
1 October	Franco installed as head of army and government. Cortes passes Basque statute of autonomy.
3 October	Franco forms first cabinet.
7 October	Aguirre elected president of Euzkadi at Guernica.
10 October	Popular army decree ends independent militias.
12 October	First arrival of Soviet aid for the Republic.
14 October	First international brigaders arrive at Albacete.
15 October	Commissar system established in army.
25 October	Spanish gold reserves arrive in Russia.
29 October	Nationalist bombing raids on Madrid begin.
1 November	Nationalist troops reach outskirts of Madrid.
2 November	Brunete, west of Madrid, falls to Nationalists.
4 November	Russian fighter planes appear over Madrid. CNT enters government.
6 November	Republican government moves from Madrid to Valencia.
7 November	Battle for Madrid begins.
8 November	Nationalist assault on Madrid checked. International Brigades arrive in Madrid.
15 November	Condor Legion sees first action.
18 November	Germany and Italy recognize Burgos government.
20 November	Durruti killed near Madrid front line. Execution of José Antonio.
23 November	Franco calls off assault on Madrid.

13 December	Nationalists launch offensive on Coruña Road northwest of Madrid.
17 December	Communists insist on POUM expulsion from Catalan government.
18 December	Germany and Italy recognize Franco government.
22 December	Italian troops arrive in Spain.
23 December	Valencian government recognizes Council of Aragón.

1937

6 January	United States bans export of arms to Spain. Nationalists commence attack in the Jarama Valley.
8 February	Fall of Málaga to Nationalist forces.
21 February	Caballero asks for Soviet recall of Rosenberg.
8 March	Italians launch attack on Guadalajara.
18 March	Battle of Brihuega. Italian retreat.
31 March	Mola begins northern offensive. Durango bombed.
19 April	Franco merges Falange and Carlists. NIC establishes naval patrols and border observers.
20 April	The land offensive begins in Vizcaya.
26 April	Bombing of Guernica by Condor Legion.
2-6 May	May events in Barcelona over telephone exchange.
5 May	Assault Guards dispatched to Barcelona.
17 May	Largo Caballero ousted. Negrín forms government.
24 May	Italian warship *Barletta* bombed at Palma.
29 May	Battleship *Deutchland* bombed at Ibiza.
31 May	German warships shell Almería.
3 June	General Mola killed in plane crash.
16 June	POUM outlawed; leaders arrested.
19 June	Fall of Bilbao to Nationalists.
23 June	Germany and Italy withdraw from NIC naval patrols.
30 June	Portugal ends border control.

1 July	Collective letter from Spanish bishops.
6 July	Republican Brunete offensive continues until 24 July.
12 July	France ends NIC frontier control.
August	Italian submarine offensive begins.
11 August	Council of Aragón dissolved.
15 August	SIM established.
24 August	Republican offensive in Aragón begins. Battle of Belchite. Santander falls to Nationalists.
28 August	Vatican recognizes Franco regime.
1 September	Nationalist Asturian campaign begins.
7 October	Papal legate appointed to Burgos junta.
21 October	Nationalists capture Gijón. End of the Asturias campaign.
31 October	Republican government moves to Barcelona.
15 December	Republic begins Teruel offensive.
29 December	Nationalists counterattack at Teruel.

1938

6 January	Teruel falls to the Republic.
16 January	Heavy aerial bombardment of Barcelona begins.
30 January	Burgos government constituted.
22 February	Nationalists recapture Teruel.
6 March	Loss of Nationalist cruiser *Baleares*.
9 March	Nationalists promulgate Labor Charter. Nationalist offensive on Aragón front begins.
12 March	Blum again opens French border.
16 March	Barcelona bombed by the Italians.
25 March	Yagüe enters Cataluña.
28 March	Prieto calls for peace negotiations.
5 April	Nationalists revoke Catalan autonomy statute.
6 April	Prieto resigns as minister of war.
15 April	Nationalists reach Vinaroz. Cataluña isolated.

22 April	Law of press censorship established.
1 May	Negrín announces his thirteen points.
3 May	Nationalists welcome back Jesuit Order.
13 June	Daladier closes French frontier.
5 July	Nationalist offensive toward Valencia.
25 July	Battle of the Ebro begins.
21 September	Negrín announces withdrawal of International Brigades.
11 October	POUM trials begin; continue until 1 November.
8 November	Republican army withdrawal across Ebro River.
15 November	International Brigades leave Spain.
19 November	Franco gives mining concessions to Germany in exchange for military aid.
23 December	Nationalist offensive on Cataluña begins.

1939

15 January	Tarragona falls.
26 January	Nationalists enter Barcelona.
27 January	French open border to women, children and elderly.
1 February	Last meeting of the Cortes in Figueras.
5 February	Azaña and other leaders cross frontier into France. Fall of Gerona. Republican soldiers to cross frontier.
14 February	Franco government issues the retroactive Decree of Political Responsibilities.
21 February	Franco signs the Anti-Comintern Pact.
27 February	France and Britain recognize Franco government.
28 February	Azaña resigns presidency of Republic.
3 March	Negrín appoints Communist officers to all key posts.
5 March	Casado's National Defense Council established in Madrid.
10 March	Mera's troops surround Communists in Madrid.
27 March	Nationalist troops enter Madrid.
31 March	Valencia falls to Nationalists.

1 April	Civil war ends. United States recognizes Franco.
20 April	NIC dissolves itself.
23 August	Nazi-Soviet Pact signed.
1 September	World War II begins. Franco declares neutrality.
1940	Germany invades France.
1945	End of World War II.
1946	Spain boycotted by the United Nations.
1947	Franco declares Spain a constitutional monarchy.
1953	Agreement on U.S. air and naval bases in Spain.
1955	Spain joins United Nations.
1960	Death of Francisco Sabaté.
1975	Death of Franco.

PRIME MINISTERS OF THE SECOND REPUBLIC

1931	Niceto Alacalá Zamora (April–October). Provisional government.
	Manuel Azaña (October–September 1933).
1933	Alejandro Lerroux (November–October).
	Martínez Barrio (October–November). Caretaker government to preside over elections of 1933.
	Alejandro Lerroux (November 1933–April 1934).
1934	Ricardo Samper (April–September).
	Alejandro Lerroux (October 1934–October 1935).
1935	Joaquín Chapaprieta (September–December).
	Portela Valladares (December 1935–February 1936). Caretaker government to preside over elections of 1936.
1936	Manuel Azaña (February–May).
	Casares Quiroga (May–July).

Martínez Barrio (18–19 July).

José Giral (July–September).

Largo Caballero (September 1936–May 1937).

1937   Juan Negrín (May 1937–1939).

PRESIDENTS

1931–1936   Niceto Alcalá Zamora (Julián Besteiro, temporary president, 13 October–9 December 1931).

1936–1939   Manuel Azaña.

Places named in the text.

OVERVIEW

Spain entered the twentieth century primarily as an agricultural society that lagged decades behind most of industrialized western Europe. The contrast in social conditions, most apparent in the southern regions of Andalucía and Extremadura, was vast: At one extreme, a desperately poor, totally illiterate landless population lived in villages in gloomy flea-ridden, earthen-floored adobe hovels and toiled for a daily pittance barely enough to purchase a loaf of bread. Most went to bed hungry every night. For many months of the year there was no work and no pay. The parish priests of the Roman Catholic Church lectured on the acceptance of poverty as part of the divine plan; and if that did not avert outbreaks of rebellion, the police or the army did. At the other extreme the wealthy aristocrat who owned the land the peasants worked might have a castle, several country houses of palatial dimensions, a luxury apartment in Madrid or Sevilla, a half dozen chauffeur-driven automobiles and an immense income of thousands of dollars a day.

Industrial development in the hands of magnates was mostly confined to certain sections of the country that were hotbeds of worker agitation for better pay and conditions. Barcelona, a major Mediterranean seaport, the northern Basque port of Bilbao in a rich iron-mining district and Oviedo in Asturias surrounded by coal deposits were important manufacturing cities.

Millions of farm laborers on grand estates, quasi-serfs fettered by medieval customs and factory workers and miners laboring long hours in dangerous circumstances for meager pay found hope for a brighter future in the creation of the Second Parliamentary Republic on 14 April 1931. It seemed to offer greater freedom from local oppressive bureaucrats, the Church, landowners and factory owners, the military and the police.

The moderately left-of-center government of the new Republic had an ambitious agenda for political and social reform including more equitable distribution of land, improvements for workers, an overhaul of the educational system (taking it out of the clutches of the Church), prohibiting the Church and monastic orders from enriching themselves through capitalistic enterprises, plans to make the military accountable to civilian control and a certain amount of self-rule for the provinces.

These reforms threatened the power of conservative vested interests in whose grasp most of the wealth of the country was amassed. Ordinary Catholics of the upper and middle classes and even some peasants, who might have supported the Republic's ambitions, were alienated by moves to disestablish the Church, while high-ranking army officers feared loss of prestige and influence in state affairs and the breakup of the country. Landowners felt threatened by peasant demands for a greater stake in the rural economy, and industrial oligarchs were alarmed by workers' clamor for higher pay and for labor unions.

Among the population of 24 million, support for the new government of the Second Republic or reaction to it was broadly divided along class lines, with workers and landless peasants generally endorsing its programs and the elite, landowners and industrialists considering it inimical to their interests. Mutually hostile positions were also manifest among the laboring classes. Anarchists loathed the authoritarian and centralized policies of the Republic, the Communists and the Socialists; some Socialists supported the central government; others aspired to regional autonomy.

Political polarization intensified as the Republican government sought to realize its policies. Extreme left-wing organizations were determined to bring about economic, social and political change beyond that which the Republic envisioned—in short, a revolution—while right-wing conservative forces resolved to maintain the status quo. Strikes, parades, street fighting, rural uprisings, peasant occupation of farms, church burning, assassinations and brutal police retaliation became commonplace, with the liberal government, caught in the middle, unable to effectively control either left-wing or right-wing violence.

The center-left Republic shifted to the center-right in the 1933 elections, with the new government undoing previous Socialist legislation and leading to more intense leftist agitation. Outbreaks of violence were swiftly squashed by government security forces that further alienated the extreme Left and lent credence to the extreme rightist contention that a democratically elected government was incapable of governing.

In the 1936 elections, by a narrow majority at the polls, a moderate Socialist government, backed by a Popular Front coalition of leftist parties, again took center stage. But with disturbances in the cities and in the countryside growing worse, a coterie of generals planned to overthrow the Republic and take charge of government in order to end the political and social chaos, avert the possibility of left-wing extremists taking over the country and dispense with a government that sanctioned military reform detrimental to the officer class.

On 17 July 1936 the military seized control of Spanish Morocco, and in the following days, army units rose on mainland Spain and succeeded in taking over in many cities and towns; in others, notably Madrid and Barcelona, thwarted by an angry populace, they failed. The result was a patchwork of localities, some loyal to the Republic and others that fell victim to or supported the military uprising. The nation became engulfed in civil war.

The rebel side, which soon became known as the Nationalists, included military and police units, conservatives of many persuasions—those who supported a return to some form of monarchy, Fascist organizations, landowners and industrialists who saw in the Nationalists the only hope of retaining their wealth and position and millions of Catholics shaken by the anticlerical attitude of the Republic. Opposed to the uprising were intellectuals, Socialists, Communists, Anarchists, many peasants and workers, much of the middle class and a sizable portion of army officers and police with left-wing sympathies. While the officers of the navy went over to the Nationalists, sailors generally remained loyal to the government, as did the officers and men of the small air force.

The democratically elected parliamentary Republic represented equality, human rights and freedom of speech, religion and assembly. The Nationalists displayed the trappings and ideology of the Nazi and Fascist movements of the 1930s in Germany and Italy with their philosophy of order, duty and obedience and the elimination of political dissidents. Adopting the Nazi salute the antiparliamentarian Right saw the Republic as a dangerously corrupting pack of scheming politicians ready to sell out the country's traditions and heritage and turn the nation into a godless, libertine state. They portrayed the struggle as a titanic clash between Christian civilization and satanic forces bent on destroying it.

The civil war encompassed a social and political rebellion by hundreds of thousands of peasants and workers (Anarchists for the most part) who found the time opportune to liberate themselves from the centralized parliamentary government. With their own agenda, they plotted revolution and by persuasion or force collectivized much of the land and many of the factories in Republican-held territory. They took control of industrial resources through workers' committees and management of rural collective farmland through peasant assemblies.

They created their own societies, administrations, armed workers' squads to police the streets and militia units to fight the Nationalists. Ideological conflicts among the leftist groups, however, often led to violent internecine fighting among themselves that weakened their effectiveness and benefited the Nationalists.

The terror began immediately as left-wing organizations and individuals in Republican-held territory rounded up and murdered those suspected of right-wing sympathies, and as towns and villages fell to the Nationalists, Republican advocates were ferreted out of hiding and shot.

During its first weeks, the war acquired international political and ideological significance reflecting in microcosm the polarization of much of the Western world into left and right camps. Nazi Germany, Fascist Italy and autocratic Portugal provided massive support to Nationalist strength. The USSR sent weapons and advisers to the Republicans; the Comintern organized thousands of anti-Fascist liberals and leftists into volunteer International Brigades and sent them to Spain. Under these ideologically charged circumstances, both sides engaged in bloody atrocities in the name of anticommunism or antifascism.

The Spanish conflict served to hone the tools for the war machines of Germany and Italy, while for Britain and France, it was a period of dithering, indecisiveness and burying the head in the sand. The Non-Intervention Committee, established to deny arms to both sides and signed by all the European powers, was the epitome of hypocrisy and contemptuously disregarded by some of the signatories. The Soviet Union gave hope to the Republic through aid and the sale of arms but not enough for it to win the war. Serving as an axis proving ground for new weapons, the civil war would later become known as a dress rehearsal for World War II.

Not unlike Britain and France, the United States also pursued a policy of nonintervention and embargoed arms shipments to both sides. These actions represented a great blow to the loyalists who, fighting for Spain's legal government, expected aid from the democratic Western powers.

Major battles were fought around the capital, Madrid, in attempts to take or surround and starve the city into submission; other battles were successfully waged by the Nationalists in the south, in the north, then in Aragón and Cataluña, culminating in the conquest of most of the country, leaving the demoralized Republicans isolated in the center zone—in Madrid and in Valencia—between hostile forces.

Unlike their comparatively unified and well-disciplined opponents under Nationalist command, the Republican forces remained beset by internal strife. The Communists, an insignificant force at the beginning of hostilities, through discipline and organization became feared by other left-wing groups. As the conduit for Soviet aid, they became increasingly influential and, as their numbers mounted, led a drive to repress rival leftist groups. Through secret police, control of Russian arms and their successful internal war against Anarchists and other anti-Stalinist groups, the Communists came to exert powerful control over the Republican army and government. Communist policy in Spain appears to have revolved around three concepts: (1) maintain a stalwart, united Popular Front to defeat the Nationalists; (2) work to present Republican Spain to the rest of Europe as a democratic bourgeois state rather than a leftist revolutionary regime (in the hope of winning support from France and England); (3) infiltration of political parties, labor unions, the police, the military, youth movements and the government that would lead to eventual Communist control.

For the peasants and working class, who hastened to support the Republic, the war was a struggle to save Spain from stifling dictatorship, from a police state in which the worker and peasant would be reduced even further into abject slavery by capitalistic enterprises. For others, it offered the chance for a long overdue revolution against class exploitation and a tyrannical Church and for the creation of an egalitarian, decentralized free society. For the Nationalists, it was a crusade against despised atheism, communism, freethinkers and international Freemasonry.

Until late in 1938, the Spanish civil war dominated foreign policy concerns of European nations. As it was by this time obvious that the Nationalists would win, and World War II hovered ominously over Europe, the focus on Hitler's intentions took precedence. On 1 April 1939 the war ended with the total, unconditional defeat of the Republic. Of the four western European dictators, Hitler, Mussolini, Salazar of Portugal and Franco, the latter two maintained their repressive regimes throughout their lives. Remaining officially neutral during World War II, they did not incur fatal Allied retribution. For some who supported the Republic, as long as Franco remained in power, the Spanish civil war was never over, and even in the twenty-first century, it still generates emotional debate.

CHAPTER 1

PRELUDE TO CIVIL WAR:
A CENTURY OF CONFLICT

Countercultural ideas of liberty and equality, generated from the French Revolution in 1789, and more remotely from the American Revolution of 1776, began to impact Spanish society at the end of the eighteenth century. The conservative monarchy, the aristocracy and the Catholic Church gradually awoke to new and threatening voices among the lower classes. Awareness of a more just social system was reinforced among the Spanish population by relatively liberal-minded French and English soldiers who arrived in Spain to fight each other in the Peninsular War between 1808 and 1814. The Spanish working classes became aware that their miserable and subservient role in a profoundly class-stratified society was not necessarily ordained by God, as they had been led to believe by those who wielded power.

CORTES OF 1812

While the French controlled most of the country, and the king, Fernando VII, was held captive in France by Napoleon, the Spanish Cortes (Parliament), formerly only a rubber-stamp body that did the king's bidding, met at Cádiz in 1812, an area outside of French control. The 303 delegates sat together in a single chamber. Referred to as liberals, many of the deputies were activists and reformists, imbued with ideas of justice and equality. This Cortes formulated a new Constitution for the country. The document they created was the second written Constitution in the world after that of the United States. It placed sovereignty in the hands of the nation and reduced the authority of the king. Universal male suffrage was espoused, and noble privileges were abolished. The Holy Office of the Inquisition was suppressed.

Restored to the throne in 1814, Fernando VII rejected the Constitution and engaged in a campaign of persecution of anyone professing liberal ideas. When the king died in 1833, his daughter Isabella II became queen, championed by liberals and by the army. Her reign was troubled by intrigues, civil strife and political instability. Conservatives hostile to change and to parliamentary government rejected what they considered the liberalizing policies of the Bourbon monarchy and a woman ascending the throne. They supported Don Carlos, brother of Fernando VII, who claimed the throne of his niece. Carlists (supporters of Don Carlos), fervent Roman Catholics, were most numerous in the Pyrenean region, especially in Navarra, and championed the *fueros*, the traditional local liberties still retained by the Basque provinces and Navarra. (The *fueros* varied from region to region but might include exemption from taxes or from military service and the right to levy customs duties). A violent insurrection in favor of Isabella's uncle led to the First Carlist War. The struggle raged until the Carlists were defeated by General Espartero in 1839; Don Carlos went into exile, renounced his claim to the throne in favor of his son Carlos, count of Montemol, and the Carlist movement lived on.

THE ARMY IN POLITICS AND THE FIRST REPUBLIC

To maintain order, General Espartero set himself up as head of government and was the first of the generals who were to dominate Spanish politics. He was ousted in 1843 by General Narváez, who ruled for the next decade. To keep the army loyal, he created an oversupply of officers with an inflated budget, making it a caste apart, contemptuous of civilian politicians. In the following years, coup followed coup (*pronunciamientos*) by one general after another with monotonous regularity. The liberal generals Juan Prim and Francisco Serrano forced the queen into exile and announced the overthrow of the Bourbon monarchy in 1868. A provisional government was declared, and a new Constitution was drawn up the following year proclaiming Spain a constitutional monarchy with an elected bicameral legislature. The Catholic Church was recognized as the official religion, but much to the chagrin of the ecclesiastics, toleration for other religions was acknowledged. Meanwhile, there were regional voices that clamored for local autonomy—the most vociferous in the province of Cataluña.

In 1870 the Cortes invited Amadeus I, son of Victor Emmanuel, king of Italy, to assume the throne of Spain. The day he arrived in Madrid, General Prim was assassinated in the street, a not-very-encouraging sign. Amadeus attempted to exercise his constitutional authority, but opposed by all factions, unable to control the violence between Liberals and Conservatives or form a stable government, he abdicated in 1873.

With the retirement of the king, the First Republic was instituted and aspired to a federal form of government with substantial autonomy for the provinces. In the north the Carlists rose again, while in the south and southeast, cities such as Alicante and Cartagena declared themselves independent cantons. The Cortes was hopelessly divided. Three Republican presidents resigned within four months. Denounced by Conservatives and from the pulpit, the First Republic lasted less than a year. In 1874 the captain general of Madrid, Manuel Pavía, with the troops at his disposal, closed down the Cortes and sent the delegates home. General Serrano assumed the presidency and formed a new government until General Martínez Campos, backed by his soldiers, issued an ultimatum reestablishing the monarchy on behalf of Alfonso XII, son of Isabella. General Serrano stepped down, and Alfonso XII was proclaimed king. A new Constitution was promulgated in 1876 confirming a constitutional monarchy, the Carlists were defeated and Navarra and the Basque country secured for the government. The northern provinces were then deprived of their *fueros* and came under direct rule from Madrid—a move that did not sit well among the Basque people.

Governments alternated between Conservatives and Liberals, each political party taking turns in power. Generals continued to engage in politics alongside civilians, and their backing of a candidate was often the deciding factor. The army considered itself the guardian of order and tradition in Spain.

A pressing problem throughout the period was educational development. New public schools were opened but made only limited progress owing to lack of funds. Literacy doubled between 1840 and 1860 but only reached a level of 25 percent of the population in some regions. Higher education improved little. Universities continued to use poor translations of French textbooks.[1]

In November 1885 Alfonso XII died, and in May the following year, his wife, María Cristina of Habsburg, gave birth to a son, Alfonso XIII, the future king.

LOSS OF MILITARY PRESTIGE

In 1895 a Cuban rebellion began against Spanish rule. The United States supported the rebel island, and in February 1898, when the American battleship *Maine* blew up in Havana harbor under mysterious circumstances, the United States demanded the independence of Cuba and blockaded the island. As a result, Spain declared war on the United States on 24 April 1898. American troops landed in Cuba while the navy devastated the outclassed Spanish fleet. American soldiers also descended on the Spanish-held Philippine Islands, where they were supported by local insurgents. At the end of the short war, Spain lost both Cuba and its Philippine possessions, along with Puerto Rico and Guam, bringing to an end its once-glorious overseas empire. The Spanish military felt humiliated by the defeat and betrayed by civilian governments that they thoroughly mistrusted. For most Spaniards the defeat, swift and consummate, was distressing. Instead of a modern European power, Spain seemed to them now to be a weak, backward nation.

Alfonso XIII's mother, Queen María Cristina, acted as regent until Alfonso attained his majority in 1902. Under her somewhat liberal regime the military was treated none too kindly by those who were disgusted with its performance. In 1906 the army demanded and was granted a Law of Jurisdictions from Alfonso XIII that allowed it to court-martial civilians who published or uttered unflattering, derogatory or comic remarks about military life. In an attempt to maintain some semblance of prestige the military establishment was determined to keep a hold in North Africa, the only remaining fragment of imperial possessions.

MOROCCO, TRAGIC WEEK AND WORLD WAR I

By the first few years of the twentieth century, spheres of interest in most of Africa had been carved out by European powers. The sultanate of Morocco still lay open for exploitation, but the Spanish government, perhaps demoralized by its disastrous defeat, seemed content to maintain only its historic economic enterprises in the northern third of the country where it had held the Mediterranean coastal cities of Melilla and Ceuta for several

centuries. In 1904, Spain and France divided Morocco into zones of influence whereby Spain kept the section opposite her shores, and France
took most of the rest. (Tanger became an open international city.)

The rich Moroccan iron mines were one of the attractions for Spanish
industrialists, and expansion of commerce soon followed. Land was
bought through a Spanish colonization company, and troops were sent to
protect it. Moroccan tribesmen then began to resist further encroachment,
which led to bloody skirmishes that plagued the 40,000-man Spanish
army.

Riff tribesmen annihilated a column of Spanish troops on their way
to protect mines bought by the count of Romanones, a friend of the king.
The government called up reserves. Antimilitary feeling ran high, especially in Barcelona whence many of the recruits were drafted. The idea of
young men being killed for the financial benefit of the upper class set off
a wave of violence and destruction. In July 1909, the working class took
out their anger on the government, the army and the Church—the latter
identified with the upper class. Trade unions called a general strike, barricades went up in the streets and the ensuing clashes between workers
and government forces became known as the "Tragic Week." About 120
people were killed and sixty government buildings and churches burned.
On a reckless rampage of destruction the rioters chased nuns from their
convents, burned their possessions, smashed holy icons and despoiled
Church cemeteries.

Alfonso's reign was marked by revolutionary, antidynastic uprisings,
notably in Madrid and Barcelona, from 1909 to 1911. Workers in the
urban industrial areas lived in crime- and disease-infested slums, and miners in the north of the country often lived in bunkhouses with the enduring
odors of sweat and urine, strong tobacco and putrefying food. They slept
on sacks stuffed with corn shucks. Men ill with typhus or smallpox
moaned in their miserable beds until they were removed to a hut to await
death. In one case disobedient miners were locked in the kennel, a room
under the school. The children could see them through the cracks in the
floor, and some added to the prisoners' discomfort by urinating or pouring
water on them from above, reinforcing the teacher's view that they were
criminals and needed to be punished.[2] When men or their widows grew
too old to work, the only alternative, with no family backing, was begging
on the streets.

The country pursued a neutral policy in 1914 and throughout World

War I and prospered selling raw materials, textiles and ships to both sides. High inflation hurt the poorest classes, and the gap between rich and poor widened. The Left was mostly pro-Allies; the Right, mostly pro-German.[3]

Before the world war, revolutionary ideas had made inroads into working-class circles, and two major trade unions had developed, the Socialist General Union of Workers and the Anarchist National Confederation of Labor. The Russian Revolution of 1917, looked upon as the panacea of the working classes, prompted widespread labor unrest, and strikes were broken by the army and police, alienating workers from the government. When the war ended In 1918, economic depression and rising unemployment set in. From 1919 to 1923, Barcelona was ruled by martial law under generals determined to keep the peace in the troubled industrial quarters of the city.

Alfonso XIII was blamed for Spanish setbacks in Morocco. A military defeat at Annoual in 1921, costing the lives of 10,000 Spanish soldiers, led to a public outcry and a parliamentary investigation. In 1923, as the results, detrimental to the king and the army, were about to be published, Alfonso XIII, in collaboration with the army, replaced the parliamentary monarchy with a military dictatorship.

MONARCHY AND DICTATORSHIP

With defeat in Morocco, and rumors of scandal at court, the flamboyant General Miguel Primo de Rivera, the scion of an influential military family, took over the reigns of government. He dissolved the Cortes and proclaimed himself dictator, taking immediate steps to suppress social discontent and political liberties.

Primo de Rivera's government achieved victory in Morocco in 1925, supported labor arbitration, built public works, and stimulated tourism, commerce and industry. In his efforts to substitute order and prosperity for democracy, he modeled his government on that of Benito Mussolini in Italy. After 1927, however, Primo's arbitrary decisions, his rough handling of intellectuals (he deemed professors lazy and students frivolous— he was no doubt not pleased by the fact that when he received an honorary degree, a student group gave one to a donkey)[4] and his mounting budget deficits alienated many of his supporters. The worldwide economic depression of 1929 brought his grandiose public works to a halt. The efforts of his finance minister, Calvo Sotelo, to stabilize the currency was of no avail, and the peseta fell 20 percent on world markets. Primo polled the army garrisons of the country in January 1930 asking for a vote of confidence. The results were disappointing, and he resigned, retiring to Paris, where he spent his last days frequenting bars and brothels.

The king, with rapidly waning popularity, appointed the aging General Dámaso Berenguer to take charge of an interim government that would prepare the way back to a constitutional monarchy. By dispensing with the dictatorship, the king hoped to redeem and preserve royal authority. Opposition to the Berenguer government came in the form of Republican leaders, Liberals, Socialists and Catalans who met in August 1930 and in the Pact of San Sebastián, pledged to establish a constitutional Republic. By promising to prepare a statute of regional autonomy, they won the support of the Catalan Left.

REPUBLICAN CONVICTION: INSURRECTION AT JACA

As sentiment for a Republican form of government grew, the abolition of the monarchy became a major factor in the thinking of many junior army officers. In December 1930, Captain Fermín Galán and Lieutenant García Hernández staged a revolt at the garrison at Jaca in Aragón. Marching their troops on Zaragoza, both were captured on the road and died before a military firing squad. The uprising failed, but the executions raised public indignation among Republicans. In January 1931 the government announced parliamentary elections. General Berenguer resigned in February 1931, and Admiral Aznar, appointed by the king, took over the reigns of the temporary government. Supporting the monarchy, the Catholic Church proclaimed that to vote liberal was a sin. In the campaign of 1931, clerics referred to Republican candidates as Communists and atheists.

SECOND REPUBLIC, ELECTIONS

On 12 April 1931 elections for municipal offices were held first. Monarchists gained the majority of the rural votes where political bosses, landlords or their agents (*caciques*) dictated the manner of voting to the peasants. They sent out armed gangs to convince dissenters to vote in the manner they were told. If things did not go well, ballot boxes were destroyed or phony ballots substituted. Peasants who did not behave as ordered faced eviction and subsequent starvation.

The result of the elections in nearly all the large towns and provincial capitals was a solid backing of Republican parties. Mobs gathered in the streets of Madrid and outside the palace proclaiming hostility toward the king. Alfonso, who heard the message loud and clear, abdicated and fled Spain for Italy on 14 April 1931. At 5:00 P.M. that very day the Republican flag was raised over the Madrid city hall, and shortly after Niceto Alcalá Zamora declared the Second Republic.

There was great rejoicing in the streets of Madrid, Barcelona and other capitals. A new transitional central government took office in Madrid consisting of a committee of leaders of several small recently formed parties.[5] Alcalá Zamora, an Andalucian lawyer, devout Catholic, large landowner and a minister of the king before the dictatorship (and former Monarchist politician), became leader of the Provisional Republican Government made up of the members of the Pact of San Sebastián.

Meanwhile, right-wing forces gathered strength to oppose the Republic. Two weeks after the proclamation, the archbishop of Toledo, primate of the Spanish Church, Cardinal Segura, published a violent, militant letter in praise of the monarchy and against the Republic, declaring that the victory at the polls was a triumph for the "enemies of the kingdom of Jesus Christ."[6] Shortly after, crowds attacked and burned a new Jesuit church in Madrid, and the following day churches and convents were destroyed in many other parts of the country. Over one hundred churches were burned under the banners of red flags identifying the arsonists as leftist.

The inability and unwillingness of the government to preserve order even though the minister of the interior, Miguel Maura, in charge of the police, was conservative and Catholic, alarmed opponents of the Republic. Church persecution was getting out of hand, and Catholic forces began to unite in the face of what many considered a demonic threat to Christianity itself.

Elections for a constituent Cortes, the first Republican Parliament, were held in June 1931, and leftists and Liberals were again victorious. Conservative groups, suffering from the collapse of the monarchy, had not recovered sufficiently to organize an effective campaign.[7]

Apart from Alcalá Zamora and Miguel Maura, the members of the first cabinet were anticlerical. Five were Freemasons and suspected by their conservative enemies of being disloyal to Spanish traditions.[8] A daunting task before the government was the transformation of a country in which many sections were still living in the Middle Ages eking out a living with obsolete agricultural equipment, the majority illiterate; understaffed schools with worn-out books available for less than a quarter of the student population; not enough doctors and hospitals; and a child fatality rate around 50 percent in country villages. Children were born at home, and the best the peasant could expect was the help of a neighbor with some experience in childbirth. To turn a backward, desperately poor, class-ridden, mostly agricultural society used to arbitrary justice into a modern nation-state with a progressive parliamentary government would be nothing short of a Herculean endeavor.

The major goals of the government were several: (1) to reform and reduce the size of the army and bring it under civilian control; (2) to separate church and state, curb church privileges and modernize education; (3) to modify the structure of the state, permitting a degree of Catalan regional autonomy; (4) to achieve broad social, economic and agrarian reforms.

MILITARY REFORMS

Manuel Azaña, minister of war, was more than a little dissatisfied with the role of a military that was inefficient, independent and overstaffed with an officer corps that intervened freely in politics. First he decreed that all officers swear an oath of allegiance to the Republic; then, in April 1931, he set about reducing the numbers by retiring as many officers as he could (with full pay). If, after thirty days, the number of voluntary retirements was not sufficient in the view of the government, officers would be forced out. By these means the officer corps was reduced by about 40 percent.[9] Azaña's decree satisfied neither the Left, unhappy by his failure to purge Monarchist officers or others with questionable loyalty to the Republic, nor the Right, who complained about the arbitrary nature of the act and the ensuing loss of military morale. Azaña further offended the officer class by reducing the number of military academies from six to three and by declaring that 60 percent of places in them be taken up by the recruitment of noncommissioned officers (NCOs) and by requiring that officer cadets serve at least six months in the ranks.

Perhaps more onerous than other measures for the military establishment was the effort to bring it under civilian control and remove the army from nonmilitary affairs. Azaña tried to stop the practice of military courts trying soldiers for crimes committed in the civilian sphere and trying civilians that committed so-called crimes against the military such as publicly ridiculing the army in newspaper cartoons or editorials. The abolition by decree of the position of captain-general, the supreme military authority in the eight military regions of the country, superior to civilian officials, also rankled the army. These men had been able to use their position to impose a military solution on social or political problems.

The effectiveness of Azaña's efforts to place the maintenance of public order in the overall hands of civilians was compromised by the government's continued use of the military and the militant police force, the Civil Guard (*Guardia Civil*), to quell disturbances, especially in rural communities. Commanded by General Sanjurjo, the 30,000-strong force instilled fear and hatred. Recruited in one region, Civil Guards always served in another and were forbidden to fraternize with the local population. They were often considered foreign occupiers who protected the interests of the upper classes.

The government created the Assault Guards (*Guardia de Asalto*) in October 1931 as a loyal Republican police force also organized along military lines. These paramilitary riot police were intended to be the urban equivalent of the Civil Guards. Military men were generally in charge of these units. Offenses such as maligning the army, the Civil Guard or Assault Guards, even the murder of civilians by a soldier, in spite of laws to the contrary, continued to be punished in military courts.

A law for the defense of the Republic was passed giving the prime minister extraordinary powers to act against anyone defaming the Republic. Punishment might include exile to North Africa, prison, suspension of the publication of newspapers or censorship. Many people all along the political spectrum deplored the government's arbitrary act and dictatorial law.

CHURCH, STATE AND EDUCATIONAL REFORM

Millions of Spaniards felt alienated from the Catholic Church; many despised it. Many felt that the Church was not in tune with the times of the 1930s. It still insisted, as it had always done, that the state allow it a monopoly in matters of religion and education and that it be the sole judge of moral standards. The government was not prepared to allow such generous provisions. On the contrary, it wanted to limit the role of the Church in society. The Church countered by claiming that the atheistic, anti-Catholic government was attacking religion and hence the very soul of Spain. Plans for thousands of new primary schools were published, and on 6 May 1931 the government decreed that from then on religious instruction was no longer obligatory in state schools. The revolutionary change further incensed already irate churchmen.

Religious clauses in the new Constitution under preparation aroused the most fury. Article 26 separated church and state, and state payments to priests were to cease after two years in spite of the fact they were paid in compensation for the confiscation of church lands in 1837. All religious orders had to register with the Ministry of Justice and would be dissolved if considered incompatible with the state.

On 13 October 1931 Alcalá Zamora resigned, along with Miguel Maura, in disagreement over the religious clauses, and the speaker of the Cortes, Julián Besteiro, assumed the temporary rank of president and named the moderately leftist Republican, Manuel Azaña, prime minister. Azaña shocked the Church and its followers when he reported to the Cortes that "Spain is no longer Catholic."[10]

The state reserved the right to approve public religious processions such as Holy Week, and cancellation of Church parades in the army caused much fury. Divorce was to be granted with petition of each party, while civil weddings would be the only valid ones. The government passed a law requiring all elementary school teachers to have a university education (most nuns who taught in Church schools did not meet this qualification) and announced freedom of religion. Whatever little tolerance the Church had for the Republic disappeared altogether.

Thus, for the first time in the history of the country, clauses were added to the Constitution affirming that Spain had no official religion ending financial support for the Church and declaring that religious orders could own no property other than that which they required for daily living. They could not be involved in education, commerce or industry and were obliged to submit their accounts to the government. All Church holdings that generated income were to be declared and taxed. Further legislation secularized cemeteries and also included mandatory civil funerals unless the deceased had asked for a Catholic ceremony in the will. The Jesuit order, which demanded a vow of obedience other than that given to the state, was disbanded on 23 January 1932 and their property seized by the government.

THE QUESTION OF REGIONAL AUTONOMY

Madrid, in the center of the country, was primarily an administrative capital, the home of the central government and surrounded by generally poor agricultural land. The leading industrial and consequently richer regions were situated on the geographical periphery of Spain such as Cataluña and the Basque regions.

As these regions grew economically, local movements, dissatisfied with government in far-off Madrid, grew accordingly. Too much of the wealth generated from industry was perceived as going to support the distant bureaucrats with little return to the provinces. The outlying regions had also a distinct cultural orientation. Their languages, Catalan and Basque, were different from the Castillian spoken in the center of the country. These economic and cultural rumblings turned into political movements demanding home rule and even independence from Spain.

The provincial councils of the four Catalan provinces had merged some functions in 1913 in preparation for autonomy from Spain. Primo de Rivera had cut short such intentions, and some Catalans had in vain called for a declaration of war on Spain. Among a multitude of politically active groups in Cataluña in 1931, Colonel Francisco Maciá headed a separatist group, the *Esquerra* (Left). Its members comprised intellectuals, small businessmen and the lower middle classes.[11] His able lieutenant was Lluis Companys, a young lawyer. When the results of the 1931 municipal elections were announced, three members of the government made a hasty trip to Barcelona and persuaded Maciá to wait until the Cortes, soon to be elected, could decide on home rule for Cataluña.

The notion of any regional autonomy was anathema to conservative groups that feared, through a breakup of the state, loss of political and economic power, but the most vehement opposition to provincial autonomy came from the army, the defender of unity and tradition. With a centralist view of government, officers were fearful that local autonomy would diminish their importance, their budgets and their prestige. It was also argued that autonomy granted to one section of the country would lead to other regions clamoring for similar status, a fact not long in coming.

AGRARIAN ISSUES

Of major concern was the issue of land, especially in the south of the country where large estates dominated. Peasants lived in heatless shanties on the property administered by a foreman. Gruel and a few vegetables made up most of their sustenance. They cooked over an open fire on the floor; tried to keep warm around a brazier of charcoal, taking in its noxious fumes; and slept on the ground or on wooden boards. There was no indoor running water, toilets or electricity. Generally prematurely old, the laborers worked all the daylight hours in the planting and harvesting season for a few pesetas a day and might have no work at all for most of the year while subject to the whims and brutality of powerful landowners or their agents. Working on the large estates, agricultural laborers had to accept whatever was paid since the supply of the unemployed was inexhaustible.

Entire families not only lived on the edge of starvation, but poor diets and lack of hygiene led to endemic diseases such as trachoma.[12] It was small wonder that rebellious farmworkers viewed their landlords as oppressive tyrants. While about 200,000 landowners and rich peasants owned 40 percent of the cultivated land in the country, there were 3 million peasants who owned a small parcel or leased a small plot and 2 million landless laborers who owned nothing.[13] A visitor to the south of Spain wrote:

> I recall an incident during a visit (in 1935) to an experimental pig farm in an out-of-the-way part of Andalucía. From the darkness at one end of the building came a red glow. I went along and found a labourer's family crouched on the floor round a twig fire with smoke so thick that breathing was difficult. The malodorous squalor contrasted with the carefully washed sites that I had been seeing [the pig stalls]. To my query an old woman mumbles: "Yes, we live here. Worse than the pigs." At which the owner beside me exclaimed indignantly: "You have a roof over your head. What more do you want?"[14]

Compounding the agrarian situation, hostility was also directed toward the Church—an important landowner with some 11,000 estates—who supported the large land proprietors. In nearly every village a church towered over the houses like the medieval castle of bygone days.[15] For many landless peasants the Church was an instrument of oppression teaching acceptance of poverty while it amassed wealth. In some areas the

Church stopped teaching children to read so that they later would not be able to read leftist propaganda. Catechisms were recited instead.[16]

To ensure their continuation of authority over the peasants, landlords could rely not only on the Civil Guard but also on freely rigged elections for their own benefit and had powerful influence in the system of justice. The courts were manipulated from the top right down to the village level. Any man or woman with a grievance, such as the seizure of their land, but without financial means, could expect never to have their case heard in court, let alone obtain justice. The times were propitious for the introduction and spread of revolutionary ideas against which the landlords banded together to thwart, through legislation and police control, any movements to put them into practice.

The peasantry was not a homogeneous group, and many peasants did not support the Republic. Local conditions such as access to markets, type or size of land tenure, degree of piety and living comfort dictated their politics. Often social relations were bad, and peasants engaged in fratricidal conflicts. For many, however, the most pressing issue was to have a stake in the land.

Short-term land reforms were introduced by Minister of Labor Largo Caballero in May 1931. Laws made it more difficult for landlords to evict tenant farmers, and an eight-hour day was instituted with overtime pay for longer hours among farm laborers. Arbitration boards of landowners and laborers would decide wage disputes. Landowners had to offer jobs to locals before calling in outside workers, as they might have done in case of a strike. These and other decrees prompted thousands of farmworkers to join the agricultural section of the Socialist trade union, the General Union of Workers (*Union General de Trabajadores* [UGT]), so that by 1932 there were 450,000 mostly landless farm workers in the union.[17]

CONSTITUTION OF 1931

The Constitution was a controversial political document that aroused the anger of the Right. It began by proclaiming that "Spain is a democratic republic of workers of all classes organized in a regime of liberty and justice." It further stated that "government emanated from the people" and all citizens were equal. No titles of nobility would be recognized. Both sexes would have the vote at age twenty-three. The powers of the president were limited by a six-year term. The president would nominate the prime minister, but the president could veto laws of which he did not approve. He could be removed if he dissolved the Cortes twice. Once the Constitution was approved, on 9 December 1931, Alcalá Zamora was elected the first president of the Second Republic. Azaña remained prime minister.

It still remained for the government to enact all its clauses of the Constitution. Ministers first occupied themselves with a law for the defense of the Republic. The Constitution provided for a suspension of guarantees of freedom of speech for thirty days in cases of emergency, and the minister of the interior was empowered to suspend public meetings. An income tax was introduced for the first time.

The new religious legislation, obstructed by the Conservatives in the Cortes, was not passed into law until spring of 1933. The Church, meanwhile, responded by threatening to excommunicate deputies who had voted for the new law, and the pope condemned the new legislation.

The medical profession showed strong signs of anticlericalism. Church accusations of doctors practicing sorcery were not appreciated, and not forgotten were the fines levied on doctors in the nineteenth century if they failed to advise their patients on the first visit to attend Confession.[18] Some people resented the dispensations to eat meat during Lent sold by the Church to those who could afford it and the fact that priests often picketed theaters but encouraged bullfights.

POLITICAL DISSENSION

Azaña served the Republic in the capacity of prime minister from 1931 to 1933 (and from February to May 1936), but cracks were beginning to show in the fragile structure. Alejandro Lerroux, the corrupt leader of the Radical Republican Party, displeased with Azaña's appointment, which he felt should have been his, passed with his ninety followers into opposition. Lerroux, who held the center of the political spectrum, opposed both socialism and the Church. In an inflammatory speech Lerroux once said to his followers: "Go storm the nunneries and elevate the nuns into the exalted rank of motherhood."[19]

His constituency consisted of middle-class and Republican right-of-center voters. Opposition from further Right came from the Progressive Party of Alcalá Zamora and the new Conservative Republican Party of Miguel Maura. Also opposed to the Azaña government was a wing of the Radical Socialists composed of disenchanted intellectuals who advocated expropriation of the lands of the nobility and the abolition of the Civil Guard. Anarchists, who spurned all forms of centralized government, had no elected representatives in the Cortes.

During its first three years in office, the Republican government, struggling under the impact of the worldwide depression, raised wages, providing some relief for many hungry rural workers, and continued the projects begun under Primo de Rivera in dam building and irrigation canals. The new Constitution proclaimed compulsory education, but lack of schools prevented its implementation even though many new schools were built throughout the country. University facilities were improved. The government tried to advance military technology while reducing the bloated officers corps. Regional autonomy demanded by the Catalans in culture, administration and education was granted. In the area of land reform, however, government policy was negligent and far from adequate.

NOTES

1. Payne, *A History of Spain and Portugal*, 2:482.
2. Ibárruri, 44.
3. Thomas, 21.
4. Pierson, 132.
5. First cabinet of the Second Republic (April 1931): Niceto Alcalá Zamora, leader (Catholic, Republican Right); Alejandro Lerroux, foreign minister (Radical); Diego Martínez Barrio, speaker of the Cortes (Radical); Fernando de los Rios, minister of justice (Socialist); Indalecio Prieto, minister of finance (Socialist); Largo Caballero, minister of labor (Socialist); Manuel Azaña, minister of war (Republican); Miguel Maura, minister of interior (Catholic, Republican Right); Nicolau d'Olwer, minister of national economy (Catalan Left); Santiago Casares Quiroga, minister of marine (Republican). A minister of agriculture, Marcelino Domingo (Republican), was added in December.
6. Crow, 307.
7. The PSOE (Socialists), 117 seats; Lerroux's Radical Party, 89 seats; Radical Socialists, 59 seats; Catalan Esquerra under Lluis Companys, 33 seats; Azaña's Republican Action Party, 27 seats; Alcalá Zamora's Right Republicans, 27 seats; Galician Republicans of Casares Quiroga, 16 seats; the non-Republican Right, 57 seats.
8. Thomas, 42.
9. Esenwein and Shubert, 71.
10. Ibid., 37.

11. Thomas, 45.

12. Gallo, 21. Between them, thirty-eight high nobles owned over half a million hectares as hunting preserves; 51,015 hectares belonged to the duke of Medinaceli alone.

13. Ibid., 20. Thousands of peasants from the south migrated to Barcelona looking for work in industry, where they swelled the ranks of the labor force.

14. See E.H.G. Dobby, "Agrarian Problems in Spain," *Geographical Review of the American Geographical Society*, April 1936. Quoted by Brenan, 121, and Gallo, 21.

15. Gallo, 22.

16. Beevor, 28.

17. Thomas, 83.

18. Beevor, 28.

19. Artiles, 18.

CHAPTER 2

THE SECOND REPUBLIC, 1931–1936

Opposed to the extreme Left and extreme Right, many politically moderate men and women supported the Republic, desiring only law and order under a competent and democratic government. They lamented the trend toward political polarization and the concomitant rhetoric and violence that came with it.

AGRARIAN REFORM LAW, 1932

The elected, mildly Socialist, Republican government of 1931 began work on the thorny problems of agrarian reform, distributing the land in a more equitable fashion by breaking up the large estates of the wealthy. Progress was painfully slow. The government's preoccupation with other matters such as education, the Church and the secession of Cataluña often overshadowed the debates on land reform.

Other reasons also account for the snail's pace toward a new agrarian policy. The government could not decide whether or not to collectivize the land confiscated for distribution among the peasants or parcel it out to individuals; it could not determine how much to pay the landowners in compensation; and it did not have the money to buy the land for anywhere near its market value. In two years the government had bought up enough land to resettle less than 1 percent of those in need.[1] The version of reform when passed on 9 September 1932 was watered down by the opposition and often ignored in sections of the country, leaving many peasants disillusioned.[2]

HOME RULE FOR CATALUÑA AND THE BASQUE PROVINCES

A plebiscite in Cataluña in the summer of 1932 resulted in 592,961 votes in favor of home rule and 3,276 against.[3] The four provincial councils were then organized into the Catalan government with the name of Generalitat. While it had no control over foreign affairs and national defense, the Generalitat had limited powers in matters of education, justice, public order and communications. It could initiate legislation in matters of local administration, health and civil law; Spanish and Catalan were the official languages.

Basque local rights had been abolished in 1876 after the defeat of the Carlists, and many Basques wished to see those privileges reinstated. A statute was brought forward demanding similar rights to those granted to Cataluña. The Basque provinces' pursuit of self-rule was motivated by reasons different from those of Cataluña. Basque industrialized regions retained their fervent Catholic traditions but feared Spanish cultural domination. The traditional way of life was being disrupted by mass immigration of workers from the poorer areas of Castilla that threatened to obliterate the Basque language, culture and ethnic cohesion. In June 1932 three Basque provinces, Alava, Guipúzcoa and Vizcaya, agreed to press for self-rule as one unified region. The province of Navarra, with only a quarter of the population Basque speaking, declined to follow the path of the other three. The Navarese, deeply conservative Carlists, fearful of Marxist revolutionary influences, and in vehement disagreement with the Republic's anti-Church legislation, espoused the ideals expressed by the rightist politicians, the military and the Church.

The Republic promised home rule to the Basque provinces in 1936 (it was granted on 1 October after the outbreak of civil war). These provincial successes prompted a similar movement in Galicia where a statute for autonomy was being planned by Casares Quiroga, minister of the interior in Azaña's government. Murmurings were also heard in Valencia and even in Castilla of separatist longings.

SOCIALISTS

The Spanish Socialist Workers' Party (*Partido Socialista Obrero Español* [PSOE]) came into being in 1879. At first it consisted mostly of the members of the Madrid union of typesetters under the leadership of Pablo Iglesias, son of a poor widow who washed clothes for a living in the Manzanares River.[4] The party had about 1,000 members in 1881. Iglesias called a strike (something not seen in many decades) to protest the failure of legal commitments of the printing industry toward the workers. The strike leaders were jailed for three months. In 1886 the weekly paper *The Socialist* (*El Socialista*) was founded.

The Socialist trade union, the UGT, took shape in 1888 with a membership of 3,300 workers. Founded in Barcelona for the benefit of industrial employees, it achieved little and moved its headquarters to Madrid the following year. By the turn of the century, UGT membership, spreading throughout the country, rose to 26,000.[5] The PSOE won its first seat in the Cortes in 1910.

Socialists were fairly united in 1931, and both Indalecio Prieto, journalist and influential member of the party, and Largo Caballero, secretary-general of the UGT, were in favor of the Socialists entering and collaborating with the Republican government. The apathy of the government to enact land reform, however, disillusioned younger members with the Republic, and under Largo Caballero, who was becoming more radical, they moved further left. Fearful of losing ground to the rebellious Anarchist movement that already outnumbered the Socialists, he and his followers felt the only hope for the masses was a Socialist revolution. Prieto, on the other hand, and the more moderate right wing of the PSOE preferred to work toward a Socialist state within the government: evolution, not revolution. The two leaders who strongly disliked each other vied for control of the Socialist party. Largo Caballero had the UGT and the Socialist youth behind him. Irreconcilable differences in the Socialist camp did not bode well for the country and the party but played into the hands of right-wing organizations as more and more people became alarmed at Largo Caballero's revolutionary rhetoric.

ANARCHISM AND ANARCHO-SYNDICALISM

The Republican government faced mounting threats to its existence from within the leftist camp, especially from the growing numbers of Anarchists[6] whose philosophy rejected all forms of hierarchical authority— social, economic and political.

Unlike Karl Marx, who sought an authoritarian centralized state controlled by the proletariat, Mikhail Bakunin, his Russian revolutionary rival, appealed to the peasant communities by his opposition to all participation in politics, seeking destruction of the state, the bastion of privilege and exploitation, through the development of self-governing communes with local control and maximum liberty. In 1862, the Italian Anarchist Giuseppe Fanelli, a disciple of Bakunin, set up a cell in Madrid consisting of twenty-one converts. As the doctrine was preached from village to village by itinerant apostles, anarchism took root and spread among the rural poor. The antiauthoritarian political philosophy gave the peasant hope that landowner, police and priest would one day disappear and the land would be equally owned and worked by free men. Anarchism also flourished among the miners of Asturias and among the industrial working class of the cities in Cataluña and Valencia where the workers styled themselves Anarcho-Syndicalists. Their objective was to nullify government by direct means such as general strikes, boycotts and sabotage, while the workers took over the ownership and management of industry, creating their own syndicates (trade unions) and forming the basis of a new society. By 1874 there were 30,000 Anarchist members primarily in Andalucía and Cataluña, represented by the National Confederation of Labor, or the CNT (*Confederación Nacional de Trabajo*).

By 1920 the Anarchist movement had 700,000 members and was climbing. While battling the conservative establishment, Anarchists also clashed with proponents of socialism and communism, rejecting their view of centralized government and state. From 1919 to 1923, Barcelona was the scene of massive strikes, lockouts, open class warfare and gangs fighting in the streets.[7] Forced underground during the Primo de Rivera dictatorship of 1923 to 1930, a radical, militant group of Anarchists met secretly in Valencia in 1927 and organized the Iberian Anarchist Federation, or FAI (*Federación Anarchísta Ibérica*), which assumed leadership of the movement.

When the Anarchists were again able to organize freely, the membership polarized into *Cenetistas* (CNT) and *Faístas* (FAI). *Cenetistas* were the relatively moderate members of the organization, dedicated to improving wages, working hours, conditions and education among the working class. The *Faístas*, younger and revolutionary, carried out propaganda programs to encourage revolutionary spirit and consistently worked toward the overthrow of the Republic. The most influential FAI group was the Indomitables (*Los Indomables*) in Barcelona. It included Juan García

Oliver, strike organizer, and Buenaventura Durruti and Francisco Ascaso, who were strike leaders and strong-arm men for the organization.[8]

In June 1931 the CNT held a general congress attended by spokesmen for 511 syndicates representing more than half a million members. The congress was balanced between moderates (*Cenetistas*) and militants (*Faístas*). In the months following, the FAI gained the upper hand, and sudden and violent strikes flared up. Barricades were erected in the streets of Barcelona during a building strike, and battles broke out. The army was called in, and workers were gunned down even as they tried to surrender.

On 19 July 1931 a worker was killed by strikebreakers in Sevilla. At his funeral two days later a pitched battle broke out in the streets; three Civil Guards and more workers were killed and hundreds injured. A general strike was called throughout the region, and the governor responded by instituting martial law and closing down the offices of the CNT syndicates. On 27 July, an Anarchist meeting hall was reduced to rubble by army artillery fire, killing twenty and wounding one hundred.[9]

Policies and actions of the CNT-FAI were directed by an administrative junta for each syndicate consisting of a president, secretary, treasurer and council members. Representatives of syndicates were sent to participate in higher organizational levels of the confederation: the district, the regional and the national. Committees worked for the release of political prisoners and raised money for the relief of their families. A defense committee stockpiled weapons and organized shock troops for the struggle ahead.

At their peak, Spanish Anarchists numbered well over 1 million, primarily in rural Andalucía (where Anarchist principles appealed strongly to landless laborers), industrial Cataluña, the mining districts of Asturias and sections of Madrid and Valencia. Barcelona became the headquarters. Members of the militant FAI probably numbered around 200,000.[10]

The Federation of Iberian Libertarian Youth, or FIJL (*Federación Ibérica de Juventudes Libertarias*), was formed in 1932 by the FAI to enlist young militant members into the Anarchist ranks. Members of FIJL vociferously condemned the capitalistic state, its army, police and the ownership of property. They styled themselves Libertarian Communists or simply Libertarians. In accordance with their views, Anarchists shunned a political party with a relationship to the CNT similar to the Socialist Party (the PSOE), with its trade union (the UGT).

ANARCHIST INSURRECTIONS

In Castilblanco, a remote village of 4,000 inhabitants in eastern Extremadura, some 500 peasants took to the streets on 1 January 1932 in a demonstration against the feudal conditions in which they worked. A shot was fired by a Civil Guard. The enraged farmers struck back, leaving four dead guards, cut to pieces by scythes. On 5 January 1932, revengeful Civil Guards in the northern town of Arnedo in La Rioja fired on peaceful demonstrators, killing seven, among them four women. Two weeks later, in the mining area northwest of Barcelona in the Catalan Pyrenees, the CNT took over the town of Sallent, raised a red flag, declared Libertarian communism and abolished money and private property.[11] The government recaptured the town five days later, and terrible repression followed. The police and the army filled the cemeteries and prisons with working-class victims. The head of the Civil Guard, General José Sanjurjo, was dismissed by Azaña as a result of the brutal repression at Castilblanco and Arnedo. Sanjurjo, a Monarchist, staged a military uprising 10 August 1932 in Sevilla and Madrid. The poorly planned operation failed, and Sanjurjo, whose life was spared, went to prison and then into exile in Portugal.

In November 1932 the Indomitables in Barcelona (Oliver, Durruti and Ascaso) intended to use a railroad strike as a signal for an Anarchist uprising. The strike would prevent police and troops from reaching the centers of upheaval, encouraging the populace to join the revolution. The Socialist UGT controlled many of the workers, however, and opted out of the strike, leaving the Anarchists to go it alone. There was no love lost between the Socialists and Anarchists; the former accused the latter of undermining the Republic, thus aiding and abetting the Right, while the Anarchists accused the Socialists of supporting the suppression of their movement by participation in government. A few weeks before the expected revolt the police began uncovering stores of arms and explosives, depleting CNT arsenals. The strike and the revolution failed to take place. Events in some towns, however, continued to spiral out of control.

On 8 January 1933 Anarchist insurrections took place in Madrid, Barcelona and Valencia but were rapidly put down. Three days later, on 11 January, trouble broke out in the impoverished Andalucian village of Casas Viejas in the province of Cádiz. Landless peasants paraded through the streets proclaiming Libertarian ideals. This led to an exchange of gunfire at the Civil Guard barracks where two guards were killed. More detachments of police arrived at the village and had to deal with the implacable resistance of a group of Anarchists holed up in the house of a peasant nicknamed Six Fingers (*Seis Dedos*). The hut was set on fire by the Civil Guards, leading to the death of the eight men and one woman inside. The inhabitants of the town were then rounded up, and a dozen men were shot as a lesson to the rest. News of the incident reverberated throughout the country. The Left was outraged and the Right took it as another example of the inability of the government to rule effectively.[12]

COMMUNISM AND THE COMINTERN

In March 1919, following the Russian Revolution, Lenin, the Communist leader of the new Soviet government, organized the Third International (two prior Socialist Internationals were held in 1864 and 1889). It consisted of national Communist parties outside the Soviet Union and was popularly known as the Comintern (Communist International, dissolved in 1943), designed to promote world revolution on the Russian model. For Stalin, Lenin's successor, the Comintern was a means of increasing Soviet influence abroad, and shifts in Comintern strategies reflected Stalin's foreign policies.

The advent of the Republic in 1931 found the Communist Party of Spain, the PCE (*Partido Comunista de España*), weak and ineffectual, with at best a couple of thousand members.[13] Throughout the next several years, it remained small and hostile toward the Socialists and Anarchists. Late in 1933 it developed a paramilitary organization known as the Peasants and Workers Anti-Fascist Militias, or MAOC (*Milicias Antifascistas Obreras y Campesinas*), led by Juan Modesto, a former noncommissioned army officer. Both Socialists and Communists viewed the Republic as only a transitional step to full implementation of socialism or communism.

RIGHTIST ORGANIZATIONS

Powerful forces arrayed against the government, in whose hands most of the wealth of the country was amassed, reacted strongly to liberal polices and left-wing threats. Intense opposition originated from the Agrarian Party, which represented the landlords of Castilla, from the Conservative regional parties such as the Catalan League of Industrialists, from

Monarchist movements and from others who opposed the antireligious, military and land reform policies of the Azaña government.

The Agrarian Party launched a campaign for the reform of the Constitution. Calls for its revision, the rallying cry of the Right against the Republic, were disseminated in newspapers and public meetings throughout the country. The Agrarian Party in the Cortes had already impeded legislation by introducing 143 amendments in 1932 to block land reform. Four months of debate led to the approval of only four of twenty-four articles.[14]

In February 1933, forty-two right-wing organizations, representing three quarters of a million voters, met in Madrid and formed the Spanish Confederation of Autonomous Rights, known as CEDA (*Confederación Española de Derechas Autónomas*), a right-wing umbrella organization led by lawyer Gil Robles. He stressed the themes of national unity, religion and traditional military values and introduced the notion of "accidentalism," signifying an indifference to forms of government that were accidental as long as intrinsic Catholic concerns were protected.

An admirer of Hitler and Mussolini, Gil Robles visited Germany in 1933 to attend the Nazi Nuremberg rally. In speeches he talked about the dangers of a social revolution, the clashing forces of Marxism and anti-Marxism throughout Europe, the necessity to defeat socialism in Spain, the need to establish unity through a totalitarian regime and the need to purge the country of Jews and Freemasons.[15] The CEDA youth movement, Youth for Popular Action, known as JAP (*Juventudes de Acción Popular*), was made up of well-off antiparliamentarian young men, who preached the view that an assembly (i.e., the Cortes) elected by the unstructured and ignorant masses could not benefit the common good.

THE JONS

Two men who revered the Nazis, Ramiro Ledesma and Onésimo Redondo, both of whom had founded small publications glorifying Nazi achievements, had drawn together in 1931 to announce the genesis of a Fascist-style movement called the National Syndicalist Juntas on Offense, or JONS (*Juntas de Ofensiva Nacional-Sindicalista*). For lack of finances its activity was ineffective, although it gave rise to the Spanish Syndicate of University Students, or SEU (*Sindicato Español Universitario*), a group of university students about 500-strong, organized to fight leftists in the streets.

MONARCHISTS

High-ranking military officers, career civil servants, judges and attorneys, landowners and the high clergy often favored the system of monarchy. A hereditary and authoritarian figure at the apex of the social hierarchy for many meant stability and order. For the two groups the Carlists and the Alfonsine Monarchists (supporters of the deposed king Alfonso XIII) the Cortes no longer served any purpose and was taken as living proof that democracy in Spain would not work. The Monarchist leader José Calvo Sotelo, who had been finance minister under the dictatorship of Primo de Rivera, stated that he was proud to call himself a Fascist. In a later speech in the Cortes he warned of the Left's intention to destroy the bourgeois and the conservative classes. The right-wing press never ceased to proclaim that the Republic was ungovernable. Army officers were publicly insulted for not dispensing with it.[16]

MILITARY UNIONS

The secretive military union, the Spanish Military Union, or UME (*Unión Militar Española*), was established in 1933 and composed of mostly junior and middle-ranking officers. It was a decentralized association of men with no exact agreement on goals but with no love for the current politicians. Some wanted to protect the country from leftist elements; others wanted to restore the monarchy or maintain the Republic under new leadership. The common denominator was disdain for the current state of affairs. UME grew rapidly and began to form strong associations with the Falange and with Monarchists. Not all officers were rightist, however. Founded by a Socialist officer in 1934, in response to the UME, the Military Union of Anti-Fascist Republican Officers, or UMRA (*Unión Militar Republicana Antifascista*), consisted of army officers sympathetic to the Republic.

THE ELECTIONS OF 1933

The municipal elections held in April 1933 returned about an equal number of councilors on the Left and on the Right.[17] The Republicans did not fare as well as expected. President Alcalá Zamora dismissed Azaña and the cabinet on 3 September 1933, whereupon Lerroux formed a short-lived government. On 2 October the Socialists, disillusioned with the prospect of coming to power by parliamentary means, abandoned support for the Republicans, and the government fell. Martínez Barrio filled in a caretaker government to prepare for elections to the Cortes, which took place on 19 November 1933.

The Left, in disarray, was poorly prepared to fight the general parliamentary elections. Instead of forming a united front, the Socialists refused to cooperate with the government, and the Anarchists as expected, refused to vote. The Right went into the elections united, and the Left suffered overwhelming defeat. The rightist parties (CEDA) took 207 seats; government parties, 99; and centralist parties, 128.[18] The Communists with 200,000 votes elected one deputy. The small party was viewed with some alarm due to its massive propaganda machinery and its connection with the Soviet Union.

THE FALANGE

The Spanish Falange (Phalanx) made its political debut in October 1933. José Antonio Primo de Rivera, its leader, contemptuous of political parties, was the son of the former dictator of the 1920s. With views similar to the JONS and to the Italian Fascists, the Falange attracted upper-class members and advocated strong authoritarian leadership to replace Parliament. Rejecting capitalism, socialism and communism, José Antonio, nevertheless, found it intolerable that masses of people lived in poverty while a few enjoyed great luxury and that so many peasants were landless. He called for a more even distribution of the country's wealth and state aid for those involuntarily unemployed, all within the framework of a totalitarian regime. The paramilitary Falange was in the forefront of demanding the overthrow of the government and provided a terrorist wing to carry out acts of assassination. Lack of funds hindered the party's early growth, however.

Street battles were a common occurrence between young fanatics of the SEU and the Federation of University Students, or FUE (*Federación Universitaria Escolar*), the latter, the students' union, controlled by left-wing members. Militant Anarchists and Socialists, both workers and students, engaged in guerrilla warfare in the cities with Fascists and

Monarchists. Shots were often fired and someone killed, inviting the inevitable retaliation. Strength in numbers was the best protection.

On 11 February 1934 the JONS and the Falange merged and adopted the JONS' symbol of the yoke and arrows (dating back to the sixteenth-century Catholic kings). The Falange had less than 5,000 members, but José Antonio placed it at the disposal of the minister of the interior to help in the repression of leftist agitators. He solicited Mussolini for support of his Fascist movement and received welcome money from the Italian government. Establishing similar links with the Nazis in Germany was unsuccessful.

CEDA IN POWER

The new center-right government repealed or diluted most of the legislation of the previous administration, and state money again flowed back into the coffers of the Church. On 4 April 1934 a bill introduced by Gil Robles was passed that gave to all priests over the age of forty pensions of two-thirds of their salary. The laws prohibiting the religious orders from teaching were reversed in December, and other laws restricting the activities of the Church were ignored. Church holidays were again celebrated. Left-wing protests led to street violence and strikes, followed by the usual police repression.

CEDA was the strongest party in the chamber, but its leader, Gil Robles, refused to declare loyalty to the Republic. CEDA deputies demanded that he be appointed prime minister, but the president of the Republic, Niceto Alcalá Zamora, although a conservative Catholic, refused because of his dislike for Gil Robles and the fact that CEDA was organizing Fascist youth groups. Gil Robles had stated openly the year before that democracy was not an end for him and his party but a means to arrive at the conquest of the New State. When the moment came, he predicted, "parliament will either submit, or we will make it disappear." Moderate Socialists like Prieto, remembering these words, warned the president that they would take it as a declaration of war on the Left if CEDA members were appointed a majority in the cabinet.[19]

The governments of successive center-right prime ministers Ricardo Samper and Alejandro Lerroux did little to appease the Left or the Right. When Samper resigned in the first days of October 1934 the president again called on Lerroux to form a government but with three cabinet posts, justice, labor and agriculture, going to CEDA. This decision set off another leftist explosion. The Socialists voted to call a general strike throughout the country. The government declared a national emergency to deal with the unrest, censorship was imposed and the police given wide powers of arrest.

ASTURIAN REVOLT, 1934

With the entry into the government of CEDA, heralding a Fascist takeover in the view of some center-left and leftist organizations, a revolt broke out in Barcelona on 5 October 1934 under Lluis Companys, leader of the Catalan Left. The CNT did not participate, and the revolt fizzled out in a few hours. About the same time, the Socialists in Madrid under Largo Caballero staged a revolt that also soon collapsed. The situation in Asturias was more serious.

The 50,000 or so miners, armed with guns and dynamite, attacked Civil Guard barracks, town halls and other official buildings along with churches and convents. The Socialist UGT, the Anarchist CNT and the Communists, in a rare moment of cooperation, combined forces. The small number of Communists joined in belatedly owing to a change in Comintern policy directed by Moscow. Stalin now thought it best to establish a common popular front coalition with bourgeois governments to resist the growing menace of European fascism and Nazism that threatened Communist Russia. From here on, Communists spoke of the need to preserve bourgeois parliamentary democracy until it could be replaced by proletariat democracy.[20] The Soviet Union had a good reputation in Spain among leftists. The details of Stalin's bloody agricultural collectivization program in Russia were as yet not widely known.

Within three days of the outbreak, much of the province of Asturias was in the hands of the miners including the capital, Oviedo. As each town fell into their grasp, a revolutionary committee took charge and assumed responsibility for the welfare of the citizens. The local arms factories were commandeered by workers' committees. While the miners contemplated a march on Madrid, the Lerroux government, under pressure from CEDA leaders, called on General Francisco Franco (then in Madrid as adviser to the General Staff) to coordinate the quelling of the uprising. Franco orchestrated the bombing and shelling of the working-class districts of the mining towns and sent the ruthless Spanish Foreign Legion under Colonel

Yagüe and Moorish Moroccan troops to Asturias. Conscripts of the regular home army might not have been a match for the tough miners and, besides, might have sympathized with the rebels.

The rebellion was crushed within two weeks. The last mining villages surrendered on 18 October 1934. Atrocities were not lacking as some Civil Guards, along with some priests, were shot or hanged out of hand. The right-wing press had a field day reporting the rape of nuns (a matter later denied by the Mother Superior of the convent where this incident was supposed to have occurred), the flesh of priests sold for the stewing pot and children's eyes gouged out. It was a matter of indifference to the press if the stories were authenticated or not. Violence against civilians amounted to twelve priests and fifteen businessmen killed during the uprising.[21] Repression in Asturias was swift and savage. The Lerroux government could not control the vengeance taken out on the people by the Civil Guard, the Assault Guards and the Foreign Legion. Prisoners by the hundreds were tortured and arbitrarily shot in groups or after a five-minute summary court-martial. Thousands were locked up in makeshift prisons, their wives and daughters raped and mutilated. Total censorship accompanied the brutalities inflicted on the Asturian "reds" by the Moroccan troops who reputedly castrated captured enemies. Major Doval of the Civil Guard seems to have delighted in brutal treatment of prisoners during his quest to discover arms caches. Prisoners, male and female, died or went mad as his torture squads went about their gruesome task.

Political prisoners, including Azaña and Largo Caballero, arrested for their part in the Madrid disturbances, numbered about 30,000 at the end of October. In Barcelona, Lluis Companys was sentenced to death, and CEDA insisted on his and other executions. But President Alcalá Zamora resisted these demands, claiming that General Sanjurjo and other Monarchists had been spared for their uprising against the Republic two years earlier.

As 1934 came to a close, it was abundantly clear that parliamentary government was ineffective in maintaining order. Local demands for regional autonomy were on the increase; armed uprisings rocked the country. Many on the Left resented and criticized the government's use of detested foreign Moorish troops to quell the insurrection in Asturias, and the specter of more revolutionary violence was everywhere. Fascist ideas heralding a new antidemocratic order were becoming more vocal, increasing the hatred of already deadly opposed factions.

The rebellion of the miners gave the rightist government the excuse to condemn and suppress leftist movements. Socialist municipal governments were suspended along with the Catalan Parliament as subversive, plotting against the Spanish state and contributing to the Asturian insurrection. The jails overflowed with prisoners awaiting trial on cloudy charges of conspiracy. In June 1935 the seven members of the Companys government received sentences of thirty years each for inciting revolution in Barcelona. Largo Caballero was acquitted of charges of creating disorder in Madrid. Government repressive measures of censorship and persecution further radicalized Left and Right ideologies. Young Socialists finding their inspiration in Largo Caballero turned more and more toward revolutionary rather than reformist ideas to bring about an egalitarian and collectivized society.

Fascist organizations competed along with Monarchists, Catholic youth organizations and the youth movement of CEDA (JAP) for the minds of peasants, workers and students. Some were anticapitalist, but all were anti-Marxist and nationalistic, concerned with traditional values and an officially Catholic Spain. Both Left and Right had one thing in common: They despised the government.

In April 1935 five CEDA ministers entered the cabinet, unleashing a new round of street violence. Alcalá Zamora still prevented Gil Robles from becoming prime minister, but he took the office of minister of war. Azaña's military reform came to a halt, and Gil Robles made the army a repressive instrument of social agitation. Liberal officers were replaced by anti-Republicans in the highest posts. General Franco became Chief of Staff; General Mola, commander in Morocco; General Goded, inspector general; and Monarchist General Fanjul, undersecretary. The military academy in Zaragoza, closed by Azaña, was reopened.

FALL OF THE CONSERVATIVE GOVERNMENT, 1935

On 29 October 1935 the Conservative government fell. The corrupt Prime Minister Lerroux resigned over the *Straperlo* gambling scandal in which a Dutch adventurer persuaded certain ministers to agree to a new type of roulette wheel called a *Straperlo* that guaranteed good profits. Joaquín Chapaprieta, a Republican, became head of government but lasted only until December. The president appointed Portela Valladares to take his place, and Gil Robles was removed from the war ministry, nearly provoking a military uprising in Madrid. With little backing, Valladares could only preside over a caretaker government until new elections scheduled for 16 February 1936 were held. CEDA hoped to attract the moderate Left and the moderate Right, both tired of militant turmoil, and form a new center-oriented government with greater support, thus giving Gil Robles the power to strengthen the right-wing position and continue to undo previous leftist legislation.

POUM FOUNDED

Former Anarchist Andreu Nin was a major figure in the Communist circles of the 1920s. His friendship with Leon Trotsky prompted Stalin to veto his nomination of secretary-general of the Spanish Communist Party in 1927. After ten years in Russia, he returned to Spain dismayed with the Communist Party over Stalin's persecution of Trotsky and formed the Communist Left, a small anti-Stalinist group. His ex-Anarchist colleague Joaquín Maurín, who also deplored the Communist leadership, formed a new small and anti-Stalinist group called the Worker and Peasant Bloc, or BOC (*Bloc Obrer i Camperol*). Both Nin and Maurín, operating in Cataluña, inhibited the Stalin Communists from finding adherents in the province and incurred the wrath of the PCE and of Stalin.

The Workers Party of Marxist Unification, or POUM (*Partido Obrero de Unificación Marxista*), was founded in 1935 with the union of the BOC Under Maurín and the Communist Left under Nin. It was often described by the Communist Party as Trotskyist, a convenient label of disapprobation. (Trotsky disowned it.) The little-known party established headquarters in the hotel Falcón on the Rambla, a main street in Barcelona, and agitated for a government of workers only, plastering its propaganda on walls, cars and buses in the city. The anti-Stalinist revolutionaries of the POUM attracted members who opposed both Stalin's and the Anarchist's brand of communism. Its numbers grew rapidly, and it attracted many foreigners who came to Spain to fight in the civil war, the most famous, perhaps, being George Orwell.

The Communist Party spent much energy in trying to discredit and destroy the POUM, whose youth movement, the Iberian Communist Youth, the JCI (*Juventud Comunista Ibérica*), was the more radical and dangerous of the leftist groups, callously gunning down so-called enemies of the people.

In the province of Cataluña and in much of Aragón, committees were formed to administer the towns and villages, and power resided in the hands of the strongest party. The POUM dominated in the province of Lérida and the CNT elsewhere. Some local authorities abolished religious festivities, prohibited the wearing of a crucifix and required a tax on the ringing of church bells. One priest was fined for being a Monarchist since he alluded to the Kingdom of God, and another for saying Mass in a public place, although it was in a church whose roof had been destroyed by lightning.[22]

THE POPULAR FRONT

As the election scheduled for February 1936 drew near, the Spanish atmosphere was heavily charged with highly emotional political issues. Both the Right and the Left had learned the value of coalitions to win seats in the Cortes. In the run-up to the balloting, the Communists joined forces with bourgeois Republican parties and when possible with dissident Communist groups. The new political anti-Fascist coalition composed of sixteen parties and called the Popular Front was headed by Azaña, now out of prison. The largest component was his Republican Party.[23] The Popular Front promised amnesty to political prisoners of the October 1934 uprising and a return to the leftist programs begun in 1931. The Communists increased their numbers from about 1,000 in 1934 to about 30,000 in 1936 (it would have a quarter of a million members by the end of the year and 400,000 by the summer of 1937),[24] still a small figure compared to the 1.5 million Socialists and a larger number of Anarchists. The Comintern used its influence and efficient propaganda to promote Largo Caballero as leader of the militant Spanish workers. Largo Caballero, suspicious of the center-left alliance advocated by Azaña and Prieto, had become even more militant and soon began to embarrass his Communist benefactors with rousing revolutionary speeches around the country.

During the campaign, the Right characterized the election as a choice between good and evil, the latter referring to revolution, communism and destruction of church and state. Its pamphlets portrayed the Popular Front as armed rabble intent on burning churches and private houses, dividing up private possessions, collectivizing the land and planning to make women common property. Children would be taken from their families.

THE NATIONAL FRONT

CEDA formed coalitions with other right-wing organizations such as the Monarchists, including Carlists, in what was known as the National Front. Calvo Sotelo, once finance minister under Primo de Rivera, again appeared on the national stage with an anti-Republican and antidemocratic campaign and argued that the Constitution was dead and a Marxist revolution imminent. If the country did not vote for the coalition of the National Front, a red flag, symbol of the destruction of the Spanish past and ideals, would fly over Spain. According to the Church, a vote for the National Front was a vote for Christ.

On 4 January 1936 the Cortes was dissolved pending the elections. Under the temporary government of Portela Valladares, censorship was lifted. Words and cartoons in newspapers and pamphlets kept the pressure up. Some leftist publications talked about Vatican fascism, and bishops responded by explicitly demanding that Catholics vote against the Popular Front. Largo Caballero declared that if the Right won, he would initiate a civil war.

THE ELECTION OF 1936 AND RIGHTIST REACTION

About 72 percent of the eligible 13.5 million voters cast their ballots. The Popular Front obtained 48 percent of the vote; the rightist bloc, 46 percent (the remainder went to the central group). For the Left this resulted in 263 seats (55 percent) of the 473 seats in the Cortes. Most Republican support came from the big cities; the Right did best in the rural areas of Castilla. Numerically, the country was almost evenly divided into two opposing blocs.[25]

When the results of the election became public, Chief of Staff General Franco tried to persuade Portela Valladares not to hand over power to a Popular Front government. A group of Monarchists asked Gil Robles to overthrow the government, but he declined and even turned on CEDA's financial backers, attacking landowners and employers who, when the Right came to power in 1933, had lowered wages, raised rents and carried out unjust evictions, sealing their own doom in the 1936 elections.

Portela Valladares resigned on 18 February 1936, and President Alcalá Zamora asked Azaña to form a government. The victorious Left engaged in prolonged victory parades in major cities, carrying banners and adopting revolutionary slogans, thoroughly alarming right-wing opponents. On 26 February the Generalitat under Lluis Companys was restored in Barcelona.

José Antonio had promised that his Falange would disregard a leftist victory. The organization now numbered about 10,000 members but had no deputies elected to the Cortes in the 1936 elections. The Falange stepped up its attacks on Socialists in the press and in the streets, and on 15 March, José Antonio and his Falange leadership were arrested and the party's offices and newspaper closed. From his cell José Antonio called on the army to rebel.

On 25 March some 60,000 laborers in Extremadura, impatient for land reform, began plowing the fields left idle by landlords. Landowners thought it wiser to remain in the cities rather than show themselves in the countryside. The government refrained from calling in the Civil Guard for fear of a major bloodbath and scandal. Near the town of Yeste, however, the Civil Guard shot twenty peasants who resisted an order to stop gathering firewood on private land.[26]

GOVERNMENT CONCERN

A main concern of the government was public order in the streets, and it tried to tone down the noisy victory parades that stirred up hostilities. Municipal elections scheduled for April were postponed owing to the current climate of agitation. On 7 April the Cortes voted overwhelmingly to impeach Alcalá Zamora for having dissolved Parliament twice (grounds for impeachment), for having authorized the use of Moorish troops in Asturias and for fear that he would block left-wing legislation. The Right abstained from supporting him because he had refused power to Gil Robles in 1934.

On 15 April 1936 a bomb was hurled during the Republican anniversary parade in Madrid, and a Civil Guard was shot by an Assault Guard for allegedly pointing a pistol at Azaña. On 17 April the funeral of the officer provoked a demonstration by members of the Falange who, shouting slogans, lined up behind the hearse. Socialist youth with clenched fists and singing the anthem "The International" sprayed the demonstrators with bullets. At the cemetery Falange and Assault Guards engaged in running gunfights. About a dozen people were killed.[27] The war of propaganda, rumors and slander was as uncontrollable as the street fighting. It seemed to many that a civil war had already begun.

On 10 May Azaña became president and hoped to make Prieto, head of the moderate Socialists, prime minister. This move was blocked by Largo Caballero and his left-wing Socialists, and instead the Galician Casares Quiroga became head of government.

On 20 May Catholic schools were closed, owing to tips that arsonists would burn them if they remained open. Church festivities were again prohibited and Jesuit property confiscated. The president was besieged by protesting Catholic parents, but rising anti-Catholic agitation was reaching a level the government was unable to control. In the countryside, landless peasants defiled churches, smashing religious icons.

Youth groups that once championed Gil Robles enlisted in the ranks of the Falange, and many young people with leftist leanings joined the Socialist or Communist Parties. In both cases they spent their free time in paramilitary training under the supervision of army officers holding similar points of view. Prominent political figures trod carefully lest they be assassinated. As the violence escalated, Indalecio Prieto, who traveled with a bodyguard and had shots fired at him, warned the Azaña–Casares government that continued disorder and strikes would not bring socialism but instead military dictatorship.

Investment came to a halt as capital looking for safer markets fled the country.[28] Industrialists, frightened by extreme left-wing rhetoric, which they thought would soon be put into practice, had no faith in the Azaña government to prevent a revolution. The degree of violence perpetrated by the Left was denounced by Gil Robles in the Cortes when he spoke on 16 June of 269 homicides in four months and 170 churches burned.

PLANS FOR AN UPRISING: REBEL GENERALS

Key generals including Goded, Fanjul and Franco, working with the UME, met in Madrid on 20 February to discuss the state of affairs. Some were ready to act against the government, but Franco urged caution as they could not be sure of sufficient support. Their contacts continued afterward, and right-wing political leaders were kept informed of plans. The conspirators agreed on the impending dangers of a leftist revolution, territorial breakup of the nation and the suppression of the Catholic Church. It was decided that General Sanjurjo in exile in Portugal would head the insurrection, as he had done in 1932.

That the army might be a dangerous rival for political power was not unknown to the Azaña–Casares Quiroga government, which took the pre-caution of removing senior officers from Madrid who might lead a military uprising. On 21 February 1936, General Franco was shipped out to the Canary Islands, and the Monarchist General Goded was sent to the Bal-earics. General Mola was stationed in Pamplona. The Republican leaders thought these men conveniently isolated from conspiratorial plots. The planning continued, however, by messenger and coded phone calls. While Franco demurred, General Mola emerged as the major planner with the sobriquet *El Director*, director of operations. Mola hated Azaña for the latter's military reforms. Colonel Galarza served as liaison between Mola and Sanjurjo, while Foreign Legion Colonel Yagüe served as the link to Franco and to the Falange whose leader, José Antonio, remained in jail.

The civilian Monarchist leader, Calvo Sotelo, agreed with Mola's in-tentions and brought into the plot Gil Robles who, distrusted by the army, was thought nevertheless to be an asset due to his wide following. Gil Robles ordered his followers to be ready to assist an uprising when it should occur. Links were forged to Carlists in the north. The officers' union UME reported to Mola on the morale and loyalty of the army, and the chief of police in Madrid kept him informed of government sentiment. Mola planned for key positions to be taken over by the army at the moment of insurrection. The rather unimportant post the government had assigned him in Pamplona facilitated his purpose since the province of Navarra was the most anti-Republican, reactionary and conspiratorial region in the country. Along with Falange recruits from other conservative northern towns such as Burgos and Valladolid, the Navarese Carlists would supply Mola with needed manpower. Mola intended to swoop down on Madrid through the Guadarrama mountain passes and capture the city. Franco in the Canary Islands remained uncommitted.

Meanwhile, the Carlists in the north, under the national leadership of the uncompromising lawyer Manuel Fal Conde and the local Navarese aristocrat and Carlist chief the count of Rodezno, gathered arms—some purchased in Germany and shipped in champagne cases by private yacht—while officers were trained in Italy, courtesy of Mussolini.[29] The Falange, aware of the conspiracy, worked to establish ties with high-ranking officers and to become the political force behind the insurrection. As CEDA disintegrated in the early months of 1936, the Falange increased its membership to about 30,000. Gil Robles did little to arrest the decline of CEDA since he was fully briefed on the impending military coup d'état.

On 12 July 1936, Calvo Sotelo was murdered by government Assault Guards, casting grave suspicion on the role of Republican high officials in the event. The assassination was in retaliation for the killing earlier in the day of José Castillo, a popular Socialist Assault Guards officer shot down in the streets of Madrid by members of the Falange. In the view of the army and many of the right-wing politicians, the time had come to save the country from the red menace. General Franco by now had committed himself to the insurrection.

The military junta planning the takeover expected a quick victory in a *pronunciamiento* so familiar to Spanish history in which the military decided what kind of government would rule and took charge to implement it. The generals had at their command most of the infantry and artillery officers, along with reliable Carlist regiments (*Requetés*) that had been secretly drilling for some months in the north, and the Foreign Legion in North Africa along with a division of Moroccan Moorish troops. A good portion of the Civil Guard, under the command of army officers, could be counted on to cooperate in the uprising. Naval officers were also expected to support the insurrection. Foreign aid, planes, arms and munitions, from the Italian Fascists, were promised.[30] The government, on the other hand, could count on Republican Assault Guards, a small and poorly armed air force and some of the army that would undoubtedly remain loyal.

Prime Minister Casares Quiroga and President Azaña refused to take seriously that an insurrection was imminent. They sent some naval vessels to guard the Strait of Gibraltar against a possible incursion of the African Foreign Legion into Spain and ordered the police to break up a few rightist parades in Madrid but did precious little else. Indalecio Prieto implored Casares Quiroga to distribute arms, laying in government arsenals to the people so that they might defend the Republic when the time came. But Casares Quiroga and Azaña were less concerned about a rightist military coup than they were about a leftist revolution. They felt that to arm the Anarchists would be tantamount to self-destruction by the Republican government. When news reached Madrid during the night of 17 July 1936 that the Spanish Foreign Legion in Morocco had revolted, it was scarcely credible. Its commander, Colonel Juan Yagüe, had been considered loyal to the Republic. The matter was urgent but apparently not desperate. It seemed only a matter of containing the insurgents in Morocco.

NOTES

1. Beevor, 32.
2. For agrarian problems, see Thomas, 83 ff., and Carr, *Spanish Tragedy*, 33 ff.
3. Thomas, 86.
4. Brenan, 215.
5. Ibid., 217–218.
6. The term derives from the Greek *an archos*, "without a ruler."
7. Esenwein and Shubert, 80.
8. Mintz, 144.
9. Beevor, 33.
10. Thomas, 70.
11. Ibid., 78.
12. See Mintz for a treatment of the subject.
13. Thomas, 120.
14. Esenwein and Shubert, 16.
15. Preston, *The Coming*, 71.
16. Beevor, 41.
17. For figures, see Thomas, 106. Figures differ a little among historians.
18. The way votes were translated into seats did not necessarily reflect the strength of the parties. In each province the slate with the majority of votes received 80 percent of the seats. A small difference in voting numbers could lead to an enormous difference in the number of seats. The 1.6 million votes for the Socialists overall gave them 58 seats, while the Radicals with 800,000 votes captured 104.
19. Beevor, 36.
20. Ibid.
21. Ibid., 37.
22. Thomas, 105.
23. The Popular Front was an attempt to align Western powers into an anti-Nazi coalition. Popular Front policy was introduced at the Seventh World Congress of the Communist International in 1935 in response to the rise of Hitler and the fear that Germany's growing military power would be unleashed on the Soviet Union. Stalin was aware that commercial and political interests in the West, including the United States, did not view this as a bad thing. Communism would be wiped out by a victorious Germany that would itself, after the conflict, be a spent force and no longer a threat to the democracies. See Boloten, *Grand Camouflage*, 91.
24. Beevor, 122.

25. Ranzato, 47. Although prominent Anarchists were bribed by the Right to campaign not to vote as in 1933, thus helping the Right win the elections, some Anarchists, who had abstained in previous elections, voted for the Socialists, prompted by the fact that a number of their comrades remained political prisoners.

26. Beevor, 44.

27. Thomas, 172.

28. Beevor, 41.

29. Ibid., 43.

30. Brenan, 316.

CHAPTER 3

CIVIL WAR, 1936

MILITARY UPRISING

The military uprising scheduled to take place on Saturday, 18 July 1936, throughout Spain and its Moroccan territory began in Spanish Morocco at 5:00 P.M. on 17 July, when the garrisons of the colonial army of Africa, the Foreign Legion, seized the public buildings in Melilla, Ceuta and Tetuan, arresting or shooting anyone who opposed them. The Legion acted prematurely because the plan was discovered and nearly thwarted by officers loyal to the Republic.

The Canary Islands were taken over the next day, and the military governor, General Franco, flew to Tetuan early on 19 July to take command of the uprising. An enthusiastic crowd of rebel officers met him when the plane touched down. Meanwhile, General Goded in Mallorca quickly took control of the island and departed in a seaplane to lead the insurrection in Barcelona.

In Pamplona, according to schedule, General Mola rose at the head of some 6,000 Carlist troops, took command of the city and shot the head of the Civil Guard, who refused to join them. Insurgents in Valladolid met some resistance from railroad workers but were in command of the city within twenty-four hours. Salamanca and Burgos fell easily to the rebels, while in Zaragoza, the capital of Aragón, resistance to the insurrection by about 30,000 mostly unarmed CNT members resulted in a massacre. Owing to poor coordination and unexpected resistance, the rebellion failed in the major cities of Madrid, Barcelona, Valencia, Bilbao and Málaga.

EVENTS IN MADRID

In Madrid, President Azaña first reacted to the news of the military rebellion by refusing to believe it, just as he had ignored or dismissed the warning signs. As the news came in of one town after another falling to the rebels, Prime Minister Casares Quiroga panicked, shouting orders and then countermanding them. He sent the director-general of the air force, Nuñez de Prado, to Zaragoza in an attempt to convince General Cabanellas, in charge of the garrison, to remain loyal to the Republic. Upon landing, Nuñez de Prado, his aide and pilot were arrested and later shot. As a result, the air force lost its able commander, and the rebels gained an airplane.

Meanwhile, the plotters in Madrid were in a state of confusion. General Fanjul, commander in charge, received no word from his superior General Mola in Pamplona, although the uprising had already started. In the afternoon of 19 July he went to the Montaña Barracks, addressed the officers and men and then attempted to march out and take over the city.

At the same time, the CNT and the UGT directed their members to the barracks, and a member of Parliament, Dolores Ibárruri (La Pasionaria), made stirring speeches in the capital exhorting the people to rise up and defend the Republic from those who wished to destroy liberty and plunge the nation into a reign of terror. Crowds paraded through the streets clamoring for arms and converging on the barracks. For the government a major dilemma was whether or not to distribute arms from the military arsenals to the trade unions for their thousands of members who demanded them. It was argued that given arms the masses would use them in indiscriminate shooting rampages, and some, like the Anarchists, would employ them on the government and mount their social revolution.

General Fanjul, hesitant about taking troops into the hostile streets and with communications to other garrisons around the city cut off, withdrew his men back into the safety of the Montaña Barracks. The building came under siege by workers (some armed) and loyal military forces.

Under enormous strain and suffering from tuberculosis, Casares Quiroga resigned on 18 July, and a new government was formed by Martínez Barrio, who telephoned Mola in Pamplona and offered him a cabinet position as minister of war if he would call off the rebellion. Mola refused, and Martínez Barrio resigned after only a few hours at his post. General Miaja, loyal to the Republic, was named minister of war.

Reports continued to come in of cities and towns falling into the hands of the insurgents. Sevilla, Córdoba, Jerez, Algeciras and Cádiz had all gone over to the rebels. In the chaotic situation, officers still loyal to the Republic took it upon themselves to break into the arsenals and distribute arms to the people. Thousands of rifles were secured, but for most the bolts necessary to fire them were in the Montaña Barracks. Rebel sympathizers in the city fired on the crowds in the streets from concealed positions on rooftops and windows. The mobs, out of control, burned churches, convinced that priests and Fascists were shooting at them from church towers. Hordes broke into buildings where snipers were hidden and killed them on the spot, then swarmed into bars, demanding free drinks in the name of the Republic.

The new prime minister, José Giral, a member of Azaña's Left Republican Party, was sworn in and with the reluctant president belatedly agreed to hand over arms to the people. Some cannons were brought into play by loyal officers around the Montaña Barracks as the civilian crowd surrounding the military establishment in the heart of the city grew to many thousands. Fighting was fierce. Soldiers wanted to surrender and waved white flags from the windows, but when the crowds surged forward, they were cut down by machine-gun fire by others who continued to resist. Enraged by the seeming deception, the people stormed the barracks, resulting in the slaughter of the officers, who were hanged or thrown from windows onto the patio below. Many other combatants, some of them Falange units, were also brutally killed. The besieging workers obtained numerous rifles but in most cases still had to learn how to use them as they went looking for anyone suspected of Fascist sympathies. In other barracks around the city, surrenders took place and Madrid remained in Republican hands. Many newly armed workers marched off to neighboring towns such as Alcalá de Henares and Guadalajara to the east and Toledo to the south to help resist insurgent takeovers.

By the fourth day, the rebels held about one third of the country. Besides the failure of the coup in the major industrial cities, a setback for the rebels occurred in the navy where sailors formed committees, arrested and killed their insurgent officers and made sail for the Straits of Gibraltar, which they intended to blockade, preventing Franco and the Moroccan army from crossing to Spain. The government in Madrid, meanwhile, lost its authority, and power passed to the streets, where armed self-appointed anti-Fascist committees composed of members of the trade unions set up roadblocks and made house-to-house searches looking for enemies of the Republic to liquidate.

THE BATTLE FOR BARCELONA

General Goded planned to take Barcelona using the 12,000 troops quartered in and around the city. News of the impending coup reached the Catalan government the night before, and the rebels' plan to take the city lost the element of surprise. President Lluis Companys refused, nevertheless, to distribute arms to the people, and the defense committees of the CNT and the FAI seized armories and confiscated the weapons. Along with members of the POUM, the Socialist Party and the Communists, they commandeered cars and trucks and hastily converted some of them into armored vehicles. As in Madrid, they took control of the streets.

In the early morning of 19 July, soldiers from the Pedalbes Barracks in Barcelona marched on the main square, the Plaza de Cataluña, where they were to link up with units from other barracks. They were met by crowds of armed workers supported by Civil Guards, Assault Guards and city police (*Mozos de Escuadra*) who had remained loyal to the Republic and to the Generalitat. The soldiers took refuge in the telephone exchange and in the hotels Ritz and Colón around the square. The workers erected barricades in the surrounding streets, and fighting became intense. General Goded arrived in the city from Mallorca to find a full-scale battle in progress. By evening the sheer numbers of civilians and security forces had overpowered the soldiers. The Atarzanas and the San Andrés Barracks held out until the following day when they were stormed by a fierce mass attack by Anarchist militias. The ill-coordinated assault cost heavy casualties including Francisco Ascaso, the Anarchist leader. General Goded was taken prisoner, tried the following month and shot.

REBELLION IN OTHER CITIES

Spontaneous fighting broke out in all the major cities and towns. In the southern cities of Málaga and Jaén the municipalities passed out arms in spite of orders to the contrary from the central government. In Badajoz the loyal General Castelló squashed the incipient rebellion.

Insurgent Nationalist General Queipo de Llano arrived in Sevilla on the night of 17 July and the following day personally arrested the commander of the garrison, then the civil governor and chief of police. Backed by a few soldiers, he threatened to shoot anyone who opposed the take-over. Queipo de Llano later became infamous for his vulgar radio broadcasts to the nation. In one of many similar broadcasts, he stated in reference to workers and peasants:

> The people are swine. They must be killed like swine! . . . We do not want to be bothered again in our lifetime by Bolsheviks. These seducers of the people must be made to feel the pangs of hell before they die. . . . Spain must again be made a country fit for caballeros [gentlemen] to live in.[1]

In the northern provinces of Santander and Asturias, towns remained loyal to the Republic, although Oviedo, the capital of Asturias, was taken when the commanding officer, Colonel Aranda, pretending to be loyal to the Republic, supplied a train for the militant workers to go off and defend Madrid. When they had gone, he seized the city on behalf of the rebels.

The Basque provinces of Vizcaya and Guipúzcoa with their respective major cities of Bilbao and San Sebastián declared in favor of the Republic. The surprise element was lost in Bilbao when the government listened in on telephone calls to the barracks, and the rising was aborted. Navarra, the Basque province of Alava, the northwest regions of Galicia and León and much of Old Castilla fell under control of General Mola. Half the province of Aragón, including Zaragoza and Huesca, was in insurgent hands or soon to be so, along with much of Teruel including the capital. A besieged rebel garrison held out in Toledo.

On 20 July, the conspirators in the north awaited the appearance from Portugal of General Sanjurjo to take charge and led the march on Madrid. A small plane was dispatched to fly the general to the rebel-held city of Burgos. More than a little overweight, and accompanied by a heavy trunk containing his dress uniforms and medals, the general squeezed into the rear seat of the aircraft. Taking off with its ponderous burden, the plane struck the top of a tree, nosed into the ground and burst into flames. Sanjurjo was killed even though the pilot walked away from the wreckage.

THE FIFTH REGIMENT

In Barcelona, Valencia and Madrid, civilian workers formed columns of about 300 militiamen. Some were organized by the Ministry of War

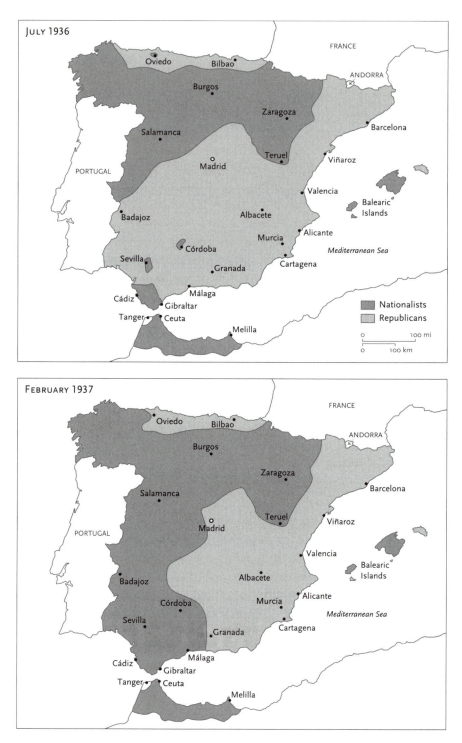

Republican and Nationalist-held territory, July 1936 (top) and February 1937 (bottom).

Republican and Nationalist-held territory, April 1938 (top) and March 1939 (bottom).

and led by regular army officers, but the majority of the militias were organized by the trade unions and trucked off to the front lines in Aragón west of Barcelona (near Zaragoza) or the Guadarrama mountains north of Madrid to stop Mola's advance.

The most famous unit in Madrid was the Fifth Regiment formed by the Communists, many of the men recruited by Dolores Ibárruri. With its own artillery, supply units and reserves, the detachment was self-contained and adopted the use of political commissars to explain to the soldiers the purpose of their fight and instill Communist ideology. By the end of July, its 1,000 members were on the Guadarrama front. Some outstanding officers gained their experience in the Fifth Regiment such as Enrique Lister (an ex-quarryman) and Juan Modesto (an ex-woodcutter). The Communist force was noted for its discipline and obedience to commands, in sharp contrast to the Anarchist militias who elected their own officers and, after a discussion, voted by a show of hands whether or not they would obey orders!

MOLA'S ADVANCE ON MADRID

From his headquarters in Pamplona, General Mola assembled his troops, the *Requetés*. Wearing red berets, they hastened to Mola's banners along with blue-shirted Falange from neighboring towns. With great fanfare and priestly blessings, they all set off for Madrid. Mola boasted that he would be having coffee in a Madrid café in a few days, that his four columns would push through and take the city with the help of a fifth column, meaning the rebels would still be holed up in Madrid and carrying out sabotage and sniping.

The city was vulnerable from the north by two passes through the Guadarrama mountains and from the northeast via Guadalajara. Colonel Francisco García Escámez, one of Mola's devoted officers, was to lead a unit south from Pamplona to Guadalajara and swing west into Madrid. From other Nationalist-held northern towns, Segovia, Avila, Burgos and Valladolid, troops were to storm the mountain passes and descend on the city.

Early in the morning of 21 July the roads leading out of Madrid to the northern mountains were packed with cars, trucks, buses and bicycles laden with armed militiamen. Republican soldiers too were moving north to fight, inspired by Dolores Ibárruri and her Communist colleague Enrique Lister, both of whom had gone to the Madrid barracks and promised the new recruits, mostly young peasants, that they would get their own land after the Republic won the war.

Cipriano Mera, a bricklayer by occupation, and his Anarchist followers raced for Guadalajara to retake and hold the town then in the hands of the rebels and give Mola an unpleasant surprise. Mera, one of the most influential Anarchists in Madrid, a prominent member of the militant FAI and head of the CNT construction union, had been jailed for strike action shortly before the revolt. He was released from the Model Prison by Anarchist throngs who were angry because the government handed out weapons to the Socialists upon presentation of a UGT trade union card. Still fearing a revolution, the government was reluctant to hand over weapons to the Anarchists. Mera was willing to temporarily support the government, however, and impose discipline on his Anarchist militia in order to crush the insurrection.

Guadalajara was seized after bitter fighting. A POUM militia then spearheaded a drive further to the northeast to take the town of Sigüenza, crushing rebel resistance there before Mola's troops arrived. The old cathedral town was held until 15 October when Colonel García Escámez's units recaptured it. Meanwhile, the Guadarrama passes changed hands several times, but finally militiamen dug in and held their ground, encouraged by another Communist leader, Valentín González, a road contractor by occupation and known as El Campesino (The Peasant), notorious for his great beard and physical strength. All along the northern front, Mola was stopped, however, and Madrid remained secure but chaotic.

FRANCO CROSSES THE STRAITS

Realizing that the uprising had fallen short of its intentions on mainland Spain, Franco in Morocco desperately needed aircraft to transport his elite African army across the Strait of Gibraltar guarded by the Republican navy. The few Republican air force planes and Italian Savoias that Franco possessed were inadequate for the numbers of men, but the crisis was solved when Hitler supplied Junkers (Ju 52) transport aircraft, greatly enhancing the capability, begun on 27 July 1936, of the first airlift of troops in history. German pocket battleships later arrived to escort the army of Africa across the straits by boat, effectively reducing the threat from Republican warships whose loyalist seamen were far from efficient without their officers.

During the late summer and early fall, heavy fighting took place in southwestern Spain as Franco's forces moved north from Sevilla to Badajoz and Mérida and then up the Tajo valley toward Madrid, the major prize. The advance took on a familiar pattern. Soldiers were transported in trucks and lived off the land, taking what they needed. When a village appeared, they dismounted and entered it on foot with fixed bayonets. Loudspeakers ordered that the doors of the houses be opened and white flags displayed. If resistance was met, the village was leveled by artillery. Anyone caught with a weapon or with bruise marks on the shoulder from having fired a rifle was summarily shot. Ironically, men and women loyal to the Republic were considered traitors for not supporting the military takeover. The Republican militiamen who made a stand were no match for the highly trained African army and took flight when the fighting heated up. With little perception of coordinated military tactics, they were mowed down in batches by Nationalist machine guns as they fled. The dead Republican defenders would then be looted for anything valuable—gold teeth, watches, jewelry, clothes—which often found their way back to the families of Moroccan soldiers. The piles of the dead were then burned. Town after town along the route fell in the same way, and every day the objective, Madrid, drew closer.

MASSACRES AT BADAJOZ AND MADRID

The walled town of Badajoz, capital of the province of Extremadura near the Portuguese border, suffered severely for its resistance. The town was important to the insurgents, for here Franco and Mola could link up their southern and northern armies. It had also undergone revolutionary land seizures and was a Socialist stronghold. Mass killings of Republicans took place in the bullring on 14 August where several thousand men were enclosed and machine-gunned in a orgy of hatred and blood by Nationalist troops.

Meanwhile, the prisons in Madrid were packed. The Model penitentiary contained about 2,000 men considered dangerous Fascists. With the massacre at Badajoz in mind, guards at the prison machine-gunned the prisoners who were taking exercise in the courtyard. That night people flocked to the prison from around the city and threatened to kill the inmates. Among other leaders, Indalecio Prieto rushed to the site to try to calm the crowd. No one paid attention. Inside, guards examined lists of prisoners, deciding whom they would murder and dragging the victims off to the cellar for execution. Two who died this way were Fernando, brother of José Antonio, and Pedro, brother-turned-Falangist of the Anarchist Buenaventura Durruti. The killing went on all night, and at dawn the crowds drifted away.

On 27 August 1936 the first bombs fell on Madrid, further inciting the militias to seek out and destroy the enemy fifth column in the city. Suspects were shot on the least suspicion. Those found with radio sets in their rooms had no chance to even explain, although, in one case, an old man was found with earphones hooked up to an alarm clock. A militiaman thought it was a radio set. The concierge explained that the man was deaf and needed to hear the clock. The militiaman, not to be denied his victim, insisted it was a radio set, and the deaf man was taken out and shot.[2]

NATIONALIST ADVANCE AND POLITICAL CHANGES

On 5 September the Nationalists under Mola captured the frontier town of Irun, cutting off the Basque region from France. The following day, Franco's troops advancing from the south captured Talavera de la Reina sixty miles southwest of Madrid. With the fall of Talavera, the road to Madrid, littered with the debris of retreating Republican soldiers, was open, while Mola's forces north of the city, now better equipped, threatened to break through the mountain passes.

Prime Minister Giral, an unimaginative former pharmacist, inspired little confidence, and Largo Caballero, popular among the masses, wanted him out and himself in. Giral resigned on 4 September, and President Azaña, with few options, appointed sixty-seven-year-old Largo Caballero prime minister. Caballero also reserved for himself the post of minister of war. Largo Caballero's new cabinet consisted of Republicans, left- and right-wing Socialists and two Communists.

Socialist Julio Alvarez del Vayo, with strong ties to the Communists and considered by some members as little more than a Communist stooge, became foreign minister. He was kept on over the objections of Indalecio Prieto and another moderate Socialist, Dr. Juan Negrín. The former took over the Ministries of the Navy and Air Force, and Negrín assumed the Ministry of Finance.

Largo Caballero, who had opposed Giral's attempt to create a unified Republican army, preferring the discordant, divided and uncoordinated revolutionary militias, immediately called for an attack to retake Talavera and put General José Asensio Torrado in charge of it. The attack failed. Prieto appointed Major Hidalgo de Cisneros, soon to become a Communist, head of the air force. His outmoded planes were swept from the skies by the newer German and Italian fighters. Madrid was now extremely vulnerable to Nationalist air attacks and ground forces.

SIEGE AT TOLEDO

A little south of Madrid, the city of Toledo underwent vicious fighting among the narrow twisted streets of the old town in the first few days of the insurrection. Republican militiamen gained the ascendancy, and Nationalist forces of Falangist, Civil and Assault Guards, along with a few cadets from the military school, retreated into the stone fortress above the river Tajo. They numbered about 1,000 and took with them several hundred women and children as hostages, among whom were members of the families of known leftists. Under Colonel Moscardó they prepared for a long siege. Tunnels were dug by the Republicans in an effort to penetrate the fortress underground, and one heavy gun was secured that shelled the stout walls intermittently with little effect. The young son of Colonel Moscardó, held by the Republicans, was ordered to telephone his father in the fortress and convey the message that he would be put to death unless Moscardó surrendered. The colonel told his son to commend himself to God and die bravely. The threat was later carried out.

The town fell on 27 September to advancing Nationalists under General Varela who had been diverted by Franco from attacking Madrid for that purpose. The long siege of the fortress was lifted. The episode soon became an inspirational propaganda piece for the Nationalists that covered up the fact that the one hundred or so leftist hostages taken into the fortress were never seen again.[3]

FRANCO BECOMES HEAD OF STATE

Franco's decision to lift the siege of Toledo bought time for Madrid and may have cost the Nationalists the capital, but it appears to have had psychological benefits for Franco, who became a Nationalist hero. When a junta of officers met in Burgos, insurgent headquarters, in September 1936, they agreed that Franco would be not only the commander in chief (*generalissimo*) of the Nationalist armies, replacing the deceased General Sanjurjo, but also head of government of the Spanish state. On 1 October Franco assumed absolute power as president, prime minister and king all wrapped in one. Soon after, Franco moved his government to Salamanca, where he took up residence in the bishop's palace.

DEFENSE OF MADRID

The people of the capital now began to erect defenses. On 28 September Largo Caballero finally agreed to Communist demands to militarize the militia units and make them into 3,000-strong mixed brigades, each composed of three or four battalions.

While career officers were available in Madrid, their loyalty to the Republic was questionable. A system of political commissars was thus introduced under Alvarez del Vayo to indoctrinate the soldiers and keep an eye on the officers to guard against any signs of Nationalist sympathies. Only the Anarchists refused to give up their cherished columns and accept military discipline. They feared Communist control over the army.

The Communist Party itself had grown from about 10,000 to 50,000 members during the months leading up to the military insurrection as thousands of radical Left Socialists of the PSOE and the Union of Young Communists merged into the Unified Socialist Youth, the JSU (*Juventudes Socialistas Unificadas*), controlled by the Communists under the leadership of Santiago Carrillo, later to become the head of the Spanish Communist Party. They foresaw the need for military training and discipline and hoped for Soviet aid. The Communists undertook a systematic defense. Trenches were begun around the city and barbed wire laid down on the approaches by thousands of civilian volunteers. Dolores Ibárruri on the radio and in speeches exhorted the people to resist. "They shall not pass," [*No pasarán*], the old French battle cry, made famous at Verdun in World War I, became the watchword.

REFUGEES

By mid-October Nationalist troops closed in on the southern and western approaches to Madrid. Compounding the problems, the city became a seething mass of humanity as hundreds of thousands of refugees streamed into it ahead of Franco's army. Exhausted parents, grandparents and children piled high on carts, along with whatever household belongings they could take with them, and pulled by scraggy mules plodded in endless processions through the streets. Cows and chickens grazed in the parks and along the margins of the sidewalks, the homeless camped on every available piece of open ground.[4] The gaiety of the bars and cafés subsided as hunger and fear in the swollen city began to take effect.

On 20 October the Republican general José Asensio failed in an attack near Illescas, south of the capital, and was replaced by General Pozas, who was also more amenable to the Communists. On 29 October German and Italian bombers began air raids on the city. Mola now boasted he would celebrate the anniversary of the Bolshevik revolution, 7 November, in Madrid. On 2 November, Brunete, a village a little west of Madrid, was taken by the Nationalists, and two days later, Getafe and its airport just south of the capital fell. General Varela was optimistic enough to tell journalists that they could announce to the world that Madrid would fall this week. Some Russian fighter planes appeared over Madrid the same day, relieving some of the gloom and offering encouragement to the population.

Meanwhile, the Anarchist movement was caught in an agonizing dilemma: to remain aloof from government (as their philosophy dictated), and risk being crushed by Fascists or Communists, or join it and fight for their own survival. On 4 November four Anarchist ministers joined the Caballero government.[5]

BATTLE FOR MADRID

On 6 November Nationalist troops entered the open stretches of the Casa del Campo west of the city while the CNT and UGT militiamen went to meet the threat. The same day the government of Largo Caballero abandoned Madrid for Valencia. General Miaja was left behind to surrender the city and chose capable Vicente Rojo as his chief of staff. Rounding up the officers of the various military units, the general expressed his determination to fight on in the defense of the capital. All concurred and that very night began the transformation of Madrid into a bastion of resistance. Houses were turned into fortresses, and war committees supervised the work. The militias would now take orders from the General Staff. Next,

Miaja called the trade union leaders to his office and demanded 50,000 men and all the arms the unions were hoarding for their own interests.

Colonel Vicente Rojo and Major Manuel Matallana organized the civilian population in the rapid construction of barricades, medical centers, soup kitchens and communication posts. Women and children continued to dig trenches around the city, but the situation appeared grim. Some 20,000 poorly armed militia manned the new trenches and barricades. The outside world waited for the outcome of this epochal battle between the forces of light and darkness. Which was which depended on one's point of view.

On 7 November, Moorish mounted troops entered Carabanchel, the southern suburb of Madrid, making for the Toledo bridge over the Manzanares River toward the center of the city. They were driven back. That evening an Italian tank was destroyed, and operational orders for the assault on Madrid, issued by General Varela, were found on the body of the tank commander. Colonel Rojo accordingly moved his best troops into the designated area to counter the attack set for 8 November that focused on the west sections of the capital, through the Casa del Campo, the old royal hunting ground that partly bordered the university campus. Nationalist troops numbered about 25,000, of which 5,000 were employed in the initial assault. Miaja told his commanders that the only order was to resist. When asked where to retreat if it became necessary, he replied, "To the cemetery."

On that day telegrams began to arrive at Franco's headquarters congratulating the general on his entry into Madrid. The great triumph had already been published in the Portuguese press. The citizens of the capital, however, had other ideas. Banners announced that Madrid would be the tomb of fascism.

The elite African army of General Varela clashed with the ragtag worker soldiers under General Miaja over a twenty-mile front at the approaches to the city. German planes bombed the Republican front lines. Unarmed Republican militiamen, as artillery shells rained around them, sheltered behind the lines until needed, then rushed forward to snatch up the rifles of their fallen comrades and continue the battle. General Miaja himself, waving a pistol, stemmed the retreat of his soldiers at a point where the Moors had broken through the line.

The Nationalists inched forward toward the Manzanares River running through the western suburbs of Madrid and the Casa del Campo but

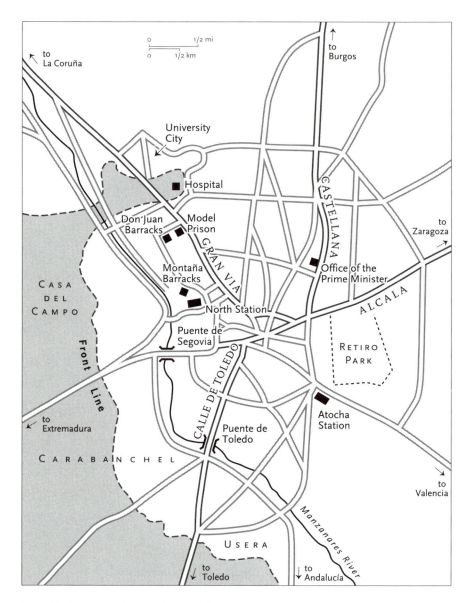

Madrid: front line, November 1936.

at a great price in casualties. They crossed the river in one sector and entered University City, where the battle raged from building to building and from room to room. Here they were stopped again.

Also on 8 November, a Sunday afternoon, the first units of the recently formed International Brigades (foreign volunteers) appeared in the city. About 2,000 strong, they consisted mostly of anti-Fascist Germans, Italians and French. Many were veterans of World War I. They had been training at Albacete and were now committed to battle. Marching through the city in precise formations and singing revolutionary songs, they immediately infused a new optimism into the inhabitants. The following day they took the full brunt of the rebel attack in the university sector of the city, and in the next ten days, most of them were dead or wounded. Foreign reporters in Madrid sent out their dispatches to the world extolling the bravery of the Spanish people and the International Brigades.

With the government absent from Madrid and the enemy at the gates, reprisals became more common. The political inmates in the Model Prison, supposed to be transferred to Valencia by order of the government, were instead trucked out of the city to the northeast, on two consecutive nights, shot and buried in mass graves, nearly 1,000 men.[6]

On 14 November, Buenaventura Durruti, the Anarchist militia chief, brought his column, about 3,000 strong, from a relatively quiet sector of the Aragón front to Madrid. He demanded an active sector of the front to make a Catalan-Anarchist contribution to the defense of the city. His militiamen took up positions in the university where the Nationalists were making a do-or-die effort to capture the sector. Waves of Moorish troops attacked and gained entry to the philosophy building and then reached the medical building and the nearby hospital, creating a salient right up to the Madrid suburbs. They were finally stopped, both sides fighting twenty-four-hour hand-to-hand combat in the buildings where each side occupied different floors.

As winter approached, icy winds descended on the city from the northern mountains, and tens of thousands of refugees from the working-class section of the capital, where concentrated Nationalist bombs had destroyed their dwellings, along with refugees from outlying villages, packed into the underground subway tunnels, abandoned shops and the cellars of houses. Coal was nearly nonexistent, and while some people froze to death, all the wood in the city was torn loose to make fires. Meat and potatoes were nonexistent. Nourishment was derived from garlic soup, peppers, the occasional cabbage or cauliflower, a little macaroni and rolled oats.[7]

On 17 November, in an all-out effort to break Madrid's resistance, the Nationalists fired 2,000 artillery shells into the city every hour.[8] The working-class sections were ablaze. Only the Salamanca district, the home turf of many upper-middle-class and presumed Franco supporters, was spared. Coming over at night, to avoid Russian fighter aircraft, waves of German bombers, guided by the fires, dropped high explosive and incendiary bombs. There were few antiaircraft guns to protect the city and no bomb shelters.

On 19 November, Durruti was struck by a bullet near the front and taken to the Ritz Hotel in downtown Madrid that had been set up as a clinic. He died the next day, and his body was returned to Barcelona for a massive funeral. Meanwhile, Franco, in frustration, poured more bombs and shells into the unyielding metropolis. Generals Franco, Mola and Varela, along with German advisers, met a few miles south of Madrid on 23 November 1936 to discuss the failure of the attack. Madrid had refused to crack. Now it was time to surround it and starve it into submission while making gains on other fronts.

On 29 November, west of Madrid, General Varela struck northward toward the Coruña highway. From there a swing to the east would cut the city off from the Guadarrama mountains and its water and electrical sources as well as the Republican militias holding back Mola's advance. Unsuccessful at first, renewed efforts, culminating on 3 January, reached the village of Las Rozas on the Coruña road where the offensive was stopped, failing to encircle Madrid. Both sides lost about 15,000 men. Republican ammunition was so low that front-line troops were issued some 20 rounds instead of the usual 300, and some were given blank cartridges to fire off to keep up morale along the line by hearing friendly fire.[9] The remainder of the 1,300-mile front remained quiet as neither side had the resources to launch more than one full-scale battle at a time.

BATTLE FOR MÁLAGA, 1937

With a population of about 100,000, Málaga, situated on the Mediterranean coast south of Córdoba, was a bustling commercial city. The front line at the beginning of 1937 ran from the coast about fifty miles southwest of Málaga north to Ronda and turned east through the mountains to Granada. The only road linking Málaga to the rest of Republican Spain ran east along the coast to Almería. The city was already partly destroyed by Nationalist bombs and by workers who ravaged the fashionable section in a frenzy of looting and killing. The inevitable Nationalist offensive began on 17 January 1937 under Queipo de Llano. A thrust eastward along the coast was followed by an attack south from Granada. Both met little resistance. Mussolini's recently arrived mechanized Italian Black Shirts assembled 10,000 men just north of the city prepared to continue the offensive.

The Republican commander at Málaga, Colonel Villalba, with about 12,000 troops, was short of rifles, ammunition and artillery.[10] On 3 February the all-out attack came both along the coast and down from the mountains, accompanied by naval bombardment from the sea. With morale low and dire shortages, the city fell as the Italian army penetrated the outskirts on 7 February.

Hundreds of people had been killed in Málaga[11] by left-wing organizations, churches burned and private houses pillaged. Nationalist retaliation was swift. Thousands of Republican sympathizers were rounded up and shot on the beaches with or without trial. On the long twisting coastal road to Almería the slaughter continued as masses of refugees fleeing the city were indiscriminately gunned down from the air or by pursuing Nationalist tanks.

JARAMA VALLEY, 1937

With the fall of Málaga the Nationalists began another offensive southeast of Madrid in the Jarama river valley. With artillery and air support, the attack commenced on 6 February 1937, embracing a ten-mile front beginning along the Madrid-Andalucía road directly south of the capital, the objective to cut the Madrid-Valencia highway further east. The attack came as a surprise to the defenders.

On 8 February, Miaja, commander at Madrid, sent the Eleventh Division under Enrique Lister, along with other hastily organized units, to General Pozas commanding the army of the center and the defense of the Jarama Valley. The following day Republican defenses were stiffened along the heights on the east side of the Jarama river, but two days later the Nationalists crossed and stormed the heights. In spite of hard and bloody fighting, they made little further progress. The front line stabilized on 16

February when the Nationalists were forced to take defensive positions. Russian planes generally controlled the air, and Russian tanks and artillery were deciding factors on the ground.

On 17 February the Republican army including International Brigades mounted a counterattack while the battle in the air between Russian, Italian and German fighter planes seesawed back and forth. The counterattack failed to dislodge the Nationalists, as did further costly assaults on 23 and 27 February. American volunteers of the 15th International Brigade saw their first action here. The bitterly contested battle with appalling losses on both sides settled down into a stalemate among rolling hills and olive trees and a monotonous existence in mud-filled trenches, wet clothes, cold stew and interminably hungry lice and rats.

GUADALAJARA OFFENSIVE, 1937

In March 1937, Nationalist commanders arranged for the Italians to attack Madrid from the northeast. Their immediate objective was to capture the town of Guadalajara thirty miles east of the capital. If the Jarama offensive could be sustained, the two armies could link up at Alcalá de Henares, about twenty miles east of Madrid, and nearly surround the capital. The 35,000 Italian troops under General Roatta were supported by the Fascist Black Shirts, 1,500 Moroccans, the Soria division under Moscardó and various Carlist units. Eighty tanks, 200 pieces of artillery and 2,000 trucks were made ready.[12]

After their success at Málaga, Mussolini and the Italian high command under General Roatta were more than anxious to again prove their value. The lines of the inexperienced Republican Twelfth Division holding the front were broken by the first assault on 8 March. By late morning the weather degenerated into fog and freezing rain. Italian support aircraft were grounded, and most Italian soldiers had only light summer uniforms. The attack ground to a halt. Owing to the bad weather and exhaustion, General Orgaz failed to launch the supporting Nationalist attack in the Jarama Valley.

On 9 March the Italians resumed their offensive in spite of the weather. The situation appeared critical for the Republican defenders. At dawn on 10 March, Brihuega, a little northwest of Guadalajara, fell to the Italians. General Miaja rushed in reinforcements. On 18 March, as the weather cleared, the Republicans counterattacked with aircraft, tanks, artillery fire and infantry.

The Italian forces broke and were soon in full retreat. The attempt to encircle Madrid was thwarted once again, and the Italians suffered heavily both in casualties and in military prestige. Apart from periodic bombardments, the Madrid front after the Italian fiasco at Guadalajara remained relatively dormant for many months.

ARAGÓN AND CATALUÑA

During the first days of the war, militia units in Cataluña formed into columns and went off to the Aragón front to stop the Nationalist advance in the east. Behind the front line the streets, factories, transportation and utilities of Barcelona and other towns in Cataluña were taken over by the revolutionary CNT, UGT, POUM and the Unified Socialist Party of Cataluña, or PSUC (*Partido Socialista Unificat de Catalunya*; a Communist-dominated party, an amalgamation of Catalan Socialist groups, established in July 1936).

The eastern front line in August 1936 ran from the Pyrenees southward a little east of Zaragoza to Teruel. While the battles raged in the southwest and around Madrid, the Aragón front remained comparatively tranquil, engaging in minor skirmishes and sniping from the trenches.

At dawn on 16 August 1936, Captain Alberto Bayo and his 8,000-man Catalan force, under the jurisdiction of the Generalitat, disembarked on the island of Mallorca to take it back from the insurgents. Moving inland they were soon counterattacked by Nationalist forces supported by Italian planes and a troop of Black Shirts led by a flamboyant Italian red-bearded Fascist who called himself Count Rossi. The military governor in Mallorca, whom General Goded had left behind when he left on his ill-fated trip to Barcelona, had been dismissed by Rossi when the Italians took over the island. Rossi drove around in his own red racing car, accompanied by the local mayor and an armed priest, proclaiming the "crusade" in all the island's towns. He told a gathering of society women that he required at least one woman a day.

With opposition mounting, the Catalans fled back to their ships, leaving the beach littered with their bodies and weapons. Their wounded, who had earlier been placed in a convent, were shot. The expedition came to an ignominious end, but the Barcelona radio hailed it as a great victory.[13]

Supporters of the Republic were shot in a bloodbath sanctioned by the archbishop of Mallorca. For some months the island was the personal fief of Count Rossi, and it remained an Italian stronghold throughout the war. The other islands of Ibiza and Formentera were abandoned, the former after atrocities in which the FAI shot 239 prisoners, and the Nationalists, upon their return, shot 400.[14]

MEN AND WEAPONS

Even though a good portion of the military remained loyal to the Republic, the Nationalists commanded just over twice as many soldiers as the loyalists including the experienced and formidable 35,000-strong army of Africa. The insurgents also began the war with their command structures intact. The Republic could count on about 27,000 troops, but most of their officers and NCOs had deserted to the other side or had been shot, leaving army units in disarray. The paramilitary police units—Civil Guards, Carabineros (Frontier Guards) and Assault Guards, numbering about 100,000—were divided fairly equally on both sides.

Forced to acquire arms wherever it could, the Republic was always plagued with a variety of rifles and machine guns of at least ten different calibers. Of the half-million or so rifles in the country, some 200,000 remained with the Republic, but about a third of these were lost during the Nationalist advances in the first two months of the war. Relatively modern artillery pieces numbered 1,007 at the outbreak of hostilities, but the government retained only 387; the remainder were located in insurgent territory.[15]

The Republic hung on to ten of the eighteen small Renault FT-17 tanks, but with a speed of five miles an hour and equipped only with a machine gun or a 37-millimeter light cannon and too small to cross trenches, it was not a very formidable weapon.

The Nationalists began the war with seventeen ships compared to the Republic's twenty-seven. But in Nationalist hands were the *Canarias* and the *Baleares*, both recently built modern cruisers that more than compensated for the Republic's superiority in numbers. The Nationalists also enjoyed assistance from the German and Italian navies that, when the opportunity arose, sank cargo ships destined for the Republic.

At the onset of war there were about 550 serviceable aircraft, both military and civil, in the country and another thirty in repair hangars, but all except a few Douglas DC 2s were obsolete. The government retained most of them, thanks to General Nuñez de Prado who, anticipating the insurrection, began to concentrate the planes at airfields around Madrid. However, pilots and air crews were in short supply.[16]

NOTES

1. Quote from Kurzman, 153.
2. Ibid., 147.
3. Beevor, 103.
4. See Barea, 580, for an eyewitness account.
5. Largo Caballero brought into his government two left-wing radicals, Angel Galarza (minister of the interior) and Alvarez del Vayo (minister of foreign affairs); four Anarchists, Juan Garcia Oliver (justice), Juan López Sánchez (commerce), Federica Montseny (health) and Juan Peiró (industry); two moderate Socialists, Juan Negrin (finance) and Indalecio Prieto (navy and air); and two Communists, Jesus Hernández (education) and Vicente Uribe (agriculture).
6. Jackson, 92.
7. Zuehlke, 72.
8. Jackson, 96.
9. Ibid., 99.
10. Thomas, 585.
11. Ibid., 586. The British consul in Málaga reported in 1944 (using official Nationalist statistics) that the "reds" from 18 July 1936 to 7 February 1937 executed or murdered 1,005 persons. During the first week of the liberation (8–14 February) 3,500 were executed by the Nationalists. From 15 February 1937 to 25 August 1944 a further 16,952 were legally sentenced to death and shot in Málaga. See also Beevor, 74.
12. Thomas, 596. See also Beevor, 156, for slightly different figures.
13. Thomas, 381 ff.
14. Ibid., 384.
15. Howson, 28.
16. Ibid., 30–31.

CHAPTER 4

POLITICS AND SOCIAL REVOLUTION

In the areas that held out against the uprising, long-repressed industrial workers and farmworkers suddenly found themselves unburdened by social and political restraints. Their hatred for the ruling classes no longer simply seethed within but broke out in orgies of violence, and all vestiges of hierarchy and privilege were targets of their wrath. Peasants and workers exacted a terrible vengeance on those whom they considered their oppressors—aristocrats, their families and agents, landowners, priests, captured military officers and police—anyone suspected of sympathy with the uprising was often summarily shot. Murder and mayhem stemming from envy and revenge were often rationalized by exclaiming adherence to noble revolutionary values and goals. Both the CNT and the UGT maintained lists of suspected Fascists or their sympathizers who were rounded up and executed if they could not immediately prove their innocence. The government in Madrid called for a halt to the killings, but no one paid attention. Azaña predicted that the slaughter would so outrage world opinion that the Republic would be alienated and lose the war.

Towns that had not fallen to the rebels came under the jurisdiction of whichever political party or trade union was dominant. If the town council had been left-wing (e.g., Socialist), little change occurred, but if it had been right-wing, the mayor and the Civil Guards would have generally fled or been shot, and deep-seated social changes often took place. In some places committees requisitioned the services of local doctors and pharmacists, and many peasants received medical care for the first time in their lives—and free of charge.[1] Churches were torched, icons desecrated; even the symbolic execution of the towering statue of Christ in the southern outskirts of Madrid by firing squad was not beyond the bounds of left-wing extremist hostility. If not destroyed, village churches were converted into marketplaces, barracks or hospitals if they were near the front lines. Town halls were plundered, legal records and documents destroyed and prisons thrown open.

Symbols of bourgeois dress disappeared from the streets including felt hats and ties, and in the major cities such as Barcelona and Madrid, women came out in trousers, something unheard of before. No one dared wear a suit, as they might be identified with the upper classes; wives draped their red petticoats from the balconies of their apartments to show solidarity with the workers. Movies were popular, but tennis, considered a bourgeois pastime, ceased to be played.[2]

Hotels and restaurants were taken over by their workers and made into collectives in which all had a stake. Tipping and any sort of dress code to dine were abolished. Private homes of the rich were confiscated and turned into schools, free medical clinics or orphanages. Leaflets on venereal disease and birth control were for the first time freely distributed, and some women clamored for the right to abortion.

Throughout the summer of 1936, about 70 percent of industry was collectivized by the workers in Barcelona and throughout Cataluña, including public utilities such as tramways, gas and water companies and the electricity grid. (In Madrid about 30 percent of industry was collectivized.) Similarly, packing houses, dairies and even large markets were placed under collective control that eliminated middle men and lowered prices of products. (Offsetting this, wages rose and productivity often declined.) Tenement houses were appropriated by the municipalities and rents lowered. Workers' committees scrutinized prices and wages. The CNT dominated the collective efforts, and the large industries were managed by committees of worker technicians. Former owners and managers who remained, if not shot, were invited to work under the committees as private employees.

The unions took over small clothing and food stores, beauty parlors, shoe-repair shops and many other types of outlets. Socialists, Communists and Anarchists competed wildly for the best business or building, putting up their banners to stake their claim. Luxury hotels and office buildings served as party or union headquarters. People's kangaroo courts (*chekas*) were established to try suspected enemies of the working class and whose grim work continued day and night, filling the morgues. All private cars were "requisitioned." Automobiles, bristling with guns, men leaning out the windows, raced through the streets, horns blaring and banners of their union affiliations streaming in the wind.

Patrols of the various factions walked the streets, demanding identity papers, and roadblocks were set up to search cars for Fascist occupants or arms. The government was impotent to enforce order. It competed with the labor unions for the enemy's wealth by confiscation of suspected Fascists' bank accounts, blowing open safety-deposit vaults and taking over the largest industries needed to produce war materials.

Vouchers issued by the trade unions became common, replacing money, but often workers helped themselves to what they needed, if necessary, at the point of a gun. Communists did their best to transfer seized property to the government to make it easier to take over when, as they hoped, they eventually seized power. They engaged in running gun battles with the Anarchists who insisted that the government control no property. All assets in their view belonged to the unions. Militiamen, mad with proletarian power, dressed in their blue *monos* (coveralls), thronged Madrid and Barcelona, often returning from the front for a day or two of recuperation, and with girlfriends and prostitutes crowded the once upper-class bars, cafés and restaurants in the fashionable sections of the city.

Periodically the unions sent men around to clean out the bars and send back to the front those militiamen who decided life in the city was better than a trench in the mountains. The hectic swirl of unrestrained life was frequently disrupted by the whine of a sniper's bullet, and the militiamen would rush off to find and eliminate the source. Fascist suspects were often dispatched without benefit of even a speedy trial or five minutes before a *cheka*. Truckloads of victims were lined up against a brick wall or taken to the cemetery and shot. Fascist women fared no better. Communists had a reputation for the worst atrocities, often torturing their prisoners for more information before shooting them. Clergymen and nuns were vulnerable to immediate execution except for those who were known to have sided with the poor against oppressive tenement owners or the police. For fear of their lives, clerics hid in the city as best they could, but if caught, the families sheltering them were also condemned. Hatred toward the Church increased as reports filtered in that priests in rebel zones condoned the killing of workers.

The Republican government sought to maintain the diplomatic immunity of the foreign embassies in Madrid where people threatened by the workers' revolt could find refuge. Militiamen then would hang a sign on a building designating an embassy such as that of Siam, although Spain had no diplomatic relations with that country. Before long, refugees crowded into the building seeking asylum and paying a high price for the privilege. Each day a truck came to supposedly take them to a waiting ship at the port of Alicante. It only got as far as the execution ground.[3]

ANARCHISM IN PRACTICE

While the Anarchists eschewed centralized government of any kind, in Barcelona, attempting to keep industry operating, buy necessary raw materials, purchase spare parts often from abroad and export their products forced them to cooperate with the Generalitat. In return the president, Lluis Companys, ratified the workers' committees and their social programs and provided the required foreign exchange. In August the Generalitat created the War Industries Commission, which gradually took over and ran the factories with the consent of the workers. By October 1936 it managed most of the industry. Collaboration with the Catalan government gradually brought the revolution in Barcelona to a standstill as the government reasserted its authority, aided by the rapidly growing PSUC whose prestige was greatly enhanced with the arrival of Soviet arms in October 1936. By early 1937 revolutionary fervor in the city had vanished.

Details of revolutionary activity varied from region to region. In port cities, dock facilities were managed by committees made up of CNT and UGT members. In the north, fishermen collectivized the docks, equipment and the canning factories. The fish catch was exchanged for supplies of grain and meat. Money, often considered a corrupting influence in some villages, was abolished or confiscated by the local committee, and if the latter, it was doled out to villagers for travel needs or specific purchases of "foreign" items. Local commerce in and among villages might be carried out by means of chits or barter. In some mining districts of Asturias, committees, having taken over commerce and abolished money for local purposes, paid workers in kind, calculated according to the size of the family.

The guiding principle, however, remained the same: social equality and local economic control. In many places property records were burned and rents abolished. Land was collectivized in villages of New Castilla, La Mancha and Aragón, while elsewhere the property of absentee landlords was simply distributed among the peasants. In only two instances did

Anarchists have an opportunity to put their social ideals into practice: during the Russian civil war of 1917–1921 when the peasant partisan movement in the Ukraine tried to implement Anarchist principles and in the Spanish civil war when anarchism was a significant force in certain regions. Some village committees used their power to prevent the sale of tobacco, alcohol and pornography[4] and to shoot so-called class enemies; elsewhere they were "reeducated" or warned to leave for safer places. The collectivist revolution reached its apex during the first three months of the war, a war that for many extreme Socialists, Anarchists and members of the POUM was only worth fighting if the social revolution was first successful.

In 1936 the inhabitants of the extremely poor village of Membrilla, south of Madrid and east of Ciudad Real, lived in miserable run-down huts. Some 8,000 people clustered around unpaved streets with no newspaper, no cinema, no café, no library, no school. On the other hand, it had many remains of burned churches. Immediately after the insurrection, the land was expropriated and village life collectivized. All goods passed to the community. Food, clothing and tools were distributed equitably to the whole population. Money was abolished, work shared. An elected council appointed committees to organize the life of the commune and its relations to the outside world. The necessities of life were distributed freely insofar as they were available, and a number of refugees were accommodated. A small library and school were established. The entire population lived as a large family: functionaries, delegates, the secretary of the syndicate, the members of the municipal council, all elected, acted as heads of the family. But special privilege or corruption was not tolerated.[5]

In the small town of Muniesa, north of Teruel in Aragón, the social structure was a little different. Bread, meat and oil were freely distributed to the inhabitants, but unlike most Libertarian villages, money remained in circulation. Every male worker received a peseta a day, women and girls received seventy-five céntimos (cents) and children under ten collected fifty céntimos. This was not a wage but distributed by the town council along with other goods for the family to purchase supplementary items.[6]

COUNCIL OF ARAGÓN

The development of Libertarian societies was not supported by the central government, by the Catalan government nor by the Communists. Only the CNT and the FAI favored the growth of Libertarian communes of which the CNT claimed there were 450.[7] A conference assembled by the Aragón collectives in late September 1936 at Bujaraloz, about thirty miles east of Zaragoza, established the Defense Council of Aragón. Composed of members of the CNT, the council was presided over by the Anarchist Joaquín Ascaso, a cousin of the well-known Anarcho-Syndicalist Francisco Ascaso, killed in Barcelona at the beginning of the war. Joaquín Ascaso, a dynamic, violent, seemingly unscrupulous man, went about escorted by twenty-four armed men.[8]

The council, an authority that the Communists called a "tyranny of gangsters,"[9] eventually fixed its residence at Caspe, on the Ebro River, and exercised authority over Aragón that became for practical purposes a quasi-independent Anarchist state. The Communists, moderate Socialists and Liberal supporters of the Republic were determined to break the back of the Council of Aragón. On 4 August 1937, Indalecio Prieto ordered Enrique Lister and his 11,000-man division to crush it. Lister's tanks rumbled through the streets of Caspe, and his artillery trained their sights on nearby villages.[10] Ascaso and the members of the council were detained along with 600 other Anarchists throughout the region. Food trucks passing from one collective to another were confiscated, while Communist propaganda portrayed Ascaso as a scoundrel and traitor. CNT offices were taken over and records confiscated. Only armed force by Communists and government troops restrained Anarchist militias on the Aragón front from deserting their posts to attack Communist units in the rear. The Council of Aragón was officially dissolved on 11 August 1937 by order of the government.

Communist hatred for the cadres of Anarchists (and in the Communist view) Trotskyite POUMists, heretics from the Moscow line of Communism, knew no limitations. They accused both the Anarchists and the POUM of aiding the Fascists, of spying for the enemy, slacking in battle, of slothfulness and gangsterism. The animosity between the factions often erupted in gun battles in the streets of Republican cities. Internal warfare was a common occurrence, but in Madrid, under direct siege, the leftist parties cooperated better than in most places.

LARGO CABALLERO, PRIME MINISTER

On 4 September 1936, Left Socialist leader Largo Caballero, a man of proletariat origins and noted for his trade union work and honesty, minister of labor in the first Republican government, became prime minister. Head of the UGT, he had the loyalty of the workers. Respected and trusted by Republican military officers, he also at first cooperated with the Communists.

Largo Caballero became a unifying force for the Popular Front for which the Communists were anxious to use him and his office of prime minister for their own ends. Caballero was, however, his own man and resented advice from Russian ambassador Marcel Rosenberg and other Communists who were determined to eliminate the POUM and certain Anarchist leaders. Largo Caballero also clashed with the Communists over their attitude toward the revolution. Since Communist political strategy revolved around courting the middle classes and the foreign democratic powers, they adhered to a policy of suppressing the revolution. Contrary to this view, Largo Caballero wanted to defend the revolutionary gains thus achieved and the political liberties of the people. He refused, for example, to suppress Anarchist and POUM newspapers, deplored by the Communists.

Largo Caballero's personal habits irritated some. He insisted on not being disturbed at night, he would sign papers only during certain hours and he showed an intense jealousy toward General Miaja and the able Indalecio Prieto. He did finally call for militia units to be integrated into the Republican army for better coordinated defense but did not move as fast on this as the Communists and military officers would have liked. He also clashed with the Communists over the commissariat headed by Julio Alvarez del Vayo. Collaborating with the Communists Alvarez del Vayo appointed scores of commissars without the prime minister's knowledge. On 17 April 1937 Caballero published a decree in an attempt to wipe out this source of Communist power, stating that henceforth all nominations for commissars would be made by him and that all current commissars must have their appointments validated by 15 May 1937. An acrimonious debate ensued. The Socialist newspaper *Forward* (*Adelante*), partial to the prime minister, accused the commissars of exerting political pressure on the army, of favoritism and of assassinations. The Communist paper *Red Front* (*Frente Rojo*) labeled the decree the work of Fascist elements and demanded that the commissars not back down. Another paper, *The Socialist* (*El Socialista*), partial to Prieto, printed names of Socialist party members who had undergone torture in secret Communist prisons in Murcia.

As if the Republic did not have enough trouble, the government tried to regain control of the frontier stations along the French border in Cataluña that had been taken over by the Anarchists on the first day of the civil war. On 17 April 1937 Republican police, acting on orders of Finance Minister Juan Negrín, began to reoccupy the border posts. Carabineros seized the border station at Puigcerdá on the French frontier. A firefight broke out, and eight Anarchists were killed. Then a prominent UGT official was murdered in Barcelona, it was thought, by CNT gunmen, and his funeral brought on huge demonstrations against the Anarchists. This was not the end of trouble for the government. Plans to militarize the militias in Cataluña elicited howls of protest from the Anarchists and from members of the POUM. For them this was repression of both workers and the revolution. The Generalitat canceled the May Day celebrations for fear of open gunfights in the streets.

These self-destructive deadly rivalries, of course, diluted the military effectiveness of the Republic, undermined its credibility abroad and played into the hands of the Nationalists.

BARCELONA, MAY 1937

At the beginning of the war, the Anarchists had taken over public services in Barcelona, and in May 1937 they still controlled the telephone exchange owned by the American International Telegraph and Telephone Company. From the main building they could intercept and listen to government communications from Valencia and Madrid and calls in and out of Barcelona. In the afternoon of 3 May the Communist chief of police, Rodríguez Salas, sent three truckloads of Civil Guards to seize the telephone exchange. When the police entered the ground floor, they found themselves looking down the barrel of a machine gun. Warning shots were fired from the windows of the building. A standoff resulted. The news spread across the city. The Anarchist Libertarian Youth Movement, the Friends of Durruti (a small militant breakaway Anarchist group) and the POUM youth were eager for a fight. Arms were brought out of hiding, and the city took on a warlike atmosphere.

POUMists and Anarchists assembled at Barbastro, east of Barcelona, and prepared to march on the city in support of their colleagues and to defend against the counterrevolution. Largo Caballero, his Anarchist ministers, Lluis Companys and the Anarchist newspaper *Worker Solidarity* (*Solidaridad Obrera*) all called for calm. The revolutionaries, however, demanded the dismissal of Communist PSUC councilors, while POUM and CNT officials ordered their followers to defend themselves. The Friends of Durruti and Libertarian Youth were in favor of armed resistance to keep the revolution alive. The CNT saw itself under attack by Civil Guards and the PSUC. Armed Anarchists began to appear on the streets, barricades went up and fighting broke out as buildings were occupied and defended. CNT-FAI and POUM forces held parts of the city, and the police and PSUC controlled other sections.[11] Savage street fighting occurred as machine guns and snipers blazed away from their respective buildings, roof tops, sand-bagged balconies and barricades and threw hand grenades and sticks of dynamite at each other's positions. The opposing sides were thus:

POUM	Armed forces of the Generalitat
CNT-FAI	PSUC
Libertarian Youth (FIJL)	UGT
Friends of Durruti	PCE
Militants of Estat Catalá (Catalan state), a separatist group	

By 5 May the situation had eased, but assassinations of prominent Anarchists and Communists kept up the tension. Companys managed a truce promising to retire the PSUC councilors from the regional government, while the matter of who would control the telephone exchange was left for later discussion. The same night a UGT official, about to become a member of the cabinet, was murdered. In Valencia the Republican government now had had enough of the Catalan Left and the following day sent several thousand Assault Guards to Barcelona while the Republican navy put on a show of force in the harbor.

Prime Minister Largo Caballero appointed General Sebastián Pozas, who had recently joined the Communist Party, to command the army on the Aragón front where military discipline was imposed on the Anarchist columns. During the following several days a dozen or so anti-Communist leftists were assassinated as the Communists stepped up their campaign to stamp out anti-Stalinist leaders.

A few days later the Generalitat under Communist urgings gave CNT-FAI and POUM members in Barcelona forty-eight hours to surrender their weapons. The POUM had already received warnings that Moscow had ordered its elimination, while the CNT feared the next move would be to deprive them of the factories they had taken over.

The Anarchists controlled much of the city but agreed on 6 May to dismantle the barricades and return to work if the Assault Guards were withdrawn. The Generalitat accepted the terms, and normalcy returned. But the agreement was not honored, and the Assault Guards remained in the city, arresting CNT members. The central government now exerted and tightened control over all the Republican zone, and the Generalitat lost its semiautonomous status. The Catalan security forces became the responsibility of the central government in Valencia.

Largo Caballero had shown himself indecisive over the bloody events in Barcelona and had ignored Communist demands to suppress *Battle* (*Batalla*), the POUM newspaper, for inciting rebellion. He had resisted Communist demands for the dissolution of the POUM itself. For these reasons and the fact that he had threatened the system of commissars, the Communists mounted a verbal attack on him, and in an angry session, the Communist ministers quit his cabinet.

Already much of the moderate wing of the Socialists under Prieto had amalgamated with the Left Socialists and with the Communists. All were prepared to dispense with the revolution for the sake of winning the war and believed that they were now strong enough to oust Largo Caballero. On 17 May 1937, bereft of enough backing to form a new government, he was forced to step down from both his posts as minister of war and prime minister.

Dr. Juan Negrín became the new prime minister. Energetic and friendly, he was on good terms with everyone. But as the Nationalist zone grew stronger and more unified, the Republican zone continued to be racked with dissension. Negrín allowed the Communists nearly complete control since they alone could squeeze badly needed arms and supplies out of the Kremlin.

The Service of Military Investigation, or SIM (*Servicio de Investigación Militar*), was organized at the instigation of Soviet advisers, especially Alexander Orlov, in the summer of 1937 with the aim of counteracting Nationalist espionage activities. From the moment of inception, it served as the executive arm of the Russian secret police, the People's Commissariat of Internal Affairs, or the NKVD (*Narodnyi Komissariat Vnutrennykh*). They kept the Communist Party pure by eliminating doubters, waged war on the POUM and Anarchists and constructed private prisons for suspected enemies of Stalin.[12] Its jails filled with presumed adversaries, many of whom were not seen again. Feared SIM agents infiltrated all branches of the military and government.

One of SIM's victims was Andreu Nin. In June 1937 Nin was arrested along with other POUM leaders during the repression in Barcelona. Some six weeks later he was removed from the government prison to a secret Communist jail outside Alcalá de Henares near Madrid and was never heard from again. The Communists claimed he was a Fascist agent and had escaped to Berlin through the Nationalist zone, but everyone knew he had been murdered. Furious, Negrín had to choose between further Russian aid, the only hope for the Republic, and denouncing the atrocity. He chose the aid.

THE NATIONALIST ZONE

From 18 July 1936, the beginning of the uprising, reactionary policies in the Nationalist zones were put into place. The traditional class hierarchy and existing social and economic values were maintained and reinforced. Official reprisals carried out by the military and police spread terror. Falange and Carlist units employed their brand of fear throughout the cities and villages by executing suspect Republican loyalists and leftists not already in the clutches of the military. The celebration on 15 August in Pamplona in honor of the Sacred Virgin (*Vírgen del Sagrado*) was accompanied by mass executions, a kind of holy cleansing.

Martial law was proclaimed from the start, giving the military commander in each region under Nationalist control full authority over civilian as well as military matters. Civilian disobedience resulted in court-martial. Strikes were outlawed; land seizures and land reform programs set out under the Republic were nullified. Wages and prices were frozen and business hours regulated. UGT and CNT members were rounded up, imprisoned and subject to the death penalty for, by some perverse logic, rebellion. Priests, landowners and the wealthy were once again in control and treated with respect.

The Nationalist equivalent to the Republican *chekas* and the SIM were local village or town purge committees made up of prominent right-wing sympathizers. In Old Castilla the village purge committees generally consisted of a priest, a Civil Guard officer and a landowner or member of the

Falange. Known or suspected left-wing supporters, Freemasons and liberals were arraigned before them and sentenced. Condemnation by the three carried the death penalty. Voting registers were used when available to help ascertain guilt. Batches of the condemned, hands tied behind their backs, were led off to the cemetery wall or an open trench in the countryside and dispatched by firing squad. Many victims never saw the committee but were executed out of hand at night in front of the headlamps of a car, their bodies left in the open with their union cards, if they had them, pinned to their chests.[13] In towns where the Popular Front aldermen had arrested Fascist sympathizers, the entire town council was shot when the town was taken.

Since the prisons were full of men and women waiting for a hearing, overcrowding was relieved by Falange and Civil Guards who emptied parts of them every day by loading batches of prisoners onto trucks, driving them out into the country and summarily shooting them, the bodies left on the roads as an example to anyone who disagreed with Nationalist policies. General Mola had once ordered the authorities of Valladolid to choose less public places for executions and bury the dead more rapidly.[14]

For those people sympathetic to the Republic caught in the Nationalist zone, fear of the white terror (Nationalist repression) was pervasive. All forms of political or social dissent were eliminated, and intensive propaganda on the radio, in newspapers, circulars and posters daily exhorted conformity to the regime. They also reported the latest executions.

Republicans of all persuasions joined the Nationalist cause in large numbers out of fear for their lives or that of their families and of losing their jobs and subsequent starvation in an unforgiving society. Not unlike the right-wing bourgeoisie who, imitating the workers, wore the blue coveralls (mono azul) in the Republican zone, in the Nationalist zone everyone put on the blue shirt of the Falange, which General Queipo de Llano sarcastically referred to as their lifejackets.[15]

People living in the the Nationalist zone were better off than those in the Republican areas inasmuch as the civilian population was not subject to daily aerial and artillery bombardment. They were better supplied with food, controlling much of the agricultural regions of the country and by importing supplies bought on credit from Germany, Italy and other foreign countries. Prices were fixed, and the production of wheat, meat, olive oil, sugar beets and a host of other items were placed under government supervision. The tightly controlled, monolithic war economy allowed the Nationalists to concentrate more on the war effort than was possible among the fractious Republicans whose densely concentrated populations in big cities and towns were deprived of nearly everything throughout the course of the conflict.

FRANCO AND THE FALANGE

The leader of the Falange, Primo de Rivera, arrested in March 1936 by the Republican government, was tried in Alicante on 13 November and executed seven days later for, among other things, having offered Falange troops to General Mola in aid of the uprising. The local civil governor who had sanctioned and carried out the act of execution did so before the Madrid government could review the circumstances, as was the law in such cases. Other prominent Falange leaders caught in the Republican zones at the outbreak of hostilities were also executed.

For Franco, the rapidly growing Falange, with its mostly youthful followers, was useful yet dangerous. It was anti-Marxist, against regional aspirations of autonomy and called for a united, militant, centralized Catholic state. These views were close to those of Franco. Conversely, the Falange had leftist appeal calling for agrarian reform and more participation of the workers in the benefits of capitalism. Many Falangists were not disposed to be governed by a military dictatorship and prone to criticize the shortcomings of the Nationalist war effort after the failure to take Madrid.

The Falange had some well-known leaders such as the poet and propagandist Dionisio Ridruejo and its would-be chief, the Santander mechanic, Manuel Hedilla, who had been in La Coruña on the northwest coast when the rebellion broke out. Hedilla and the local well-armed Falangist units helped take the town, but disillusioned with Nationalist reprisals, he became a vocal critic of the killings. On Christmas Eve 1936 he told the Falange not to persecute the poor simply for having voted for the Left out of hunger and despair. He also expressed the view that work should be the only nobility and that the bosses of industry and banking and of town and country should disappear.[16] Such statements did not resonate well in right-wing circles. On 18 April 1937 the National Council of the Falange met and voted Hedilla their leader, who then dismissed his rival Agustín Aznar, chief of the party militia.

Franco congratulated Hedilla, and the two appeared together on a balcony in Salamanca where Franco gave a speech. The wily general had a surprise in store for the new head of the Falange, however. On 19 April Franco dealt with the organization that often conflicted with his own authority by fusing the various Catholic and Monarchist parties with the Falange and the JONS into a single political party under his full control. The Carlist leader, Fal Conde, had little say in the matter. The previous December he had tried to establish an independent academy for Carlist officer cadets without Franco's permission and had been given forty-eight hours to leave the country or face a court-martial for treason. He had since resided in Portugal. The count of Rodezno proved more pliable and agreed with the merger. The new party was called the Traditionalist Spanish Falange and the National Syndicalist Offensive Juntas. The new uniform was the Falangist blue shirt and the Carlist red beret.

Personal struggles within the Falange erupted in street fighting between factions favoring Hedilla, who still thought he had a leadership role to play, and those in support of Agustín Aznar. Franco used the disorders to court-martial Hedilla and sentence him to death. The sentence was commuted, but Hedilla spent from 1937 to 1941 in solitary confinement. Franco, meantime as chief of the new party, appointed his brother-in-law Serrano Súñer, a pro-Nazi lawyer, executive head.

THE CHURCH

The Catholic Church had a dilemma. The Vatican was uncertain who would win the war and was cautious at first about committing itself to Franco publicly. Not a few Nationalist officers had been outspokenly anticlerical, but Basque Republicans, staunchly Catholic, opposed the military uprising. On the other hand, priests and nuns were protected in the Nationalist zones and suffered insults, persecution and murder in Republican areas.

The position of the Church, however, was clear and could hardly have been otherwise. Franco began to speak more and more of Spain's Catholic tradition, and his headquarters in Salamanca was set up in the palace of the archbishop. On 1 July 1937, the Spanish bishops issued a collective letter supporting the Nationalist cause. The Vatican sent a nuncio to Salamanca in October of that year that underscored its readiness to accept the Nationalists as the new rulers of Spain. The pope later praised Franco for bringing honor, prosperity, order and tranquillity to the country. In return for its service to the Nationalists, the Church reaped great benefits. It was represented on civil committees where few dared disagree with the priest, and every employee was required to have a certificate of moral cleanliness from his local clergyman. Failure to attend Mass or Confession could bring a denunciation from the priest resulting in arrest for treason. A Church poster ordered no immoral dances, indecent frocks or bare legs. Girls who ignored the instructions were sheared of their hair on the street by Falange. Abortion incurred a severe penalty, and orphans of Republicans were forcibly baptized and renamed.[17]

NATIONALIST FINANCING AND MORAL SUPPORT

The gold of private citizens, even their rings, was demanded by the Nationalist government for the war effort, but the bulk of contributions came from elsewhere. The multimillionaire Juan March, who backed the Falange, contributed $15 million to the rightist cause. The exiled ex-king Alfonso XIII also contributed some $85 million to the rebel treasury.[18] Further contributions came from the wealthy upper classes, the British business community in Spain and German businessmen mostly in Morocco. The Dutch oil magnate Deterding gave to the cause, and the president of the Texas Oil Company, a Fascist admirer, diverted five tankers on route to Spain to Nationalist ports when the news of the rebellion was known. Support also came from landowners, civil servants, judges and even landowning peasants opposed to collectivization or land reform. The Catholic middle class of Castilla and Navarra, the same people who had before the war supported CEDA, favored the Nationalists along with the conservative Republicans of Alejandro Lerroux and those who had supported the Alfonso XIII monarchy or the Carlists. Lerroux and Gil Robles offered their support to Franco, but both were distrusted by the Right. Residing in Lisbon, they exercised no significant influence over the course of events.

NOTES

1. Jackson, 70.
2. Kurzman, 128.
3. Ibid., 141.
4. Jackson, 72.

5. For an Anarchist account of events in Membrilla and other villages, see Bolloten, *Spanish Civil War*, 70 ff.

6. Ibid., 72.

7. Thomas, 430.

8. Ibid., 723.

9. Preston, *Spanish Civil War*, 129.

10. Esenwein and Shubert, 236–237.

11. For an eyewitness account, see Orwell, 150 ff.

12. See Bolloten, *Spanish Civil War*, 600 ff.

13. Beevor, 75.

14. Jackson, 81.

15. Esenwein and Shubert, 181.

16. Beevor, 181.

17. Ibid., 262.

18. Ibid., 114.

CHAPTER 5

FOREIGN REACTION

The civil war in Spain caught European governments by surprise as both sides in the conflict immediately sought military support outside the country. The Republican government turned first to France.

FRANCE AND ENGLAND

On 20 July 1936 Prime Minister Giral telegraphed Léon Blum, Socialist prime minister of France, informing him that the Spanish government had been taken unawares by a dangerous military coup, and begged assistance of arms and aircraft.[1] Blum and some of his ministers recognized the urgency of the request, for if the military prevailed in Spain, France would be nearly surrounded by Fascist states. The French cabinet was split, however, with the foreign minister, Yvon Delbos, hostile to the Spanish Republic. The French right-wing press ranted about the threat to French investments in Spain by leftist revolutionaries. Blum traveled to London on 23 July to consult the British government under Stanley Baldwin, only to learn that it was against sending aid to Spain, and Anthony Eden, secretary of state for foreign affairs and admirer of the Fascist Calvo Sotelo, warned Blum to be prudent. Along with France, British investments in Spain were considerable—mining, steel, shipping, electricity, sherry production and citrus fruit, among others— which the conservative government felt would be best protected by a Nationalist victory. Prime Minister Baldwin's government hoped for a speedy insurgent takeover. Openly supportive, the English ambassador to Spain, Henry Chilton, also wished the Nationalists quick success. Aid from France sent to help the Republic might also provoke Germany, sympathetic to the rebels, and engender a widening of hostilities and even a general European war.

Military assistance to Franco from Germany and Italy alarmed the French, and on 2 August, Blum proposed that the major European countries establish a Non-Intervention Committee (NIC) to prevent all military aid to either side in the conflict. On 6 August some French planes, already promised, were secretly sent to Spain, paid for by Spanish gold, but on 8 August the French closed the Pyrenean frontier to set the example for nonintervention and confine the conflict to Spain and to Spaniards. With no outside aid to either side, Blum thought the Republic had a good chance to defeat the Nationalists.

Meanwhile, Republican agents scouted the European markets for aircraft and arms. The Nationalists were also busy purchasing whatever war material they found in other countries but abandoned their attempts to buy aircraft abroad after 15 August 1936, knowing that their needs would be filled by Germany and Italy on credit. The British banned all war material shipments to Spain on 19 August.[2]

The Republic acquired planes from financially strapped private airlines that needed the ready cash to stay solvent. Sometimes the buyers were cheated when good engines were replaced by older, worn-out ones after the purchase. Swarms of gunrunners, swindlers and con men crowded the Republican embassy in Paris to sell their wares or try to defraud the government of its money. Few people in the Spanish government had any experience with arms purchasing, and as country after country closed it doors to the Republic, smuggling—there were even fewer people with any knowledge of this—was, at first, the only source of arms.

The Republican embassies that might have performed such tasks were either deserted or staffed with insurgents. Those in London and Washington were operated with personnel who swore allegiance to the Republic but secretly sided with the Nationalists and deceived and obstructed the business of the Republican government. In spite of the difficulties, some war material got through. Small items, such as grenades or pistols, might make it across the French land frontier, but a few ships, secretly loaded in places such as Marseilles with rifles, mortars, machine guns, artillery and ammunition, were off-loaded in Republican ports.

Right-wing refugees found shelter aboard British ships in northern ports and were allowed sanctuary in Gibraltar where the rebels were permitted to use the telephone exchange for calls to Germany and Italy. The

British government also desired to improve relations with Germany, Italy and Portugal and not offend their sensibilities by signs of support for the Republic. The municipal government of the international city of Tanger refused any and all facilities to Republican ships but allowed the Nationalists open use of the port.

NON-INTERVENTION COMMITTEE (NIC)

On 9 September, twenty-seven members, one from each of the countries that were party to the the NIC, met for the first time in London.[3] After a second meeting the daily work was relegated to a committee of nine members: Great Britain, France, Portugal, Italy, Germany, the Soviet Union, Belgium, Czechoslovakia and Sweden.

The duty of the NIC was to devise ways to prevent foreign intervention and investigate alleged cases of arms smuggling to Spain. It was understood that to relax tensions in Europe accommodation would have to be made with Germany and Italy, who, it was well known, were shipping material and personnel to the Nationalists in spite of their signatures on the Non-Intervention Agreement. To confront the two nations with blatant violations, however, would lead to disputes and disrupt the unity the committee hoped to achieve. On the other hand, if the committee did not do its work fairly and investigate violations, it could not hope to prevent them. The problem was solved by devising rules of evidence that prohibited anyone—reporters, the Red Cross, individuals or any government other than a member of the committee—from submitting evidence of violations. The Republic, of course, was not a member of the NIC and had no channels through which to complain.

When Alvarez del Vayo, the Republican foreign minister, presented unequivocal photographic evidence of German and Italian intervention in the war to the British embassy in Madrid, the documents were passed on to the committee, which then rejected the evidence since it came from a source not party to the agreement and amounted to discrimination against the Nationalists.[4] Acceptance of the reports by the committee would have been tantamount to labeling the governments of Italy and Germany as liars, which no one was prepared to do. Alvarez del Vayo then presented his evidence to the League of Nations, where it was rejected and forgotten. The matter earned the Republic the hostility of the chairman of the NIC, Lord Plymouth, who thereafter employed procedural protocol to favor the

Fascist states and protect them from accusations. Discussions were dominated by the Italian ambassador, Count Dino Grandi, who denied all charges of Fascist military intervention while accusing the Soviet Union of violating nonintervention principles.

As evidence for German and Italian interference in the war became too compelling to ignore any longer, the committee finally took it up, gently rebuking Germany; but the German delegate, Prince Bismarck, explained that planes had gone to Spain to rescue German citizens and they were armed because they were in a war zone and might be attacked. Reports of German fighter aircraft in the skies over Spain, he said, were untrue. Lord Plymouth then declared that all reports were unsubstantiated. After this, all documents on the subject were brushed aside as inaccurate or fabricated. With no authority to impose sanctions on offending nations, the committee needed some kind of international system to impose control. Thus the situation stood in the early weeks of the war.

GERMANY AND ITALY

With Germany in mind, France and the Soviet Union had signed a mutual aid pact in 1935 if one or the other were attacked by a third country. Hitler realized that should he attack Russia after a Nationalist victory in Spain, France, surrounded by Fascist states (Germany, Italy and Spain), would be much less inclined to assist the Soviets. Hitler did not want a European war until Germany had sufficiently rearmed after its defeat in World War I. Nevertheless, judging correctly the timidity of France and England, and after negotiations with representatives sent to Berlin by General Franco, he agreed on 26 July to send military aid to the Nationalists. The Nazi leader also found a convenient distraction in Spain to focus the attention of European countries while Germany continued its arms buildup. Combat experience in Spain, in what the Nazis thought would be a short war, would offer invaluable knowledge for German pilots, navigators, gunners and communication units and would test the reliability of their equipment under battle conditions.

The first German aid arrived during the last few days of July and consisted of twenty Junkers 52s and a half dozen Heinkel 51 fighter-bombers. Together with Italian transport planes, they began the airlift of Franco's troops from Morocco to Sevilla and Cádiz. Ships flying South American flags to disguise their origins sailed from Hamburg for Cádiz or

Lisbon every few days loaded with fighter planes, bombers, pilots, mechanics, gun crews, antiaircraft guns, rifles, machine guns, flame throwers, antitank guns, ammunition, military radios and telephones with the appropriate personnel.

German aid to the Nationalists was conducted through two trading companies referred to as HISMA/ROWAK (*Hispano-Maroquí de Transportes/Rohstoff-und-Waren-Einkaufgesellschaft*). The companies supplied Germany with agricultural products but, more important, with copper from the Rio Tinto mines in southern Spain and iron ore from Moroccan mines in exchange for arms. On 24 August 1936, Germany disingenuously agreed to the Non-Intervention Pact.

On 4 November Germany sent an expeditionary force to Spain with the code name Condor Legion consisting of 100 aircraft, antiaircraft batteries, field artillery, tanks and technical personnel and medical units. On 18 November 1936, Germany and Italy recognized Franco's regime as the only legitimate government of Spain. The following day Franco permitted the establishment of MONTANA, the consolidation of five mining companies in Spain in which Germany held 75 percent ownership in the three largest. More than immediate payment for war materials, however, the Germans were concerned with postwar advantages with future military needs in mind such as U-boat bases on the Atlantic coasts.

German military aid went only to Franco so as to preclude dissension among the Nationalist generals. The variety and amount of material soon included the Panzer Mark I tank and the famous German 88-millimeter gun. On 5 January 1937 Franco accepted a ten-man staff of German and Italian advisers and then agreed to the creation of a German-Italian general staff in return for more arms deliveries.[5]

Not to be outdone, on 6 September 1936, Mussolini, who had also signed the Non-Intervention Pact, established air bases on Mallorca from which he intended to bomb Republican cities. The island became virtually an Italian colony. In October he sent twenty tanks to participate in the attack on Madrid. The Italian dictator supplied destroyers and submarines, and the Italian navy was ordered to assist Nationalist warships in sinking Republican ships.

Mussolini saw in the outbreak of hostilities in Spain a glorious chapter for the Italian army. Still glowing from his victory over the spear-throwing warriors of Ethiopia and conquest of that militarily backward country, he was anxious to commit Italian troops to another war for the greater honor of Italy in its imperial ambitions. He insisted that Italian troops be given a battle front of their own where they could demonstrate their valor and not be simply integrated into Spanish units.

A Hispano-Italian trading company with the initials SAFNI was organized in 1936 to supply the Nationalists with war material in exchange for Spanish olive oil, woolens and pyrites. (The Italian government never collected the value of the arms sent to Spain in spite of the fact that it threatened at times to stop shipments. The large debts to both Germany and Italy were automatically canceled when the Axis Powers lost World War II.)

Mussolini approved of another Fascist state on the Mediterranean and saw in Nationalist Spain a nation indebted to him and offering assistance in limiting the activities of the British navy there—one of his main preoccupations. A Nationalist victory and Spanish control of Gibraltar could effectively close the inland sea to British shipping.

When Franco failed to take Madrid and end the war in a few weeks as expected, Mussolini increased his commitment. On 26 November the Italians at a secret meeting with Franco in Burgos pledged stepped-up aid. Throughout the winter, as the city held out, Mussolini sent more tanks, aircraft (Savoia bombers and Fiat fighters), artillery and troops. By the end of the war he had sent to Franco over 600 military aircraft, 57 training airplanes, nearly 2,000 artillery pieces, about 150 light tanks and 72,827 troops.[6]

PORTUGAL

In the grip of the dictator, Dr. Antonio Salazar, Portugal supported the military uprising from the beginning, fearful that left-wing, Popular Front politics would spill over the border. Besides sheltering right-wing fugitives such as General Sanjurjo, Salazar gave notice on 1 August 1936 that he intended to aid the rebels with all available means including the Portuguese army, if necessary, well aware that a Republican triumph could spell his own demise. It might have been only a matter of time before the Portuguese opposition, with encouragement and material aid from Spanish leftists, toppled his police state.

On 13 August Salazar accepted in principle the idea of nonintervention. Relations with the Republican government were severed, but Portuguese roads and telephones were available to the Nationalists, allowing links between General Mola in the north and Franco in the south. Franco's older brother Nicolás was allowed to establish his headquarters in Lisbon for the purchase of foreign arms.

German supplies and armaments were off-loaded in Lisbon and shipped overland to the rebels when the Spanish ports, patrolled by the Republican navy, were too dangerous. Portuguese military intelligence and border guards worked with the Nationalists, sending back to Spain Republican refugees for execution. On 17 September Salazar announced the formation of a Portuguese legion, 20,000 strong, to fight in Spain.

THE SOVIET UNION

On 25 July, José Giral sent a message to the Russian ambassador in France (Spain at the time had no diplomatic relations with Russia) appealing for modern armaments and munitions in significant quantities from the Soviet Union to aid the struggle against the military uprising. But Stalin was cautious about sending military equipment to Spain. On 24 August, Russia signed the Non-Intervention Pact. In spite of this the Russian ambassador, Marcel Rosenberg, arrived in Madrid on 27 August 1936, along with General Jan Berzin, who came in charge of military advisers, and aided by General Vladímir Gorev, the military attaché. The major Russian diplomatic consular appointment in Barcelona was the veteran Bolshevik Antonov-Ovseenko. The writer Ilya Ehrenburg came as well as the journalist Mikhail Koltsov, the latter ostensibly as a correspondent for the Russian newspaper *Pravda*. He was one of Stalin's top agents who spied on other Communists for the Russian dictator. Arthur Stashevsky, Soviet trade envoy, who remained in Barcelona, came to advise on the economy. In September 1936, Alexander Orlov, a NKVD officer, came to take charge of the secret police that became the most feared of all organizations in Spain.

The Comintern (whose agent, the Argentinian Vittorio Codovilla, was already in place as adviser to the PCE) sent many of its people, such as the French Communist André Marty, to organize the international volunteers for the Republic and Palmiro Togliatti, the Italian Communist leader in exile, who became chief adviser to the PCE. The Hungarian Erno Gerö supervised the PSUC in Cataluña.[7]

The prestige of the Soviet Union demanded that some kind of substantial aid be sent. Food, money and clothes were collected throughout the Soviet Union and sent to Republican Spain, but on 29 September 1936 Stalin and the Politburo decided to render assistance to the Republic on a grander scale. Russian involvement in the civil war also took the spotlight off the brutal official murders of Trotskyists, Anarchists and other dissidents in Russia in what has been called the Great Terror and the forced collectivization programs that began in 1929 and cost the lives of many hundreds of thousands of peasants. The decision to send extensive aid to the Republic, nevertheless, seems to have been taken once Stalin learned that the Spanish government was willing to transfer Spain's gold reserve to the Soviet Union, and the full costs of military aid would be covered.[8]

Spain had the fourth largest gold reserve in the world, obtained during the lucrative trade years of World War I and valued at about $800 million. On 13 September most of it was shipped secretly from Madrid to Cartagena, where 10,000 cases of gold were deposited in the naval arsenal. From there, shipped by freighters, the gold arrived in Odessa on the Black Sea on 25 October 1936 and was taken by armored train to Moscow, where it was to be stored for safekeeping. The agreement allowed the Spanish government to reexport the gold whenever it wished. Orlov later recounted that upon its arrival in Moscow Stalin said the Spaniards would never see their gold again.

Meanwhile, the first Russian ship to sail via the Black Sea and the Mediterranean, with arms for the Republic, arrived at Cartagena on 4 October 1936. It carried antiquated guns of various national origins not traceable to the Soviet Union. Soviet ships transporting arms carried false papers and displayed foreign flags and near their destinations sailed at night with no lights to evade German, Italian or Nationalist interception. Barcelona, controlled by Anarchists, was excluded as a port of debarkation since Stalin forbade any arms to Anarchist militias.

The Russians charged the Republic $80,000 (1936 value) for transporting the gold, $70,000 for packing and storage and $174,000 a year for guarding it in the Russian treasury. The remainder was quickly depleted to pay for Soviet arms.

With little gold to back it, the Spanish peseta fell to half its value, costing the Republic twice as much for the arms and supplies it bought from the Soviets. The Russians charged the Republic for everything including the transportation and maintenance of the Soviet advisers in Spain and manipulated exchange rates and the cost of the weapons to ensure all the gold was spent.[9] The obsolete and sometimes worthless weapons of

World War I vintage or older and of various calibers sent to Spain in 1936 and charged for by inflated prices by the Russians clearly defrauded the Republic.[10] In addition the artillery often came with few or no shells. Some new weapons the Russians were anxious to try out under combat conditions were also sent.

For the Spanish people who knew nothing about the deceit, robbery and betrayal of the Soviets, the appearance of Russian aircraft and tanks, just as Madrid was about to be taken, gave an enormous morale boost to the besieged. Stalin decided that to send regular troops to Spain would be too blatant a move, and only tank crews, pilots, technicians, advisers and a few regular army officers were sent. To keep the war going, however, he encouraged foreign Communists living in Russia and those in other countries to go and fight in international brigades organized by the Comintern.

A very limited number of weapons came from other eastern European sources: Czechoslovakia was the largest arms exporter in the world but had signed the Non-Intervention Pact. Due to numerous intrigues and shady deals, the Republic had great difficulty procuring a small amount of arms from this source.[11] Some arms were from Poland, but much of the equipment was so antiquated as to be nearly useless, much never arrived although paid for and much was overpriced, reflecting the desperation of the Republic and its willingness to buy nearly anything. The NKVD officer Alexander Orlov would see that the arms and munitions sent from the Soviet Union were distributed according to the Kremlin's wishes. Because the aid sold to the Republic by the Soviets was nearly their only source of assistance, it was difficult for the Republican government not to allow Russian influence in its internal affairs.

Russian supplies and personnel were used to force the Republican government to adhere to Soviet policy. Russian officials sabotaged other arms deals the Republic tried to arrange, and only Communist formations such as the Fifth Regiment received air and tank support, new weapons, ammunition and often medical treatment. Military commanders were sometimes forced to become Communist Party members so as to enable their men to fight.[12]

COMMUNIST PARTY INFLUENCE

Insignificant before the war, the Communist Party grew in prestige and influence as the conflict progressed. Its central committee headquarters in Madrid took its orders from Moscow, while subordinate committees were established on the provincial and municipal levels. In a speech in 1933 Dolores Ibárruri declared, "We are advancing along the road which has been indicated to us by the Communist International, and which leads to the establishment of a Soviet government in Spain, a government of workers and peasants." Just after the outbreak of the war, in an about-face, and in accordance with Kremlin policy, she announced in the name of the Central Committee and in support of the Republic, "We Communists are defending a régime of liberty and democracy, and side by side with the Republicans, Socialists and Anarchists we shall prevent Spain from retrogressing, cost what it may."[13]

The Communists were the best organized of the conflicting parties in Republican Spain, and with the switch in policy from Marxist goals proclaiming dictatorship of the proletariat to defense of the bourgeois government and property rights, they increased their following. In their new role they promised hope to the urban and rural middle classes. Small businessmen of the towns found in the PCE protection against Anarchist takeovers, while in the countryside the small- and medium-sized farmer landholders hoped that the Communists would protect them from collectivization. It was more important to defeat fascism in Spain than achieve an immediate Communist victory, and the PCE denied its own Marxist precepts to present itself as a champion of the Republic. The deceptive political maneuvers did not persuade England or France to abandon non-intervention and lift the arms embargo.

To capture the power of the state, Communists infiltrated police organizations, making them into an extension of the Soviet police. Through efforts to control the prime minister, they achieved a good deal of political influence. All of this was facilitated by the supply of Russian arms and advisers that the Republic needed desperately. While there was a pressing need for cooperation between political rivals to win the war, the Communists were not shy about murdering members of dissident groups that opposed them.

In the drive to seize control of the army commands throughout the country, the PCE made great strides forward. Many Spanish officers were attracted to the party for its efficiency and its Soviet arms. Tank regiments and the air force (with Russian tanks and planes) were controlled by the Communists; pilots were trained in the Soviet Union and required to become members of the JSU.

The ultimate goal of Stalin and the Kremlin was to bring Spain under Soviet influence in preparation for a postwar Communist takeover that would make the country a satellite of the USSR. The policy, well on its way to fulfillment, failed when the Republic lost the war. It was also self-defeating. Unifying the military under Communist domination, inroads into the political establishment and the increasing domination of the NKVD in political matters led to the destruction of the Anarchist revolution, to crushing of the POUM and to hostility from moderate Socialists, undermining morale and popular enthusiasm to continue the war. Communism became as much feared as fascism.

MEXICO, THE UNITED STATES AND CANADA

One of the few diplomats who did not desert to the Nationalist side when war broke out was Félix Gordón Ordás, Spanish ambassador to Mexico. The Mexican government under President Lázaro Cárdenas favored the Republic but was only able to send 20,000 rifles, ammunition and food. All other Latin American countries, many under military dictatorships, sympathized with the Nationalists in one degree or another but dispatched no contributions.

Public opinion in the United States and Canada seems to have been divided. U.S. Neutrality Acts prevented any trade agreements with nations at war, although they did not cover civil wars. Some items such as oil were not covered in the acts at all. Texaco and Standard Oil of New Jersey supplied this indispensable commodity openly to the Nationalists. Later in the course of the war, Ford, General Motors and Studebaker supplied 12,000 trucks, items not covered in the Neutrality Act.[14] The companies supplied about $20 million worth of oil and gasoline on credit without which Franco's war machine would have ground to a halt.[15] Business communities were confident of a Nationalist victory. By the end of the war Franco's government owed an estimated $100 to $200 million to suppliers.

At the Spanish embassy in Washington, Ambassador Luís Caldarón, along with air attaché Ramón Franco, brother of General Franco, pretended loyalty to the Republic but sabotaged it by sending false information and inventing reasons as to why they could not procure arms and supplies from the United States. Ramón Franco was dismissed in August 1936, and Calderón resigned at the end of the month. Meanwhile, Juan de Cárdenas, the former ambassador in Paris, arrived in New York and created an alternative embassy for the Nationalists in the Ritz Carlton Hotel.[16]

As there was no law preventing arms going to Spain's civil war from the United States, President Roosevelt asked the nation to impose a moral embargo on war material, and most aircraft manufacturers observed it. There were, nevertheless, some who tried to ship arms and planes to the Republic. The usual behind-the-scenes wheeling and dealing was exerted by bank officials sympathetic to the Nationalists, holding up the transfer of Republican money, and by the State Department's red tape–delaying tactics. The U.S. Congress had adjourned, and the president intended to ask it to add new amendments to the embargo laws when it reconvened. Congress met again on 5 January 1937. Meanwhile, a ship loaded aircraft and other goods for the Republic in a race against time before Congress met. The ship, the *Mar Cantábrico*, managed to sail while one member of Congress, the only opponent to the new legislation, filibustered. After a stop in Veracruz, Mexico, to pick up more arms and munitions, its departure was reported by Nationalist agents, and it was tracked across the Atlantic by the Portuguese. Captured by the Nationalist cruiser *Canarias* off the northern coast of Spain, the ship was taken to the port of El Ferrol. The captain, ten of the crew and five Mexican passengers were executed, while the rest received life in prison at hard labor. The embargo amendments were passed in the U.S. Congress, putting an end to further legal shipments. Dupont provided 40,000 bombs, sending them to Germany first in order to circumvent the law, while planes and guns were then flown to Mexico before their departure for Spain.[17]

CONTROL OF THE SEAS

By early October 1936 the insurgent navy had gained control of the Mediterranean coasts in the vicinity of Gibraltar and the northern coast from France to Portugal. By late October its destroyers were turning back Soviet cargo ships bound for Valencia. During the following two months the Italian and German navies decided that the Italians would take the major responsibility for surface and submarine operations in the Mediterranean. Meanwhile, on 17 November 1936, the Franco government, at Burgos, announced that it would sink ships transporting supplies to Republican ports. The Nationalists claimed to be the only legal government of Spain and as such demanded belligerent rights on the high seas. In effect this meant the right to blockade the enemy coasts and to stop and search ships of all nations entering Spain's territorial waters. Britain responded by instructing its naval captains not to accompany British merchant ships into Spanish waters, as they had been doing, and thus avoid unpleasant incidents. British freighters, nevertheless, whose companies were attracted by large profits, continued to deliver food and other supplies to Basque ports. On 6 April 1937 the Burgos government announced a blockade of the north coast, although the Basques insisted that their shore batteries and armed trawlers could protect ships within the three-mile territorial limit. The Nationalist naval forces, on the other hand, told the British government that the blockade was effective, and the Baldwin government ordered British merchantmen not to sail to the port of Bilbao.

MEDITERRANEAN SEA AND NAVAL POWER

Attacks on merchant shipping in the Mediterranean posed serious problems for European peace. On 15 December 1936 the Russian freighter *Komsomol* was sunk off Cartagena. Up until May 1937, some thirty-five ships were damaged, confiscated or sent to the bottom. These were English, Scandinavian and Russian merchantmen. While it was thus difficult for the Republic to depend on supplies, the Nationalists had few problems receiving goods through their own and Portuguese ports.

Meanwhile the Non-Intervention Committee completed surveillance arrangements on land and at sea of all routes of entry into Spain. On 20 April 1937 the committee assigned Germany and Italy the task of watching over the Republican Mediterranean coast, while the northern coastline came under the jurisdiction of England and France. The surveillance patrols were to report any acts of infringement of the rules laid out by the NIC. No naval inspections or interference applied to the Portuguese coast and the port of Lisbon. The Portuguese agreed to a few British inspectors along its border with Spain, and the French agreed to international inspection of its Pyrenean frontier. The farcical arrangements did not hinder attacks on ships approaching Republican ports in the Mediterranean, and Nationalist Spain continued as before to import arms and munitions freely. Neither the Republic nor the Nationalists recognized the naval patrol, and the Republic announced it would attack any German or Italian ships entering its waters. It was not an idle threat. On 24 May 1937 planes from

Valencia bombed the Italian warship *Barletta* at Palma de Mallorca, killing six officers. On 29 May a Republican air raid hit the warship *Deutschland* in the harbor at Ibiza, killing twenty-two sailors. Two days later the Germans retaliated by a naval bombardment of the port of Almería, killing many civilians. On 15 June the Germans claimed that the cruiser *Leipzig* had been torpedoed on the high seas. The Republic denied involvement and asked the British navy to investigate the report. The Germans refused any investigation but used the incident on 23 June, as did the Italians, as an excuse to quit the naval patrols established two months before. The Portuguese then told the British to remove their surveillance patrols from the Portuguese-Spanish border that had at any rate been totally ineffective with no authority to stop or search anything as truckloads of arms passed under their very noses, some from Britain.[18] On 12 July the French, losing interest, stopped observer patrols along the Pyrenees but kept the border closed. Only the Royal Navy carried on.

During July and August 1937 some twenty-five ships, mostly Spanish (but also four English and two Russian) were torpedoed in the Mediterranean by Italian submarines, although the assailants were then listed as unknown.[19] While the Chamberlain government of Great Britain was doing what it could to appease Germany, the audacious Italian acts of war in international waters were too much. The British called a conference at Nyon in Switzerland, inviting all countries that bordered the Mediterranean to attend. They announced that British and French naval ships would patrol the Mediterranean and sink any unidentified submarines. Italy did not attend the conference, but the mysterious sinking ceased. Italian aid to Franco openly flowed through the Nationalist ports without British objections, but Italy had by then greatly reduced Soviet aid to the Republic by sinking Russian ships. The British government continued to tell the ever-questioning Labor opposition in Parliament that it had no sufficient information of arms shipments to Nationalist Spain.

Independent British merchant ships continued to supply the Republic. Between April and the end of June, after the Nationalists had cut the Republic in two and appeared about ready to win the war, Italian and Nationalist planes bombed twenty-two British merchant ships, half of which were sunk or disabled. More attacks followed in the months ahead. From time to time the British submitted damage claims to Burgos, but the Nationalists could hardly conceal their scorn for a government that seemed to want Franco's victory but asked compensation for damage done to British ships carrying supplies to the Republic.[20]

FOREIGN TROOPS

Foreign troops were a thorny problem for the Non-Intervention Committee. By spring 1937 Nationalist forces included Moroccans—or Moors—perhaps as many as 70,000 to 80,000, over 70,000 Italians, about 5,000 Germans and some 20,000 Portuguese. On the Republican side were about 35,000 volunteers making up the International Brigades and about 2,000 Soviet technicians and staff officers.[21] On 20 February 1937, after a massive recruitment of Moorish troops and a large influx of Italians, the NIC announced a ban on the recruitment of non-Spanish soldiers. General Franco consistently objected to discussion of foreign troops by the NIC. There were four times the number of foreign soldiers fighting for the Nationalists than there were for the Republic, and any interference by the committee in this regard, he claimed, was an infringement on the sovereignty of Nationalist Spain.

NOTES

1. Howson, 21; Preston, *Spanish Civil War*, 63.
2. Howson, 71, 93.
3. Ibid., 114 ff.
4. Ibid., 68.
5. Jackson, 109.
6. Howson, 118.
7. Radosh, Habeck and Sevostianov, 22.
8. Howson, 128.
9. Radosh, Habeck and Sevostianov, 424.
10. Howson, 129. See also Radosh, Habeck and Sevostianov, xvii. The Soviets faked the price of arms. The official exchange rate was 5.3 rubles to the dollar. The exchange rate of 2.5 rubles to the dollar was collected on the sale of Maxim machine guns, making them twice as expensive for the Republic to buy. On the sale of two aircraft alone, Stalin stole more than $50 million from the Republic.
11. For details, see Howson, 153 ff.
12. Beevor, 123.

13. Bolloten, *Grand Camouflage*, 88.
14. Jackson, 107, 153.
15. Howson, 74.
16. Ibid., 165.
17. For details, see ibid., 172 ff.
18. Ibid., 231.
19. Jackson, 147; Howson, 235.
20. Jackson, 148.
21. Ibid., 149.

¡Ayuda! a las Familias de los combatientes del Norte. Asturias Octubre 1934–1937. Socorro Rojo de España [Help the Families of the Fighters of the North. Asturias October 1934–1937. Red Aid of Spain]. The poster, by Cheché, was issued by the Spanish Red Aid in 1937 and depicts an Asturian miner. Aid is requested for families forced to leave the region in the civil war. The letters U.H.P. represent *Union Hermanos Proletarios* [Union of Proletarian Brothers]. (Robert D. Farber University Archives and Special Collections Department, Brandeis University Libraries)

Militiamen defending Madrid in 1936. (National Archives of Canada, PA-194589)

The search for survivors after an attack by Fascist bombers. (National Archives of Canada, PA-194402)

La aviación fascista pasa sobre la capital de la República. ¿Haces tú algo para evitar esto? Ayuda a Madrid [The Fascist airforce is flying over the capital of the Republic. What are you doing to prevent this? Aid Madrid!]. Produced anonymously, this was issued by the Council for the Defense of Madrid in 1937 and portrays two children sheltering under a bridge from an air attack. (Robert D. Farber University Archives and Special Collections Department, Brandeis University Libraries)

Belchite in the aftermath of the civil war. (Photo by the author)

Some of the outdated tanks and armored cars used to try and stop the Nationalist forces. (National Archives of Canada, PA-194597)

The 15th International Brigade's Lincoln Battalion in February 1937, composed mainly of Americans and Canadians. (National Archives of Canada, PA-194605)

New Yorker Saul Wellman, commander of the Mackenzie-Papineau Battalion when it went into battle at Fuentes de Ebro. (National Archives of Canada, C67468)

Dolores Ibárruri (La Pasionaria) visits the International Brigades at the Battle of the Ebro. (Maybee, John R./National Archives of Canada, PA-19492)

A soldier of the Mackenzie-Papineau Battalion on the front line. (National Archives of Canada, C-67469)

Los Internacionales—Unidos a los Españoles, Luchamos contra el Invasor [The Internationals—United with the Spanish, We Fight against the Invader]. Produced by Parilla in 1937, this poster shows the emblem of the International Brigades (the five-pointed star and the clenched fist representing the Popular Front) against the flag of the Republic with the symbolic *Niña Bonita* guarding the soldiers. (Robert D. Farber University Archives and Special Collections Department, Brandeis University Libraries)

¡Criminales! Socorro Rojo POUM [Criminals! Red Aid POUM]. This 1936 poster by Ras issued by Red Aid was the POUM's alternative to the Soviet International Red Aid. It portrays a grief-stricken mother holding her dead child amidst falling bombs. (Robert D. Farber University Archives and Special Collections Department, Brandeis University Libraries)

18 de Julio 1936–1937 [18th July 1936–1937]. Produced in 1937 by José Bardasano, this poster commemorates one year of war against fascism by showing a
Republican soldier in hand-to-hand combat with a Nazi at a concentration camp.
(Robert D. Farber University Archives and Special Collections Department, Brandeis University Libraries)

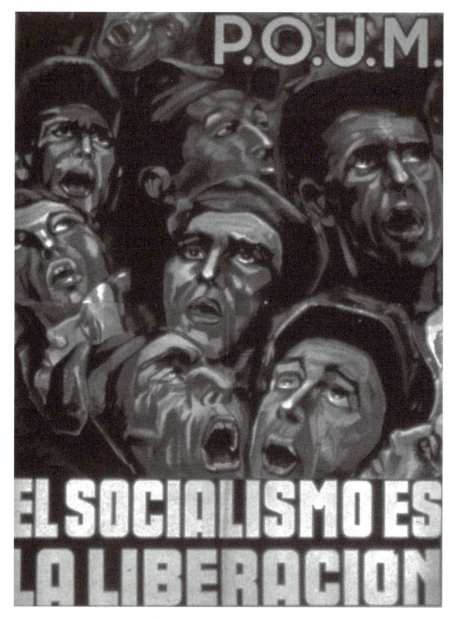

P.O.U.M., *El Socialismo és la Liberación* [Socialism is Liberation]. The POUM, a revolutionary but anti-Stalinist Marxist party, promoted progressive social change. The anonymously produced poster depicts both workers and soldiers as a unified group. (Robert D. Farber University Archives and Special Collections Department, Brandeis University Libraries)

¡No Pasanran! Julio 1936 [They shall not pass! July 1936]; *Julio 1937 ¡Pasaremos!*
[We shall pass! July 1937]. This poster by Ramón Puyol shows a worker in the
background stopping the Fascists in 1936. By 1937 he has become a soldier who
will defeat them. (Robert D. Farber University Archives and Special Collections
Department, Brandeis University Libraries)

¡Treballadors! El Feixisme es l'Explotacio i l'Esclavatge. 100,000 Voluntaris [Workers! Fascism is Exploitation and Slavery. 100,000 Volunteers needed]. This poster by José Bardasano, put out by the Popular Front of Cataluña, shows the crucifixion of a worker set against a swastika. (Robert D. Farber University Archives and Special Collections Department, Brandeis University Libraries)

Los Nacionales [The Nationalists], thought to be by Juan Antonio Morales, 1936, depicts a monocled German Nazi capitalist, an Italian general, two Moors and a Catholic bishop in front with a vulture behind. It has been suggested that the toylike appearance represents a ship of fools. (Robert D. Farber University Archives and Special Collections Department, Brandeis University Libraries)

Falangist girls in uniform, marching. (Library of Congress, Prints and Photographs Division, LC-USZ62-108330)

Symbol of the Falange: yoke and arrows. "The glorious Spanish army, with our *Requetés* and Falangists, united on the fronts to win for us with their blood! Spain! United forever under the orders of the Caudillo (head) we will build a new Spain. One, Great, Free with the impetus of youth, with traditional roots, *¡Arriba España! ¡Viva España!* Franco, Franco, Franco, Head of the Empire." (Library of Congress, Prints and Photographs Division, LC-USZC4-7521)

Weary refugees pour into France. (Library of Congress, Prints and Photographs Division, LC-USZ62-128346)

CUARTEL GENERAL DEL GENERALISIMO

SECCION DE OPERACIONES.

ESTADO MAYOR

PARTE OFICIAL DE GUERRA

correspondiente al día 1º. de Abril de 1939.- III Año Triunfal

En el día de hoy, cautivo y desarmadó el Ejército rojo, nan al-

canzado las tropas Nacionales sus últimos objetivos militares.

LA GUERRA HA TERMINADO.

BURGOS 1º. de Abril de 1939
Año de la Victoria
EL GENERALISIMO,

The last Franco communiqué: "This very day, [with] the red army captive and disarmed, the Nationalist troops have reached their ultimate military objectives. THE WAR HAS ENDED." (Library of Congress, Prints and Photographs Division, LC USZ62-125964)

CHAPTER 6

THE DIMINISHING REPUBLIC AND THE INTERNATIONAL BRIGADES

As it became obvious to Franco and his general staff that Madrid would not fall easily to the Nationalist forces and the war would be prolonged, it was decided to launch a campaign in the north of the country. Once conquered, the Republican territories in the north would yield up valuable assets including arms factories, iron and steel industries in the Basque country and the coal mines of Asturias. Through intense recruitment the overall number of Nationalist men under arms was approaching 300,000.

The Cortes, sitting in Valencia, had granted the Basque region a Statute of Autonomy in early October 1936. On 7 October municipal councilors met in Guernica under the old oak tree, the symbol of Basque tradition and independence, and elected José Antonio Aguirre president of the Basque nation. Nevertheless, the Basques were staunch, conservative Catholics with little in common with revolutionary Socialists or Anarchists, and the Nationalist junta in Burgos did not expect to encounter stubborn resistance. On 27 March 1937 Franco put the Madrid front on the defensive and began the buildup for the campaign in the north that received the bulk of the Nationalists' aircraft and as much artillery as could be spared. It was thought that the port of Bilbao, the capital of Vizcaya, would be taken in a matter of three weeks.[1]

WAR IN THE NORTH

Since the fall of Irun in September 1936 the northern front had remained quiet. Basque forces numbered 30,000 to 40,000 trained militia plus a smattering of Popular Front combatants. They held lightly defended lines to the east of Elgoibar, about halfway between Bilbao and San Sebastian, and along the hills north of Vitoria. Many soldiers were engaged in the construction of a so-called ring of iron, a (hopefully) impenetrable system of fortification around Bilbao. They were not well endowed with heavy artillery, possessing only about forty field guns. A single Russian ship arrived at the port of Bilbao in October and unloaded twelve aircraft, twenty-five armored cars and a few heavy machine guns.

General Mola amassed some 50,000 well-equipped Italian, Moroccan and Navarese troops equipped with the new German 88-millimeter gun that far outclassed anything in the Republican arsenal and a first-rate communication network under German supervision.

The offensive got under way on 31 March 1937, with advances along the entire east to west front, directed in the field by General Solchaga. The Basques resisted tenaciously but retreated before superior firepower. Heavily wooded terrain and poor roads helped slow the advance, but the Nationalist ground forces enjoyed overwhelming air superiority from the Condor Legion whose fighter aircraft were stationed at Vitoria, the bombers at Burgos. Italian planes flew support missions. Mola promised to raze the region to the ground if submission was not immediate.

On the first day of the offensive, German pilots of the Condor Legion tested their skills at dive bombing and carpet bombing on the town of Durango, a railway junction behind the front lines, killing over 200 civilians. This was the first time European civilians were targeted in systematic aerial warfare. The bombers appeared in waves, laying waste to the undefended town, while fighters swarmed in, machine-gunning fleeing civilians. On 20 April the offensive began in Vizcaya. Subject to constant bombing and artillery barrages, the Basque army fell back toward the ring of iron around Bilbao.

GUERNICA

On Monday, 26 April 1937, market day, the sacred Basque town of Guernica, a little east of Bilbao and six miles behind the front lines, population about 7,000, was crowded with farmers with their sheep and cattle, retreating soldiers and refugees fleeing the oncoming Nationalist troops.

The weather was bright and clear. At 4:30 in the afternoon a single German plane appeared in the sky, dropped bombs on the center of the town and flew away. There were no air defenses. At 4:45 as people began to emerge from the cellars of their houses to help the injured, a squadron of planes suddenly appeared over the town and dropped heavier bombs, collapsing the cellars, the only shelters available. Running into the fields the inhabitants were cut down by strafing fighters. Beginning at 5:15 heavy German bombers (Junkers 52) came over in waves twenty minutes apart for the next two and a half hours. The explosives that rained down included light to heavy bombs (500 kilograms), antipersonnel shrapnel bombs and incendiaries that started raging fires. Dust and smoke obliterated the scene in which 1,654 people died and nearly a thousand were injured.[2] The news shocked the world. The Burgos government attributed the destruction to the reds who, it said, burned their own town in order to blame it on the Nationalists and inflame passions against the advancing troops. A spokesman for the Church in the Vatican tried to lend credence to the Nationalists' story by asserting that there were no Germans in Spain.

For the next thirty years under the Franco dictatorship it remained a crime in Spain to say that Guernica had been bombed,[3] even though, as revealed during the Nuremberg Trials in Germany at the end of World War II, Guernica had offered German pilots superb laboratory conditions for testing the results of carpet bombing and of high explosives and incendiary bombs on a civilian population.

As the Nationalists closed in on Bilbao, General Mola was aware that the gun emplacements and fortifications that ringed the city, two lines 200 to 300 yards apart, were fatally flawed. Major Goicoechea, a Basque engineer who had helped build the defenses, defected to the Nationalists in early March 1937 and reported to Mola on the vulnerable places in the lines. On 3 June, General Mola was killed in an airplane accident, but it was not long before the ring of iron was penetrated. General Dávila's forces entered Bilbao on 19 June 1937 unopposed. Many of the inhabitants fled by boat to France or westward toward Santander and Gijón.

BATTLE OF BRUNETE

After the loss of the Basque provinces, and with the Nationalists poised to strike further west at Santander, the Republic launched an attack on 6 July 1937 toward Brunete, the village of 1,500 inhabitants, fifteen miles west of Madrid, taken eight months earlier by the Nationalists.[4] The objective: to cut off the forces besieging Madrid from the west and at the same time draw off Nationalist strength from the north. The Republican command hoped to accomplish the first objective before Franco's reinforcements arrived.

Fifty thousand men with their equipment were moved into the pine-covered foothills of the Guadarrama mountains about fifteen miles northwest of Madrid. Arriving at night they remained concealed among the trees from enemy observation planes. The surprise thrust along the Guadarrama river valley to Brunete eight miles to the south was to be followed by a swing to the southeast to cut off the Extremadura highway, the major supply route for the Nationalist forces besieging the capital. After heavy air strikes and artillery bombardments, the assault jumped off from the Coruña-Madrid road where the front line had stabilized after the Nationalist advance north to Las Rozas in December 1936.

The attack immediately began to go wrong. In the 100-plus degrees Fahrenheit, canteens were soon empty; thirst took over as the greatest enemy, units became lost among the numerous dry gullies of the ragged, sweltering plain, often intermingling with each other on the narrow front; and communications were mixed up and orders contradictory. Some companies were long overdue in meeting their objectives.

In spite of the chaos the Republican army advanced nearly ten miles and surrounded Brunete, surprising the 1,000 or so Moroccans and an understrength division of Falange. Brunete fell, but nearby towns held out stubbornly. Franco and his field commander General Varela reacted with alacrity. The Condor Legion and heavy artillery units were dispatched from the north, while several divisions were transferred from other sectors to the Brunete front. With the arrival of Nationalist reinforcements, the tide began to turn. By 13 July the offensive came to a halt, and the Republicans dug in to hold what they had conquered—a bulge in the enemy lines about eight miles deep. It was not long before the Condor Legion began to dominate the sky over the battle area with their new Messerschmitt ME 109 fighter planes and Heinkels 111 bombers accompanied by Italian Savoias 79. On 18 July they shot down twenty-one Chatos (the name given to Russian Republican aircraft). In the fierce heat of the summer sun, the battle continued day after day until 24 July 1937 when the Nationalists recaptured Brunete. The lines began to stabilize. Ultimately the Republicans gained a penetration of about four miles deep and ten miles long at a cost of about 20,000 dead and wounded and one hundred aircraft. The Nationalists suffered 17,000 casualties and lost twenty-three planes.[5] The battle delayed Franco's campaign in the north for a short time, but it did not achieve its goals, and the price in men and equipment was something the Republic could ill afford.

CONQUEST OF THE NORTH

Two weeks after the battle at Brunete the Nationalists continued their offensive in the north.[6] With the fall of Bilbao, their blockade of the north coast was nearly complete, and the Republican government was hard-pressed to find the ships, let alone to deliver much-needed supplies to the northern ports of Santander and Gijón, now under threat. As the enemy neared Santander, the local officials negotiated a separate peace with the attacking Italian army at the port of Santoña, just east of the city. The authorities surrendered their arms to the Italians in exchange for the maintenance of public order, no destruction of property and no reprisals against the populace or Republican soldiers. The Italian general, Bastico, guaranteed the lives of the soldiers and the emigration of officials and promised to use his influence to protect the population from reprisals. When Franco heard of this agreement, he dispatched troops to Santoña, canceled the surrender arrangements, arrested a boatload of refugees preparing to leave the harbor and began reprisals.

On 24 August 1937 the Italian victors paraded through the streets of Santander carrying portraits of Mussolini, and even though the capture of the city had entailed little fighting, it was a significant face-saving for the Italian humiliation at Guadalajara. Meanwhile, the docks and factories at Bilbao were repaired by prisoners of war, and iron was again produced and exported. Franco directed much of the ore from the mines in the Basque provinces to England, the traditional market, despite German objections, and used the foreign exchange to fill military needs. The hungry and demoralized civilian population of the north passively accepted the new regime, but Basque and Popular Front militiamen who would not give up moved further westward into the high Cantabrian mountains of Asturias.

THE ARAGÓN FRONT

In Aragón the front line ran through the treeless hills and dry gullies of vast empty spaces. Sand-bagged bunkers with views out over enemy territory clung to the prominent features with sparsely manned connecting trenches running between them. There was little to do except occasionally snipe at an enemy outpost across half a mile or so of no-man's land.

The front ran from the Pyrenees southward a little east of Huesca and Zaragoza and zigzagged on to Teruel, but it had been relatively quiet since the autumn of 1936 when the fighting centered around Madrid and then in the north. On the Republican side it was manned by Anarchists and POUM militias that had left Barcelona and Valencia at the start of war to contain the Nationalists and in a futile attempt to retake enemy-held Zaragoza.

On 24 August 1937, the day Santander fell to the Nationalists, an all-out Republican attack on the Aragón front began in another effort to draw off enemy forces in the north. The assaults, aimed ultimately at Zaragoza, were staged both north and south of the city to embrace it in a pincer movement. Some 80,000 men and 100 tanks supported by about 200 planes moved out in the immense summer heat toward the objective. The tenacity of the defenders, Carlists and Falange for the most part, surprised the attackers, but after short, fierce firefights, small towns began to fall one by one.

Some thirty miles south of Zaragoza, with a population of about 3,800, the strongly fortified village of Belchite held out as an island of resistance to the flow of advancing men and machines. The intolerable heat plagued both sides, while the stench of rotting bodies made the air almost unbearable. Water to the town was cut off. The thick-walled church, where machine guns in the belfry commanded the surrounding plain, remained the center of resistance. House-to-house fighting with bayonet and grenade continued until the town, still resisting ten miles behind the Republican front line, was taken on 6 September 1937. The campaign then slowed and came to a halt. Zaragoza remained in Nationalist hands.

ASTURIAS

Meanwhile, on 1 September 1937 the Nationalists embarked upon their offensive in Asturias. The going was slow in the rugged mountainous terrain, but the Republicans were gradually ground down. On 21 October Franco's battalions entered Gijón, the last stronghold on the northern coast. Since there was little chance of escape by sea (patrolled by the Nationalist navy), many Republican soldiers and officials took refuge in the most inaccessible valleys of the mountains. Franco now had at his disposal the rich resources of the north and another large piece of territory, freeing some 65,000 Nationalist troops to fight elsewhere. Total land domination of the northern coast allowed his navy to now concentrate in the Mediterranean.

By autumn of 1937 the Republican army was short of supplies, and much of the best armaments had been lost at Brunete. Several Russian freighters carrying war material had been sunk in the Mediterranean, making the situation even more critical. On 31 October the Republican government packed its bags and moved from Valencia to Barcelona.

BATTLE FOR TERUEL

Throughout the autumn of 1937, Franco gathered his forces for a new assault on Madrid. To impede his plans, Minister of Defense Indalecio Prieto and his staff officers chose the provincial capital city of Teruel, well south of Zaragoza and situated on a high rocky bluff at the junction of two rivers, as the place for a large-scale offensive. The high, drab, walled city with about 20,000 inhabitants, icy cold in winter, was lightly held by Nationalist forces and formed a bulge into Republican lines. Nearly 100,000 troops were moved into the area. The Republican attack was delayed a few days due to a railroad strike in Barcelona that tied up supplies but commenced on 15 December with snow falling and temperatures plummeting. Without an artillery barrage to alert the enemy, Lister's Eleventh Division surrounded the town, taking the Nationalist troops by surprise.[7] On 23 December Franco abandoned the proposed offensive on Madrid and instead rushed reinforcements to relieve Teruel.

By Christmas Day the Republicans had penetrated the city, while the 4,000 defenders took refuge in fortified buildings in the southern section. The temperature dropped to eighteen below zero, and men and machines froze. A blizzard swept in, dropping four feet of snow, and lasted four days, blocking roads, creating monstrous traffic jams and preventing Nationalist reinforcements from reaching the beleaguered city. On 29 December the weather began to clear, allowing the Nationalist air force back into the skies to bomb Republican lines. Meanwhile, house-to-house fighting in the city continued, Republican troops knocking down interior walls in one house to gain entrance to the next. On New Year's Day the temperature once again plummeted, a blizzard raged and Nationalist reinforcements were again stalled as trucks and tanks froze. The city surrendered on 6 January 1938. When the weather again cleared, Franco's forces continued their counterattack to dislodge the Republicans, now the defenders. In some places the front lines were only yards apart; artillery shells turned the air into thick powder, jamming guns and choking men; the air hummed with bullets. Nationalist planes circled above the battle like birds of prey and swooped down to unload a stick of bombs or to machine-gun Republican positions. On 22 February 1938 the Nationalists retook the city, a pile of rubble. The Republic sustained about 60,000 casualties and the Nationalists about 50,000. The latter suffered more planes lost owing to the weather than to enemy action.[8]

On 6 March the Republic received news of a victory at sea. Three Nationalist cruisers escorting some merchant ships sailed past Cartagena at midnight heading south from Mallorca. Republican cruisers and destroyers approached and launched torpedoes before turning away. The Nationalist cruiser *Baleares* was hit and blew up, with the loss of 726 men and officers.[9]

NATIONAL OFFENSIVE: CATALUÑA AND THE LEVANT

The victory at Teruel spurred the Nationalists on to launch a grand offensive toward Cataluña and the Mediterranean Sea. Along the north-south line from the French border to Teruel, they amassed 100,000 men, German and Italian planes, tanks and thousands of trucks. On 9 March the attack got under way, Belchite changed hands within twenty-four hours and before the week was out, the entire line had advanced some sixty miles, with tanks spearheading the assault and breaking through the weak points. The demoralized retreating Republicans were bombed and strafed as they abandoned their positions.

Unlike earlier tactics in the use of armor where it was spread out piecemeal among the infantry, the Germans insisted that their tanks be used in formations to batter holes in the enemy lines. They did not need to depend directly on accompanying infantry, which they often outran. Motorcycle troops and armored cars generally kept pace and served as support units. The tactic was practiced and perfected in the major battles in Spain and was later used in World War II when it became known as Blitzkrieg. The Condor Legion employed the effective Stuka dive bomber (Junkers 87) in action for the first time, and it was in Spain that the

Germans learned that pilots could black out and lose control of the plane during pullout from a dive-bombing attack.

Meanwhile, Mussolini ordered his air force based on Mallorca to bomb Barcelona, which they did time and again, beginning on 16 March. The Italians were particularly interested in seeing the results of new types of bombs that either had delayed fuses, in order to pass through the roofs of buildings and explode inside, or exploded with powerful lateral force, destroying everything within a few inches of the ground.

VINAROZ AND THE SEA

Exulted, the victorious Nationalist forces swept through eastern Aragón and into Cataluña, the end of the war now in their grasp. El Campesino's weary division made a brief stand at Lérida, less than one hundred miles west of Barcelona, but was soon pushed aside and the city taken on 3 April. A Nationalist corps then turned north and continued along the river Segre toward the Pyrenees to capture the town of Tremp northwest of Barcelona and the city's main source of electricity, severely disrupting industry. Other units moved swiftly down the Ebro River valley and on 15 April 1938 reached the Mediterranean fishing village of Vinaroz, about halfway between Barcelona and Valencia, splitting the Republican territory in two. Cataluña was now effectively severed from the remainder of the Republican territory.

The Nationalists were confident the war would be over in a matter of weeks. Some Republican officers talked of surrender, and Defense Minister Indalecio Prieto was deeply pessimistic. Thousands of Republican soldiers had been taken prisoner; civilian morale was at rock bottom, aggravated by severe food shortages. Tens of thousands of refugees, many of them farmers with their livestock, flooded into Barcelona and Valencia, reminiscent of the situation in Madrid in 1936.

After having convinced Blum, who was once again French prime minister, to reopen the border on 17 March 1938, Prime Minister Negrín, counting on arms now entering Spain from France and with the hope that the Western democracies would recognize the evils of fascism and cease to appease Franco and Hitler, was resolved to continue the fight. He fired Prieto and reorganized his cabinet, adding minister of war to his own duties. Arms from diverse sources that had been stored in warehouses in

France made it over the frontier into Republican hands. The struggle would continue.

On 1 May 1938 Negrín delivered one of his rare speeches in which he outlined thirteen points as conditions for ending the war. Some of the particulars were: a plebiscite on the form of a new Republic once the fighting ceased, regional liberties and individual freedom of conscience, agrarian reform and a general political amnesty—all considerations that Franco was certain to reject.

Some 200 heavy field guns, latest Russian fighter aircraft, crates of submachine guns and ammunition crossed the border. Cabinet changes in the French government, however, reducing the number of pro-Republican deputies coupled with Mussolini's threats and British urgings, caused the French and now Prime Minister Deladier to again seal the border on 13 June 1938.

Cataluña gained a small respite when Franco followed up his drive to the sea with an attack southward toward Valencia on 5 July instead of turning his main forces north toward Barcelona. By the end of the month the Nationalists held a strip of coast running fifty miles south from the mouth of the Ebro, but further progress was held up by stiff resistance.

BATTLE OF THE EBRO

In July 1938 Negrín authorized an attack across the Ebro River to reestablish land communications between Cataluña and the rest of Republican Spain. A new Army of the Ebro, over 80,000 strong, was constituted under the command of General Juan Modesto. He and most of the senior officers of the new command, such as Lister, now also a general in command of the V Corps, were Communists. On the moonless night of 24 July, a few minutes after midnight, crossings at numerous points along the front line of the 330-foot-wide Ebro River began. The assault took place primarily in the great arc of the river northwest of Tortosa. Ninety boats, each containing ten men, ferried the troops across the river to establish positions and allow pontoon bridges to be constructed for the tanks, armored cars and artillery, the latter in short supply owing to earlier losses. Achieving tactical surprise, by dawn most of the villages on the Nationalist side of the river were taken and a large bridgehead established. An attack further down the river beyond Tortosa by the XIV (French) International Brigade failed, leaving 600 dead and much equipment lost.

Rapid advance through the hills west of the river met only moderate resistance and advanced thirty miles as the Nationalist forces under Yagüe retreated, 4,000 of their number taken prisoner. But the following day the Republican attack stalled at the heavily defended town of Gandesa. The town held while Franco ordered all available units to the area. A shortage of tanks and field guns, the result of a rapid rise in the Ebro River washing away the pontoon bridges, handicapped the Republicans for two days. The Nationalists had opened the dams on the river Segre, a major tributary of the Ebro. By 1 August the Republican advance was contained, and the Army of the Ebro went on the defensive with a loss of 1,200 men in the first week. On 6 August the Nationalists' counterattack, with great élan and determination, began. The familiar Republican pattern of initial success, Nationalist reinforcements and subsequent stalemate or retreat reasserted itself. Republican soldiers tried to dig in, but the rocky terrain refused to yield, and stone shelters had to serve as protection against intense artillery fire and heavy aerial bombardment. Throughout August, in unbearable heat with drinking water at a premium, Republican losses mounted, reaching over 25,000 men. By September Nationalist aircraft controlled the skies. In spite of orders to fight to the death, as some Republicans did, they were pushed back. On 8 November 1938 the Republican army began to withdraw back across the Ebro River, its starting point.

THE INTERNATIONAL BRIGADES

During the first weeks of the war, foreign Liberals, leftist-oriented individuals with strong convictions and Communists converged on Spain to offer their services to the Republic. Within a month several hundred French workers along with political refugees from Germany, Italy and eastern Europe were fighting with the Republican army. The French Paris battalion, a Polish battalion, an Italian column and the German Thaelmann Battalion all saw action by September 1936. These first foreign units, were the outgrowth of spontaneous activity.[10]

With the order to aid the Republic given by Stalin on 26 August 1936, the Comintern geared up for the task, organizing thousands of anti-Fascists and Communists from fifty-three countries into volunteer brigades (or regiments) to fight in Spain. The head of the Communist Party in France, Maurice Thorez, Palmiro Togliatti (a founder of the Italian Communist Party and one of the most powerful Communists in Spain who headed the PCE) and Josip Broz (later known as Tito), leader of the Yu-goslav Communists, all became active in this endeavor. The Communist Party in countries throughout the Western world were sent recruitment quotas,[11] and recruiting centers were set up in many cities either openly or clandestinely. Nearly 60,000 men and women, moved by the struggle of the democratically elected Republic, packed their belongings and went to fight in Spain.

The choice at the time was clear for most volunteers: only a Repub-lican victory could prevent the spread of fascism throughout Europe. To do nothing was to acquiesce in its crimes of aggression and oppression. Volunteers from the United States and Canada, many ideologically moti-vated, others to escape the work camps of the Great Depression, came to take up the cause of the Republic. African Americans came for the op-portunity to fight racial prejudice espoused by the Nazis, not unlike the kind they were subjected to at home, and Jews saw in the struggle a chance to strike a blow against anti-Semitism. Some volunteers had fought in World War I, and their combat experience was welcome. The French, the largest national group, over 10,000 strong, made up about one quarter of the International Brigades, followed by expatriate Germans, Poles and Ital-ians. Just over 3,000 Americans, 2,000 British and 1,200 Canadians joined up.

About 80 percent of the volunteers were from the working class, many unemployed sailors, shipyard workers, miners and industrial labor-ers. A few were teachers, clerks, artists and writers. Apart from the few high-ranking Red Army officers who tested new weapons and tactics, advised and observed, Stalin allowed no Russian citizens to serve in the ranks of the International Brigades. The Russian dictator did not want complications with England or France and the NIC. However, non-Russians living in the Soviet Union were encouraged to join.

The Journey to Spain

Volunteers were registered at the recruiting offices, money for train tickets or passage on ships organized and departures arranged. For most, the immediate destination was Paris where the recruits of all nationalities were gathered together and normally sent in batches by rail to Perpignan near the Spanish frontier. The third-class compartments were jammed with Italian workers, German refugees, Slavs and men from the Baltic countries: "These were anti-Fascists forged from bitter alloys. . . . Everything they possessed after a half a lifetime of labor lay wrapped in small paper parcels held between their knees."[12]

From Perpignan they traveled to Figueras, just across the border, in buses at night, or if the French had closed the frontier, they walked into Spain accompanied by guides over the mountains. From Figueras the next destination was the revolutionary and chaotic city of Barcelona, again by train, and after a few days there, the recruits traveled on to Valencia. The last stop was the dismal provincial town of Albacete on the arid plateau east of Valencia, the center of the International Brigades. "The Americans quickly decided it was the most God-awful place they had ever seen."[13] Here, the Internationals were assigned large dreary barracks once occupied by the Civil Guard. Civilian clothes were exchanged for uniforms, pieces of which were thrown in heaps into a room where the recruit sorted out as best he could something that might fit.[14] All personal belongings were turned over to the authorities, including passports and other identification, often never to be seen again. Some of the passports, especially American, found their way to Moscow and were later used by Soviet agents to enter the United States.[15] For some, the camp must have been intimidating. One International Brigader, a sculptor from London, Jason Gurney, wrote:

The establishment was ruled by a tall, good-looking Frenchman known as Vidal who came out to inspect us accompanied by a dozen of his villainous looking henchmen, all heavily armed. This unsavory crew ran the barracks as they felt inclined, without any apparent control from the higher command. They lived in the guardhouse where they loafed around like a bunch of gangsters, with great pistols on the hips. They spread themselves over the guardroom with drinks in their hands and their feet on the desks, without any pretense at military discipline or any serious attempt to see that the barracks were properly maintained.[16]

Equipment such as helmets and canteens were generally World War I vintage, and training consisted of drill or simulated attacks without weapons. In the early stages, rifles and bayonets, in short supply, were issued on the day the unit was trucked to the front. Many young men had never fired a rifle until just before battle and sometimes not until their life depended on it.

The recruits were allocated to the units in which they would serve, generally on the basis of language, their jobs determined by previous skills, both military and civilian, such as artillery gunner, machine gunner, radio operator, mechanic or clerk. Part of the training was a regular harangue by André Marty, the chief of the Brigades, on the glorious reasons for the struggle. He suspected everyone of spying or of treason, spoke in a "hysterical roar"[17] in French that many recruits did not understand and held the power, which he often exercised, to execute a man on the smallest pretext, earning the reputation as the "butcher of Albacete."

Political commissars were an essential part of the units, and points of view other than communism were not tolerated. The men were taught to distrust the POUM and the Anarchists as subversives undermining the Republic. The culling of political dissidents was carried out by SIM, the political police within the Brigades staffed by Communists of various nationalities but all loyal to Stalin. While not all of the Brigade members were Communists or fellow travelers (sympathizers), all were forced to accept Communist leadership.

More fortunate than many who fell under suspicion was the Englishman Peter Elstob who volunteered to fight in Spain as a pilot and arrived in a group of twenty Englishmen at Figueras. Destined for the International Brigades, he protested that he was a pilot and had come to fly. For no reason apparent to him, he was arrested, held incommunicado for several weeks and underwent extensive interrogation. While in prison he witnessed numerous executions. The London Communist Party representative in Barcelona came to inquire about Elstob's situation, but suddenly no more was heard from him. Only through the efforts of the British Council was he finally released and expelled from Spain. Less lucky was the Englishman Robert Smillie, a member of the British Independent Labor Party and associated with the POUM (and hence a Trotskyite in the view of the Communists). Arrested, he died in a Communist secret prison.[18]

Some recruits for the International Brigades arrived in Spain by means other than the railroad journey through France. Some came by ship from Marseilles or other points to the Port of Valencia or Alicante where they were marshaled and sent on to Albacete. This was a dangerous route, as Nationalist warships and Italian submarines sometimes sank the cargo vessels bringing them and supplies to the Republic. On torpedoed merchantmen a number of volunteers lost their lives before reaching their destinations. The ship *Ciudad de Barcelona* was torpedoed off the coast of Malgrat, a village thirty-five miles north of Barcelona. Of the two torpedoes fired, one hit the target; the other missed and landed on the beach. It had

Italian markings. A young Republican soldier and interpreter, Ronald Lawrence, arrived on the scene:

> In company with a civilian, who I later learned was a Communist official, I was rushed north by car. The scene that met us at the beach was one of agonizing despair. Some men, naked and in deep shock, wandered about without purpose; others had already been taken into the homes of the village people. . . . Most of the dead had been dragged out of the water by the time I got to the scene. . . . All papers found were handed to the official.[19]

In spite of the early shortcomings of the training and the sometimes corrupt, incompetent and mean-spirited officials, the International Brigades were generally more efficiently trained and better armed than many of their counterparts in the newly created Republican army and were used as shock troops.

When the first of the Internationals were undergoing training and the Republican government had fled from Madrid to Valencia, defeat seemed certain. The newly formed 11th and 12th Brigades were rushed to Madrid on 8 November just in time to help stem the rebel onslaught on the capital.

Five International Brigades were eventually formed: the 11th or Thaelmann Brigade was German, refugees from the Nazis; the 12th Garibaldi Brigade consisted of anti-Fascist Italians; the 13th, the Dombroski, was composed of men of Slavic nationalities—Poles, Czechs, Bulgarians, Yugoslavs and other eastern Europeans. French and Belgians made up the 14th Brigade, and the 15th that included the Abraham Lincoln Battalion was mostly English speaking, although at the beginning, when first organized for the battle of the Jarama Valley, it also contained Slavic and French soldiers of the Dimitrov and Sixth of February Battalions, respectively. In its later composition, it consisted of English, American and Canadian Battalions and a Spanish Battalion made up of Mexican, Cuban, Puerto Rican and South American volunteers. A number of Irish volunteers were divided up between the British and Americans.

The Abraham Lincoln Battalion

The Abraham Lincoln Battalion formed on 2 January 1937 was composed of the first ninety-six volunteers from the United States along with

Canadians and Latin Americans. The battalion, 450 strong, saw its first action at Jarama. Their commander, Robert Merriman, a former lecturer at the University of California, had gone to Russia on a scholarship to investigate agricultural problems but took up the Republic's cause instead.

At Jarama the day before the attack, seventy new American recruits arrived—some still in civilian clothes. They were given an hour's worth of rifle instruction by a veteran of only one week, all the training they would receive before committed to combat in which many died or were wounded before the bloody battle resulted in stalemate. Most of the casualties were sustained in a futile attempt to recapture a hill called Pingarrón.

The Comintern colonel, Janos Galicz (Gal), first in charge of the 15th Brigade, was elevated to the rank of general, and the brigade then came under the command of Colonel Vladimir Čopić, a forty-six-year-old Yugoslavian, veteran of World War I. On a cold, wet day of 27 February, while the promised air, tank and artillery support for the attack had not materialized and the supporting Spanish attack on the flank was in full retreat, Čopić ordered Captain Merriman to advance through the olive groves toward the hill into a hail of machine-gun and rifle fire. The result was a massacre.

Along the Jarama line, mutinies began to occur as men refused to attack under suicidal conditions and began to desert the front. The surviving Americans were no exception, but they were rounded up behind the lines and put on trial for desertion by Colonel Čopić. They were saved from execution by General Dimitri Pavlov, commander of the Soviet tank corps, who ordered the tribunal dissolved.[20] Merriman had been wounded at Jarama, and Captain Martin Hourihan took over the battalion.

About ninety African Americans fought in the civil war, and the Lincoln Battalion made up the first totally integrated military unit in U.S. history. Oliver Law, the first black American to command a mostly white American army unit, took over the job when Hourihan was assigned to brigade duties.

The Lincoln Battalion was withdrawn from the trenches at Jarama in the middle of June 1937 after nearly four months on the line and sent to Albares, a village of 300 people east of Madrid, for rest and recuperation. On 2 July a truck convoy arrived to transport them to the next major offensive taking shape west of Madrid. As American volunteers continued to stream over the French border into Spain, a new American battalion, the George Washington, was instituted. The two battalions met for the first time at the rendezvous point in the Guadarrama hills for the battle of Brunete. The assignments given to the 15th Brigade to take Romanillas Heights, which commanded a view of the Guadarrama valley, to storm the village of Villanueva del Pardillo and to plug gaps in the lines cost the Americans, as well as other battalions, heavy casualties. Oliver Law was killed, and the Washington and Lincoln Battalions suffered such severe losses that they had to be merged. Hans Amlie from North Dakota and World War I veteran became the new battalion commander. The excessive heat and Nationalist counterattacks were so intense that the 13th Brigade of mainly Poles refused to return to battle. On 25 July the Lincolns were taken out of the line for rest at Albares. Of the 800 who went into battle, only 300 would fight again. The British battalion survived Brunete with 37 men out of 360, the Dimitrovs, 93 out of 450; other units fared no better. The French Sixth of February Battalion lost so many men that it was disbanded.[21] By the summer of 1937 the number of foreign volunteers had fallen off. Brigade strength was maintained by recruiting Spaniards into the ranks, including commanders.

Less than a month after the guns at Brunete had fallen silent, the International Brigades were again called upon in the bid to take Zaragoza on the Aragón front, scheduled for 22 August. In Aragón the Lincolns found themselves attacking fortified villages along the roads to the objective such as Belchite where the house-to-house fighting was fierce and casualties heavy. On 23 September 1937 a decree signed by Negrín incorporated the International Brigades into the people's Republican army.

The 15th International Brigade was called upon to help stem Nationalist efforts to retake Teruel, and in a night attack on 16 February 1938 in subfreezing temperatures, the brigade captured 500 enemy troops. The arrogant Nationalist commander demanded special treatment. The then–Lincoln Battalion commander Milton Wolff reported: "I gave it to him. I booted his ass down the side of the hill in full view of his troops— and I'm sure they appreciated it."[22]

Last Battle

On 25 July 1938 the 15th Brigade took up positions near the Ebro north of Tortosa to participate in the forthcoming battle across the river. Few casualties were incurred among the Lincolns as they advanced about six miles the first day. Nationalist prisoners, taken in droves, exhibited considerable fear when they learned that they had surrendered to the International Brigades. They had been told that the Internationals shot their prisoners or fed them to the lions in the Barcelona zoo.[23]

The immediate objective was the town of Gandesa to link up with Spanish, British and Canadian battalions already fighting in the outskirts, but the Lincolns were then slowed by enemy resistence in the hills and finally stopped at a fortified ridge line and pinned down for thirty-six hours. The number of casualties grew rapidly. In spite of orders from headquarters to assault the ridge, no one was ready to commit suicide. The young Spanish recruits with the battalion melted away into the countryside. The order was called off, and the Lincoln Battalion was relieved and sent into reserve in the rear where they remained for two weeks, shifted from one area to another but always under enemy artillery fire. Thirteen days after initially crossing the river, they were sent back to the town of Mora de Ebro for rest and reorganization. They had sustained about 50 percent casualties.

On 15 August the Lincolns, of which about one hundred Americans remained, were moved into the Sierra Pandols craggy granite hills south of Gandesa, where they relieved Republican troops. The rocky slopes of the hill they occupied were littered with dead. Here they endured eleven days of constant shelling, infantry attacks and air strikes. Nationalist artillery bombardments were heavy and concentrated as Franco threw everything he had into the battle. With all his big guns and bombs, he applied the tactic of *aplastamiento* (plastering)—the annihilation of an enemy by the sheer force of high explosives and steel. Day after day, the detonations churned earth and stone into a desolate landscape where nothing in the open survived. Shell-shocked men lay in their rock-constructed shelters, bleeding from noses and mouths from the concussion; others were disemboweled by red-hot shrapnel or fragments of flying rock. On 24 September, the last American tramped back across the pontoon bridge at Mora de Ebro.

Withdrawal of the International Brigades

Prime Minister Negrín spoke at the League of Nations in Geneva on 21 September 1938 proposing the retirement of all international soldiers from Spain and offering to withdraw the now seriously depleted volunteers serving in the International Brigades in the hope of convincing the Western powers that Spain was not Red and deserved their support in its fight against fascism. At the same time he hoped for a negotiated peace with Franco. Western governments, occupied with Hitler and their program of appeasement, were not listening.

Franco assured London and Paris that if it came to a general European war, he would remain neutral. To his relief the Great Powers, minus the Soviet Union, met at Munich on 29 September 1938 and agreed to Hitler's demands to annex a large portion of Czechoslovakia. This was a blow to the Republic, and its prospects for Allied support rapidly faded.

With the Munich pact, Stalin realized that he could not count on England and France in a conflict with Germany. His only option now was an agreement of friendship with Hitler. He sanctioned the withdrawal of the International Brigades. A farewell parade for the Internationals was held in Barcelona on 15 November 1938. The Lincoln Battalion was down to about 280 men, of which about 80 were Americans. By this time the unit consisted of a three-to-one majority of Spaniards.[24] The brigades were repatriated by the Negrín government in December 1938. This gesture was not reciprocated, as hoped, by Hitler and Mussolini who instead sent more men to aid Franco.

For the Lincolns, as for most other members of the brigades, it was not much of a homecoming. There were no medals, no pensions, no mustering-out pay, no military hospitals, of which about 70 percent were in need, only suspicion for having fought on the side of the Reds. The Friends of the Lincoln Brigade, a Communist organization based in New York, gave some support but generally only for those who had never wavered in their loyalty to the Party and the Cause. Others of humble backgrounds with no friends, no jobs and no money felt the truth of the adage "Nothing is too good for the working class, and Nothing is what it gets."[25]

Of the Americans that had gone to Spain, less than half returned. Similar figures apply to the other brigades. Even after the war was over, not all Americans had returned home. Some were still locked up in Franco's prisons. Life in Nationalist military prison camps was brutal with nonexistent medical facilities, little food, constant humiliation and arbitrary beatings. The threat of being shot was always present. Some were not released until 1940.[26]

FALL OF BARCELONA

Bereft of arms and demoralized after the Battle of the Ebro, the remnants of the Republican army faced the Nationalist onslaught. On 23 December 1938, Franco began his assault on Cataluña, and 350,000 men attacked along the entire front from Lérida to Tortosa, backed by the best weapons Germany and Italy could produce. On 15 January 1939 Nationalist troops entered Tarragona, and panic seized the civilian and military population of Barcelona sixty miles away. Half a million people set out on the long walk to the French border and sought asylum.

Those who remained behind passively awaited the inevitable. On 26 January, General Yagüe's troops entered Barcelona with hardly a shot fired. The fifth column, Nationalist supporters who had remained out of sight for over two years, emerged to welcome the invading troops and to exact revenge. Yagüe's Moors, the first to enter the city, were given several days' license to pillage and rape. Soldiers looted apartments and shops and shot anyone who resisted, but even after order was restored, the killing went on with impunity. In the first five days about 10,000 people were executed.[27]

In sharp contrast to the chaotic life of the city at the beginning of the war, the streets with their shuttered shop windows were now deserted except for Nationalist patrols, looting soldiers and hungry dogs. Nationalist doctors who found wounded Republican soldiers in hospitals that had not eaten in days tried to protect them, often unsuccessfully, from reprisals. To bring the city back to normalcy the military began to administer government offices, but manifestations of Catalan culture, including the use of the Catalan language, were banned; the people were ordered to speak only Castillian. Catalan books were burned in their thousands.

FLIGHT TO THE FRONTIER

Meanwhile, planes of the Condor Legion bombed and strafed the roads leading to the French frontier, along which passed some 300,000 defeated Republican soldiers and about 200,000 civilians. The ninety or so miles from Barcelona to France offered easy targets for the aviators. A continuous traffic jam of private and official cars inched their way along among heavily laden mules, men and women trudging on foot in the freezing weather carrying what possessions they could, their clothes soaked through from rain and snow, and children clutching a doll or favorite toy.

Many who avoided the machine guns and bombs of the planes perished from starvation and cold. The French government at first sealed the border, fearing its own right-wing parties who demanded it and the economic impact such a large number of refugees would have on the country. Negotiations with General Franco, in which the French government attempted to establish a neutral zone in Spain along the border for refugees, to be administered by foreign agencies, was rejected.

With several hundred thousand people waiting at the border stations, some for a week or more, the frontier was reopened to civilians and wounded soldiers on 27 January 1939. Many others crossed the mountains into France illegally, avoiding the Senegalese troops used by the French government to guard the border. The Nationalists occupied Gerona on 4 February and were approaching Figueras, the last town of any size before French territory and where the Republican government had retreated. The remnants of the Republican army fought rearguard actions that hardly slowed the Nationalist advance. On 5 February the French opened the border to everyone.

On 5 February, President Azaña, Prime Minister Negrín, Companys, president of the Generalitat, and the Basque president José Antonio Aguirre crossed into France together on foot after their car broke down. On 8 February the victors reached Figueras and the following day reached the border. By 12 February the entire frontier was sealed off by Nationalist troops. About 60,000 Republican soldiers failed to make the crossing and were rounded up by Nationalist forces.[28]

On 14 February, Franco's government issued the retroactive Decree of Political Responsibilities. People who had opposed the National Movement either in action or by grave passivity since 1 October 1934 would be held accountable. This would mean imprisonment, forced labor camps and even death for untold numbers of civilians and soldiers.

The fall of Cataluña had come swiftly. Still, some chose to fight on. Madrid and Valencia remained in Republican hands.

NOTES

1. Thomas, 612.
2. Beevor, 166. For a blow-by-blow account, see Thomas, 835 ff.

3. Jackson, 125.

4. For an account of the battle, see Thomas, 710 ff.

5. Ibid., 715.

6. Ibid., 717; Jackson, 130.

7. Jackson, 133; see Thomas, 789.

8. Thomas, 794; Beevor, 219.

9. Thomas, 797.

10. Esenwein and Shubert, 155.

11. Beevor, 124. It has been estimated that about 5,000 foreigners fought for the Republic independently of the International Brigades. According to Preston, *Spanish Civil War*, 160, a total of 59,380 International Brigaders came to Spain to fight fascism, 9,934 (16.7 percent) died and 7,686 (12.9 percent) were badly wounded.

12. From Eby, 13.

13. Ibid., 18.

14. Gurney, 54.

15. Thomas, 574.

16. Gurney, 53.

17. Ibid., 54.

18. For these examples, see Richardson, 160–161.

19. Lawrence, 76.

20. Eby, 65 ff.

21. Ibid., 141.

22. Geiser, 36.

23. Eby, 287.

24. Thomas, 851; Rolfe, 234.

25. Eby, 313.

26. For an eyewitness account of life in Nationalist prisons, see Geiser. Many Americans from the International Brigades fought in World War II but were under suspicion and were not allowed to go abroad until late in the war. In the McCarthy era, any connection with the Spanish civil war was considered subversive, and even the Abraham Lincoln Battalion itself was declared so. Former members were persecuted until the 1960s. For more detail, see Geiser, 245 ff.

27. Beevor, 249.

28. Ibid., 250.

CHAPTER 7

TRIUMPH AND DESPAIR, 1939–1945

With the final collapse of the Catalan front, and France now overwhelmed by hundreds of thousands seeking asylum, the French government was hard-pressed to improvise a coherent refugee policy. Emigrants were received by French soldiers and police, placed into some order and herded into hastily constructed camps watched over by guards who often stripped them of their few possessions.

FRENCH DETENTION CAMPS

The first makeshift camps on the Mediterranean beaches at Argèles-sur-Mer and Saint-Cyprien were open spaces surrounded by barbed wire without shelter, latrines or running water. To protect themselves from the wind, inmates dug holes in the sand with their bare hands. Later more camps were established—fifteen in all—in the Pyrenees mountains at Le Perthus and Bourg-Madame, among other places, where refugees often perished from the cold.[1] Children suffered from pneumonia and died in large numbers. The official policy was to make the prisoners want to return to Spain. The most sinister and feared camps were at Collioure, with its thirteenth-century castle, and Le Vernet, south and east of Perpignan, respectively. People identified as troublemakers, Anarchists, Communists or common criminals were sent to these detention centers.

Prisoners were confined in the dungeons of the castle and spent twelve hours a day breaking stones. The one latrine and one trough for bathing served the 400 or so men confined at Collioure, who were given about ten minutes out of the day to use them. Whippings and torture were everyday occurrences. Le Vernet punishment camp in the mountains, covering about fifty acres, held 2,000 to 5,000 men at various times, many of them from the International Brigades who had no country to return to.[2] Writer Arthur Koestler was confined there in winter 1939–1940 and considered the treatment worse than in Franco's prisons where he had also spent time. There was no heat against the bitter mountain winds, no lighting and no blankets. Each man slept on his side, confined to a space twenty-one inches wide, and if one turned over, the rest of the line in the wooden hut were forced to do the same. Nothing was provided: no tables, chairs, soap, clothes or eating utensils. Food was minimal and often rotten. Road building and camp maintenance kept able-bodied men busy working in soleless shoes and rags in subfreezing weather.

Many refugees returned to Spain, taking their chances with the Franco government rather than remain in such conditions. By early March 1939, about 70,000 had been repatriated. For many others, to return to Spain would have meant compulsory attendance before a Nationalist firing squad. Physically fit internees were often enlisted in labor battalions for work in various parts of the country or recruited into the French Foreign Legion. Civilian and military refugees remained in France in an atmosphere of hatred stirred up by the French right-wing pro-Franco press that reported that all Republicans were criminals, unclean and diseased. Newspaper editorials claimed that Communists and Anarchists would take over the country. Scare headlines set the tone.

The Army of Crime Is in France: What Are You Going to Do about It?[3]

For those confined to the camps, French officials tossed one loaf of bread for every four people over the fence into the compounds each day, as if feeding chickens.[4] Medical facilities were about as bad as if there had been none. Interned Republican army doctors who might have helped were not provided with equipment or medicines. Severely wounded men were left to die unattended. In time the French government improved the conditions in the camps, but they remained as symbols of total degradation for many Spaniards throughout their lifetimes.

THE SOVIET UNION AND REFUGEES

The Soviet Union, the only substantial ally of the Republic, condemned the French government for the treatment of refugees but itself offered little aid. It shunned the soldiers of the International Brigades that it had called to arms and only allowed across its borders those who were senior Communist Party members.[5] The Soviets took in some 2,000 Communist Party cadres, including El Campesino (Valentín González) and Dolores Ibárruri. El Campesino hated the discipline under which he was required to live in Russia, often found himself in trouble with Communist authorities, was sent to Siberia and finally escaped the country via Persia.

Among the Russians themselves who came to Spain, many fell victim to Stalin's bloody purges. The first Russian ambassador to the Republic, from September 1936 to February 1937, Marcel Rosenberg, and many of his diplomatic staff were recalled to Russia and executed. They knew too much about Stalin's murderous policies. They were not alone. Vladimir Antonov-Ovsêenko, Russian consul general in Barcelona, General Jan Berzin, chief of the Russian military mission, and Arthur Stashevsky, economic councilor, Soviet trade envoy and friend of Negrín, met a similar fate.

General Vladimir Gorev, military attaché in Madrid, and Mikhail Koltsov, Pravda representative and personal agent to Stalin, were also either executed or died in concentration camps, having incurred Stalin's displeasure.[6] General Emilio Kléber, alias Stern, of Rumanian Jewish origin, a member of the Comintern military section and first commander of the 11th International Brigade, returned to Russia in 1938, was demoted and executed. General Gal and Colonel Čopić of the International Brigades suffered the same end.

One who fared better, Alexander Orlov, NKVD chief in Spain, who spied and murdered under orders from the Kremlin and who was responsible for the death of Andreu Nin in 1937, defected to the United States in August 1938 and worked with American intelligence. Soviet agent (NKVD) in Spain Walter Krivitski fell out with Stalin and defected to the West in 1937. He was found shot to death on 10 February 1941 in the Washington, D.C. Hotel Bellevue.[7]

OTHER COUNTRIES

England allowed sanctuary to a few senior officials and a few hundred children, but others might enter the country only if they could be guaranteed by a Briton.[8] The United States was no more sympathetic. Belgium accepted some 3,000 children, and Mexico declared it would take 50,000 people. Some refugees escaped to North Africa, and others found asylum in South American countries. Republican leaders, composed of remnants of parties and organizations that had supported the Republic, Socialists, Republicans, Anarchists, Communists, and Basque and Catalan separatists were for the most part in exile. The Republican government, now in Toulouse, split apart. Negrín and Alvarez del Vayo and the Communists wanted to continue the resistance until, at least, the 250,000 soldiers still holding out in the central zone (Madrid and Valencia) were given guarantees against political reprisals. President Azaña, Diego Martínez Barrio, president of the Cortes, Companys and Aguirre opposed further resistance as futile. On 27 February 1939 France and Great Britain recognized the Franco government, whereupon Azaña resigned from office.

NATIONALIST POLITICAL CONSOLIDATION

Early in 1938 Franco had begun to establish a government and published decrees that would end civil disorder and religious dissension and set the tone for the postwar period. On 3 January 1938 he formed a cabinet made up of Monarchists, Falangists, generals, his brother-in-law, an ardent Catholic, Ramón Serrano Súñer, and his longtime friend, the industrialist Juan Antonio Suances.[9] The new cabinet was sworn in at Burgos in the monastery of Las Huelgas in an intimate and solemn ceremony.

On 9 March 1938 the Labor Charter (*Fuero de Trabajo*) was published, governing working conditions, setting wages and protecting the leases of tenant farmers from arbitrary acts of landowners. Landless workers on the large estates were left out. An organization was also established to return the land distributed by the Republic to its previous owners. Franco returned the family properties to the exiled king, Alfonso XIII, but left the question of restoration of the monarchy for the future.

On 5 April the Catalan autonomy statute of 1932 was revoked, and on 22 April, a law of press censorship was established. On 3 May the Jesuit Order, expelled from the country in 1932, was welcomed back and its property restored. The diminishing influence of the Church was a matter of concern for the government. Civil servants and military officials were required to attend religious services. Republican divorce laws were repealed. Laws and decrees were directed toward support of vested interests that existed prior to the advent of the Second Republic and toward a centralized state and government-controlled economy.

The country became a military-police dictatorship, severe, vindictive, devoid of imagination and compassion. The dictator relied on a coalition of forces, the Families as they were later called, that had been the basis of the Nationalist movement. The army was given a high position, and for Franco it was the guarantor of a united Spain. The Church was assigned a prominent role in the new order as the guiding light to a new moral and spiritual rehabilitation. Monarchists and Carlists were rewarded with government posts for their support during the war, but their dream of reinstating the monarchy was not on Franco's immediate agenda. (Martial law continued in force until 1948, shortly after the time Franco delivered his law of succession by which the monarchy would be eventually restored, but meanwhile he would serve as regent for life.)

The Falange dominated key positions in the Francoist regime and controlled the working classes through managerial posts in the hierarchically structured Spanish Syndical Organization, or OSE (*Organización Syndical Española*). This monolithic trade union presided over the means of production and was designed to ensure the organic unity of labor and management.[10] Falangists also controlled the media and the bureaucracy. Franco was careful that no one member of the Families—army, Church, Monarchists and Falange—would become too powerful.

SURRENDER OF MADRID

Meanwhile, isolated in the central zone, loyalist officers were sharply divided over whether to continue fighting. Ex-President Azaña's legal successor, Diego Martínez Barrio, refused to return to Spain, and the remnants of government in Madrid were in disarray. Few Socialists, Republicans or Anarchists saw any reason to waste more lives on a lost cause. Prime Minister Negrín, in favor of continuing the war, had lost the support of nearly everyone except the Communists. He clung to the idea that if the Republic could hang on until the breakout of a general European war, whose signs were ominous, the English and French, fighting Germany, would dispose of Hitler's ally Franco.

A faction developed in Madrid to overthrow Negrín's government led by Colonel Segismundo Casado, who in the course of the war had risen to command the army of the center. Casado was hostile to the PCE, recognizing the Communists as the power behind the government. He resolved to bring an end to the war on his own initiative. Among his supporters were the right-wing Socialist Julián Besteiro, the Socialist Wenceslao Carrillo (father of the Communist youth leader Santiago Carrillo), Anarchist commander of the 4th Army Corps Cipriano Mera and General Miaja.

On 5 March 1939, with the troops at their disposal, the plotters took over the chief government ministries in Madrid, seized control of the central telephone exchange and radio stations and announced over the radio that a new government, the National Council of Defense, had now been formed. Their goal was to achieve an honorable peace. The broadcast included a condemnation of Negrín and the Communists who it was alleged had sold out the Republic to the Soviet Union. Negrín and his advisers, in a state of despair over the direction of the war, were residing in the small town of Elda a little inland from Alicante. When Negrín heard the radio broadcast and after a telephone call to Casado, who remained intractable, he packed up and left for Toulouse in France. His Communist advisers were close behind.

In Madrid, meanwhile, the coup sparked off a mini civil war between the forces of the Council of Defense and the Communists. By 12 March 1939, Communist resistance was crushed, and the Council tried to engage in negotiations with Franco for an honorable peace. Franco, however, as before, had no interest in discussing any conditions of surrender. On 26 March the Nationalists announced a new drive on all fronts. Besteiro went on the radio to urge all, soldiers and civilians, to go out beyond the trenches around Madrid and greet the Nationalists like brothers.

On 27 March, Franco mounted his Victory Offensive and entered Madrid while Nationalist troops received the surrender of remaining Republican towns throughout the central zone. Those loyalists who could set sail from Valencia on the last boats heading for North Africa or France. Small groups of refugees continued to slip across the Pyrenean frontier. On 1 April 1939 Franco proclaimed the end of the civil war.

POSTWAR RETRIBUTION

With Nationalist victory achieved, Spain became a nation of suspects as a wave of harsh revenge and repression assailed the country. Occupied with the gathering storm of World War II, European nations allowed General Franco a free hand to deal out his brand of military justice to the losers in the civil war without embarrassing foreign inquiry. The relentlessly vindictive regime spurned any effort at reconciliation. The merciless liquidation of opponents was carried out with diligence.

Everyone who had been on the losing side was subject to persecution: Those who were active as leaders in political parties, trade unions or administrative posts or were officers in the Republican army were often executed without trial or given twenty- or thirty-year sentences in prison labor camps. Sympathizers and even those who were known to have voted for the Republic were hounded by police, brutalized and arrested to face military tribunals.

Ex-soldiers who had been drafted into the Republican army might be released from the camps, provided they could produce two guarantors who swore they were loyal to the Franco regime. Every village had a Falange representative who watched over the community for any deviations from the official policy, and teams of Falangists combed the towns and villages looking for signs of anti-Franco heresy. Falangists and priests studied lists of suspects, hunting for those who had served the Republic.

The regime settled accounts for the 7,937 members of the clergy including 283 nuns[11] who had been shot in the Republican zone and for the Republican executions of members of the Falange, beginning with José Antonio Primo de Rivera. All those who had belonged to the so-called Red Terror, that is, Communists, Anarchists or Socialists, according to the regime's skillful propaganda, had de facto committed crimes against the people. Mussolini's son-in-law Ciano, who visited Spain in July 1939, reported to the Italian dictator that there were 200,000 under arrest in Spanish prisons, and summary trials were going on every day. Shootings were proceeding in Madrid at 200 to 500 a day, in Barcelona at 150 and in Sevilla at 80.[12]

During the month of April 1939 defeated Republican soldiers were herded into hastily constructed barbed-wire compounds, football stadiums, bullrings and military barracks. In some places the names of those to be executed were broadcast over loudspeakers. Executions went on for months while prisoners were treated to the agonies of suspense waiting to hear their names called for the firing squad, as well as suffering from malnutrition and absence of medical care. Men went mad from thirst after being served salted fish and then denied water.[13]

Overcrowding was always a problem of prisoners. Marcelino Massana, for example, held the rank of captain, and along with thousands of others, he was stranded in the port of Alicante trying to find a ship to take them away into exile. Arrested there, he was transported to the notorious camp of Albatera built by the Republic to hold 800 prisoners. It housed 18,000 under Franco.

On 20 November 1939, the third anniversary of the death of José Antonio, 256 inmates were shot in a single session in the camp of the Bota in Barcelona.[14] Prisoners were lined up and forced to sing the Fascist anthem "Cara al Sol" and give the Fascist salute. Priests gave compulsory classes in religious education and asked penetrating questions in the confessional about a prisoner's activities during the war and reported the information to the military tribunals. The chief prison chaplain in Barcelona, Father Torrent, was a staunch supporter of mass executions.

Penal battalions and labor camps themselves often constituted a death sentence. On about fifty grams of bread a day prisoners built railroads, cleared rubble and rebuilt towns and villages and fortifications in the Pyrenees; later 20,000 were put to work building Franco's gigantic, austere tomb hewn out of the side of a granite mountain in the Valley of the Fallen, a little northwest of Madrid. The enormous underground cathedral would serve one day as the last resting place for Franco and the martyred José Antonio.

Franco relied on censorship to deprive the people of news and ideas, the secret police to infiltrate suspect groups and intimidation of the masses through unlimited power to arrest and detain. Many of those condemned to death by summary military courts-martial for their part in acts of defiance after the war never had the opportunity to speak on their own behalf. Relegated to solitary confinement, they ceased to exist even before the executioner performed his gruesome work. Their aspirations and provocation to commit illegal acts were not points of view the state wished to hear or divulge.

The draconian policies of the National Liberation lasted many months. Night and day, all over Spain, firing squads were at work eliminating suspected foes of the regime. Between 1939 and 1942 no figures are available of the number of men and women sentenced to death by the regime, and records of sentences were not always kept. Estimates put the figure in the hundreds of thousands. Sometimes fifty, eighty, a hundred people would be rounded up, dragged into a courtroom where the prosecutor read out the most outstanding crimes against the state, and the death sentence was immediately passed on the victims.

Eventually, perhaps due to the unfavorable image abroad that the regime created and a desperate need to rebuild the economy, the government changed tactics to persuasion and strove to enlist experienced militant working-class men into the Falangist-controlled labor syndicates. Those who refused were persecuted. The right to strike was forbidden by law and wages fixed by the Ministry of Labor.

COSTS OF WAR

By the end of the war the country had lost over three quarters of a million people out of a population of about 25 million. About 400,000 had emigrated, seeking political asylum in other lands; some 150,000 died in battle during the thirty-two months of war; around 20,000 people died during Republican reprisals, mostly in the first three months of the war; and another 200,000 through Nationalist reprisals from 1936 up to 1944 when the last of the mass executions took place.

The Franco government faced a deficit of many billions of pesetas to foreign banks and corporations that had aided the Nationalist cause. The majority of the gold reserves were in Moscow. Half the railroad stock and two thirds of the motor vehicles had been destroyed. Much of the cultivated land lay ruined. Starving people lived in bombed-out houses, in caves and even in holes in the ground for years after the war. About half of the livestock had been killed, and seed grain for future planting had been eaten. Much of the workforce had fled the country, were in prison or had been executed. With a standing army of 350,000 men maintained until 1946 and many thousands of security police consuming 30 percent of the national budget, and much of the rest going to pay back loans, there was little money for anything else. While the poor starved, trains loaded with Spanish food went to Germany to feed German workers in partial payment for help in the civil war. In depressed villages and towns, the infant mortality rate exceeded 50 percent.[15]

SPANISH NEUTRALITY IN WORLD WAR II

There were only five months between the end of the Spanish civil war, on 1 April 1939, and the onset of World War II on 1 September of the same year. With the outbreak of World War II, France opened her filthy, disease-ridden concentration camps and incorporated the thousands of Spanish prisoners into factories and labor units for the war effort.

Besides those enlisted into the Foreign Legion, others went into the regular army. About 50,000 men were organized into work brigades to construct fortifications.

Beginning on 10 May 1940 France was quickly overrun by the German army using blitzkrieg tactics developed in Spain. Aging Marshal Petain, one of France's military heroes of World War I, came to power, and an armistice with Germany was signed on 22 June. France was divided into two zones: the German-held north and west and the so-called Free France in the south, with the seat of government at Vichy. In their zone the Germans took charge of thousands of Spaniards from the labor companies and the military service who had not been able to disappear into the fabric of society and sent many of them to Germany either to work for the Reich as slave labor or to extermination camps if they had been prominent anti-Fascists. Many Republicans were sent to the camps at Oranienburg, Dachau, Buchenwald, Auschwitz and Mauthausen. Of the 12,000 Spaniards who entered Mauthausen, only 2,000 emerged alive at the end of the war.[16] Similarly, the vast majority of the 5,000 sent to Oranienburg perished. Largo Caballero, an inmate there, survived only a short time after the end of World War II and died in Paris.

Franco wanted to be in good graces with the Nazis when it looked as if they might win the war, especially after the fall of France. He met Hitler in Hendaye at the French border in October 1940 and showed a willingness to enter the war on the side of Germany in return for major economic and military aid and Spanish control of much of French North Africa. Hitler did not think Spain was worth it. No deal was reached.

Serrano Súñer still favored some kind of direct military alliance with Hitler. This resulted in the 40,000-plus Spanish Falange Blue Division being sent to the Russian front to support the Germans. Blue Division casualties on the Russian front were over 6,000 dead.

Spain provided the Germans with submarine refueling bases and intelligence, but Franco, with a wary eye on the events of the war, was careful to also maintain relations with the Allied powers and a disingenuous form of neutrality. When the tide of battle began to favor the Allies, Franco's enthusiasm for the Axis Powers waned. With the invasion of western North Africa by American and British troops in November 1942, Roosevelt assured Franco that Spanish interests were not in jeopardy. This could only have been a matter of profound relief for the dictator, fearful that an Allied victory in Europe could well spell the end of his regime, held together by the naked power of the bayonet.

Meanwhile, many of those Spaniards that found themselves in Vichy France, the unoccupied zone headed by Marshal Petain, were rounded up and sent back to the detention centers they had so recently evacuated. Lucky ones managed to become invisible in the large cities and often joined the Resistance. Spanish exiles contributed substantially to the French underground against the Nazis. They carried out their first action in southwest France in the autumn of 1940 and continued thereafter to engage in sabotage of German installations and helped organize escape routes for Allied airmen.

Members of the International Brigades who were not repatriated to their home countries were sent to concentration camps in Germany. Many died on route either of wounds, disease or a firing squad. Italian Internationals were handed over to Mussolini; others were sent back to Spain to wind up in Spanish prisons and graveyards. The government of Vichy was not unresponsive to the orders of extradition from Madrid. Such a fate befell Lluis Companys, returned to Barcelona and shot along with other distinguished men such as the ex-Republican governor of the province of Castellón, Manuel Rodríguez Martín, and the Socialist Julián Zugazagoitia, minister of the interior in the Negrín cabinet.

For all those in exile, most wanted to return to Spain and continue the fight against Franco. Hopes waxed and waned with the fortunes of World War II. Most exiles expected that the victorious Allies would oust Franco whose sympathies and material aid had supported the Axis Powers in World War II.

NOTES

1. Beevor, 268.
2. Stein, 72–73.
3. Ibid., 42. Another frivolous complaint put French cuisine at stake. What could be done with hungry women who refused to eat French rice because it was not prepared in the Valencian style, and men who rejected pureed potatoes? See Stein, 43.
4. Beevor, 268.
5. Ibid., 269.

6. Thomas, 952.

7. In 1941 General Pavlov, the Russian tank commander, was shot on orders from Stalin after he had lost his army in the first weeks of the German advance into Russia. Others shot in the same year were General Kulik, General Stern (Grigorovich) Russian officer and chief advisor in Spain who had replaced Berzin, and General Kulik, advisor to General Pozas. All Communists from eastern Europe who had fought in Spain fell under Stalin's suspicion. Hungarian Foreign Secretary Laszlo Rajk, commissar of the Rakosi Battalion in the 13th International Brigade, "confessed" at his trial in 1949 that he had sabotaged the efficiency of the battalion and carried on Trotsky propaganda. He was executed. Many other veterans of the Spanish civil war from eastern Europe were arrested, and some shot. See ibid., 953.

8. Beevor, 269.

9. See Jackson, 161, for more on the cabinet.

10. Esenwein and Shubert, 267.

11. Gallo, 66.

12. Preston, *Spanish Civil War*, 170.

13. Beevor, 267.

14. Ibid., 266.

15. Ibid., 268.

16. Stein, 108.

CHAPTER 8

WOMEN, ARTISTS, WRITERS AND EDUCATORS

The Spanish civil war captivated most Western writers and artists of the 1930s. Besides bombs and bullets, the struggle was also a war of propaganda. Poets, journalists, novelists, artists, photographers, poster designers and filmmakers participated in vital public opinion–making roles. In no previous local war were views expressed on such a massive scale through written and visual media. Writer-poet volunteers fought in the trenches, drove ambulances, served in field hospital units or commented on the events from safer ground.

REPUBLICAN WOMEN

On the battlefield, on the home front and in the war of words, women engaged the struggle, contributing their talents to the side they supported. During the period of the Second Republic, the status of women changed. An attempt was made to brighten women's social standing through legislation that gave them equal status to men under the law. They were first allowed the vote in 1933, and the legalization of divorce and abortion gave them more control over their individual destinies. With the advent of war, they broke out of their traditional roles to enter the workforce. In jobs, once the exclusive stronghold of males (many of whom had gone off to the front), women took up positions performing manual and skilled labor and managerial work in the trades, services and industry. Both sides in the civil war in different ways made appeals to women to participate in the war effort.

During the siege of Madrid, Dolores Ibárruri (La Pasionaria), the Communist deputy from Asturias, and Federica Montseny, an Anarchist, endeavored to uphold civilian morale and inspire soldiers on the front line. Federica Montseny, daughter of a well-known Anarchist family, was the first woman in the country to serve in the cabinet when she became minister of health in the Largo Caballero government from November 1936 to May 1937, a post that conflicted with avowed Anarchist principles (not to participate in government). She helped persuade Durruti to leave the Aragón front, to come to the rescue of Madrid with his militia column and to take orders from the government.

Montseny opened medical centers for women and was instrumental in the legalization of abortion. After the war she was imprisoned in France for a time by the Vichy government and then served in various posts in the exiled Spanish community, such as publisher of the CNT weekly in Toulouse.[1]

Dolores Ibárruri became an outspoken member of Parliament. Her brilliant, impassioned oratory is manifest by her parting speech to the International Brigades as they left Spain in 1938.

Mothers! Women! When the years pass by and the wounds of war are staunched: when the cloudy memory of the sorrowful, bloody days returns in a present of freedom, love and well-being: when the feelings of rancor are dying away and when pride in a free country is felt equally by all Spaniards—then speak to your children. Tell them of the International Brigades. Tell them how, coming over seas and mountains, crossing frontiers bristling with bayonets, and watched for by ravening dogs thirsty to tear at their flesh, these men reached our country as Crusaders for freedom. They gave up everything, their loves, their country, home and fortune—fathers, mothers, wives, brothers, sisters and children and they came and told us "We are here, your cause, Spain's cause, is ours. It is the cause of all advanced and progressive mankind." Today they are going away. Many of them, thousands of them, are staying here with the Spanish earth for their shroud, and all Spaniards remember them with the deepest feeling.

Then she spoke directly to the assembled brigades.

Comrades of the International Brigades! Political reasons, reasons of state, the welfare of that same cause for which you offered your blood with boundless generosity, are sending you back, some of you to your own countries and others to forced exile. You can go proudly. You are history. You are legend. You are the heroic example of democracy's solidarity and universality. We shall not forget you, and when the olive tree of peace puts forth its leaves again, mingled with the laurels of the Spanish Republic's victory—come back!

There were women in the early months of the war who took up arms, joined the militias and went off to fight. When Republicans and Communists formed into the Stalin Column in Bilbao to march to San Sebastián, seventy-five miles to the east, to help crush the Nationalist uprising, many of the contingent were women. Some of them marched off to battle wearing long dresses and high-heeled shoes. Two day's march over dusty roads brought them to San Sebastián, where on 28 July the rebel forces surrendered. The contingent then went on to attack unsuccessfully Vitoria, the capital of the province of Alava. In these battles and in further fighting, many of the women lost their lives.[2]

The POUM fighter Hippolyte Etchebéhère, leader of a small detachment, led a drive to take the small town of Sigüenza, northeast of Guadalajara, from Mola's forces during the battle for Madrid. The town was taken, but Hippolyte was killed, and his wife Mika, who fought by his side, took over his command, rallied the men and women under her and held off Mola's counterattacks until flight was the only alternative to death.[3] Many of the militia did not make it out of the town, but Mika survived to become second in command of a POUM unit fighting in the trenches before Madrid. When Commander Antonio Guerrero was wounded, she took over and crawled among the trenches, encouraging her men. The fighting was intense as the militiamen, amidst exploding artillery shells and a hail of bullets, threw sticks of dynamite at approaching enemy tanks. Mika was buried alive by a cave-in from a nearby explosion until her men dug her out unhurt.[4] They held off the Nationalists all day in this final attempt to take the city. Mika fought on until the end of war. There were others. A women's battalion mixed with regular soldiers fought bravely defending the Segovia bridge leading into the city.[5]

Militia women taken prisoner could expect the same treatment as their male counterparts. Johannes Bernhardt, the businessman and emissary of Hitler, was having lunch with Franco in the winter of 1936 when the question came up of what to do with four captured militia women. Franco's answer? "Shoot them," and he went on eating.[6] It is not known how many women served under front-line battle conditions; one estimate is a little less than a thousand.[7]

There were also foreign women engaged in front-line action such as the Russian Anna Starinov, translator for the Russian staff in Spain, who received the coveted Order of the Red Star for wartime operations. Sent by Stalin along with other Soviet advisers, she arrived in Spain in November 1936 where she helped train student guerrillas to make bombs, organized ambushes behind enemy lines, participated in blowing up enemy trains and railroad tunnels and returned home in 1937.

The practice of allowing women to serve at the front was eventually curtailed by the Republican government, sensitive to its image abroad. There remained, however, thousands of armed women in rear areas watching over security and administering the quartermaster corps.

COMMUNIST WOMEN'S ORGANIZATION

Communist-inspired Women against Fascism, or AMA (*Agrupación de Mujeres Antifascistas*), created in 1933 under the auspices of the PCE, was revitalized during the war. It was active in promoting the Spanish Communist Party, alerting women to the dangers of fascism and distributing relief to the needy. Dolores Ibárruri presided over the National Committee. The PCE did not readily attract female followers (there were 4,203 in 1938), but the AMA had about 50,000 members.[8] With government backing, they worked in hospitals for the wounded, created orphanages for children of combatants and aided families of women working in war industries. They also organized supplies for the front through various government ministries. Male hostility to women doing traditionally men's jobs, especially in the War Ministry, was never overcome.[9]

Margarita Nelken, a feminist and champion of women's rights and the landless poor, was a Socialist deputy in the Cortes whose biting articles sometimes brought her into court for inciting unrest. She was the most prominent woman in Spanish politics until Dolores Ibárruri usurped that position. With the outbreak of war, she advocated the formation of a fully professional army along the lines of the admired 5th Regiment, and she visited daily the front lines to encourage the troops and made anti-Fascist radio broadcasts. When the Republican lines faltered, General Miaja sent Nelken and Federica Montseny to rally and urge the soldiers back to the front. Her radicalism led her to communism, and the Socialists never forgave her for what they considered treason, nor did the Communists entirely trust her. She died in Mexico in 1968 at seventy-four.

Early in the war, women's initiatives led to the creation of new health and welfare organizations all over the country. Nursing care centers and blood banks in both military and civilian hospitals fell in large part to women. They worked long hours in unsanitary conditions and in field clinics near battle zones and underwent shelling and bombing. Outbreaks of disease in hospitals such as typhus were as dangerous as enemy bombardment. Training programs were developed all over Spain for war nurses who were in great demand, especially since nuns, who were often trained for medical work, kept a low profile in Republican zones. In prewar Spain the nursing profession had been inaccessible to women of the lower classes, but the demands of war gave women of all backgrounds an opportunity for status and a profession.[10]

LIBERATED WOMEN

The all-women's association called Free Women (*Mujeres Libres*), about 20,000 strong, an independent component of the Anarchist movement, was attentive to the welfare of working-class comrades whom they asserted suffered under capitalism and male domination. They demanded the abolition of prostitution, which they considered a highly degrading occupation, sticking posters on the walls in red-light districts and trying to persuade prostitutes to abandon their way of life, offering training courses in alternative work. Pimps and drug dealers, it has been reported, were often shot on the spot by Anarchist militiamen.[11]

The overthrow of the class system meant to many women the end of the patriarchal society in which they were accorded a subordinate role. The Anarchist philosophy maintained the equality of all human beings, but relationships changed slowly. Even in the Anarchist and Socialist collectives, traditional habits were hard to put aside. Women did not always receive equal pay as a man for the same job, and they were often assigned conventional tasks such as cooking, cleaning, laundry and making coffee. While these practices were contrary to Anarchist theory, the collectives were not around long enough for a new generation to grow up and eliminate them.

Still, some objected to housewife chores. Two who did transferred from the 5th Regiment to the POUM column headed by Mika Etchebéhère where it was understood that men and women carried out the same assignments. One of them, Manuela, stated her reasons for the transfer to the combatants:

I have heard that in your column the milicianas (militiawomen) have the same rights as the men, that they do not wash the clothes and the dishes. I have not come to the front in order to die for the revolution with a kitchen cloth in my hand.[12]

In the Republican zone young women were allowed for the first time to socialize in public such as in restaurants and bars without chaperones. Andreu Nin, the POUM minister of justice in the Generalitat, inserted in the new marriage code a statement that urged a husband to remember that his wife was his companion and had the same rights and privileges as he himself.[13]

On the Zaragoza front a POUM militia column had one woman. She had followed her lover to the front. In spite of her good looks she was not given any special attention by the men, who recognized that she was bound to her companion by a bond equivalent to marriage among the POUM revolutionaries. Her bravery under fire was admired. When someone with an accordion played "La Cucaracha" she danced to the music, and when it finished, all went back to normal. She became just another soldier.[14]

WOMEN INTERNATIONAL VOLUNTEERS

On the 25 August 1936, Felicia Brown, Communist and artist from London, was the first English volunteer killed in the civil war while fighting on the Aragón front.[15] The nurse Nan Green followed her husband to Spain, where he was killed in the Battle of the Ebro while she worked in a field hospital. The poet and novelist Sylvia Townsend made two trips to war-torn Spain with her lover, poet Valentine Ackland. Simone Weil, the twenty-seven-year-old French philosopher, wanted to fight and joined the Durruti column. An accident with hot cooking oil resulting in severe burns finished her front-line duties, however. Marion Merriman arrived at Albacete to unite with her wounded husband Robert. She joined the Lincoln Battalion, becoming the only female member, and worked on the battalion newsletter, typed death certificates and retyped much-needed training manuals with carbon paper for distribution to the men. Martha Gelhorn, who later married Ernest Hemingway, went to Spain to write.

Gerda Taro, the Jewish German companion of the photographer Robert Capa, was killed while taking pictures during the Battle of Brunete.

American Anarchist Emma Goldman, then sixty-seven, visited the front to chat with Durruti. In 1936, the Spanish comrades asked Goldman to direct their English propaganda campaign, designating her the London representative of the CNT-FAI. She worked tirelessly, writing hundreds of letters to supporters and editors. After Franco's triumph in early 1939, Goldman moved to Canada, where she devoted the last year of her life to securing political asylum and financial support for the women and children refugees of the Spanish war. She died in Toronto on 14 May 1940. The writers Lillian Hellman and Dorothy Parker both visited Spain and returned moved by the plight of the people in the Republican zone.[16]

NATIONALIST WOMEN

The social, political and economic advancement among women that transpired in the Republican areas was lacking in Nationalist territory, where their status continued to be defined by the paternalistic Catholic Church. Considered by the Church to be both physically and intellectually inferior to males, nothing changed. Women's supportive role in the struggle against the so-called Red Menace was to attend to the needs of men and raise a family. They were expected to dress modestly—trousers were strictly forbidden—and to use makeup sparingly. A manifesto of the Catholic ladies of Sevilla entitled "Spanish Women" contained the following advice:

In these grave moments for the country, your way of life cannot be that of frivolity, but austerity; your place is not in the theaters, the paseos, the cafes, but in the church and the hearth. Your ornaments cannot be inspired by the dirty fashions of treacherous and jewish France, but the modesty and pudeur [sense of modesty] of Christian morality. . . . Your duty is not to procure for yourself an easy life, but to educate your children, sacrificing your pleasures and helping Spain.[17]

The demands of war required some women to engage in nondomestic activities and join organizations such as the Carlist Margaritas, the feminist section of the Falange, or SF (*Sección Feminina*), Women in the Service of Spain (*Mujeres al Servicio de España*) and Aid Work at the Front (*Obra de Asistencia al Frente*). The women were all volunteers, and the organizations were approved by the Nationalist government at Burgos. Except for the Falange, they were all associated with the Church.

Young women of the Falange's Feminine Section, the largest of these groups, founded in 1934, was patterned after the Italian organization Fascist Women. During the civil war, the SF was headed by Pilar Primo de Rivera, younger sister of José Antonio, the founder of the Falange. With about 2,000 members at the beginning of the war, by the end it had enrolled some 580,000.[18] Their duties involved recruiting, propaganda and social work.

Pilar Primo de Rivera had definite views on how women should behave: "What we shall never do is put women in competition with men because women will never succeed in equaling men; if they try, women will lose the elegance and grace necessary for a life together with men."[19]

Mercedes Sanz Bachiller, the widow of the Falangist leader Onésimo Redondo, headed the Falange's Social Auxiliary (*Auxilio Social*) in Valladolid that distributed food to the needy and sent food trucks into recently captured towns with provisions for the destitute.[20] She also organized Winter Help (*Auxilio de Invierno*), a social welfare system that cared for the many orphaned children. Official reprisals in Valladolid and the "dawn patrols" of the Falange that rounded up and executed hundreds of Socialists left many children without a family. Mercedes insisted that her aid be nonpolitical, although it was supported by the Falange and by General Mola. Winter Help spread to other Nationalist-controlled cities.[21] The Carlist Margaritas, a feminist organization in Navarra, also ran a hospital and front-line organizations in aid of soldiers. They adhered to strict rules of social conduct. Those of Tafalla in Navarra

Solemnly promise on the Sacred Heart of Jesus

1. To observe modesty in dress: long sleeves, high necks, skirts to the ankle, blouses full at the chest.

2. To read no novels, newspapers or magazines, to go to no cinema or theater, without ecclesiastical license.

3. Neither publicly nor in private to dance dances of this century but to study and learn the old dances of Navarra and Spain.

4. Not to wear makeup as long as the war lasts.

Long live Christ the King! Long live Spain![22]

Women in the Nationalist zone worked long overtime hours for the cause. In Pamplona, girls worked in a foundry making hand grenades in their spare time with no pay. A bakery woman made bandages after long hours baking bread. For many women the war was a crusade, and they believed that their sons dying on the battlefields went straight to heaven. It was not uncommon for a woman to greet another whose son had been killed with the words, "How fortunate you are, you already have a son in heaven."[23]

Men and women of Navarra who owned nothing dedicated themselves to the war effort or went to fight to preserve their spiritual values and traditions. They fought and sacrificed not for material gain, as many would have been economically better off under the Republic, but for Christ and the Church.

Foreign women were conspicuous by their absence in the Nationalist camp. Only two Englishwomen volunteers supported the military uprising with their efforts in Spain: Priscillia Scott-Ellis, who served as a nurse and was often exposed to enemy shelling in near front-line field hospitals, and Gabriel Herbert, who acted as an intermediary between Burgos and the Catholic Bishops' Fund in London supplying medical equipment including ambulances to Franco's forces.[24]

ARTISTS, WRITERS AND CENSORSHIP

The sixteenth-century stage play *Fuenteovejuna* by Lope de Vega depicted a peasant uprising. Under the Franco regime it was rewritten to eliminate any such subversive elements. Not unlike an earlier period in the grip of the Spanish Inquisition, all dramatic works and films required an ecclesiastical license to be performed or shown, and the Church shared a major role in the censorship of books along with other government agencies. Novels were usually considered immoral, and all books disrespectful of the Church, the army or the goals of the Nationalist crusade were destroyed.[25] Newspapers and magazines were required to extol the virtues of the Nationalist movement, that is, the policies and programs of the Franco government.

The Republic also engaged in censorship. It came under the control of Alvarez del Vayo. Press releases for foreign consumption were not permitted to describe the internal leftist revolution. Instead, they were designed to convince the outside world that Spain was a liberal democracy where private property was sacrosanct. On the war front, like the Nationalists, losses were censored and emphasis placed on gains and ultimate victory. Both sides played up atrocities committed by the other side.

The commitment of writers and artists to present their views on the civil war for a wide audience was a distinct characteristic of the conflict. Intellectuals and artists troubled by the increasing threat of fascism and Nazism felt the time had come to declare their allegiance to the cause of democracy. Others, much fewer, feared the revolutionary turmoil and supported the Nationalists. Labor unions and political parties also had their own newspapers and, unlike in the Nationalist zone, were allowed to present differing political viewpoints.

Intellectuals were favorite targets of right-wing executioners. Arrested on 16 August 1936 in Granada, Federico García Lorca, Spain's outstanding twentieth-century poet and playwright, was taken out of the city and shot on the night of 19 August. Among other things the execution served as an example to those who, like Lorca, favored a homosexual lifestyle considered incompatible with the times and place. His execution startled Spanish and foreign intellectuals who came to identify the Franco regime as an enemy of culture.

As rector of the University of Salamanca, Miguel de Unamuno found himself at the outbreak of war in Nationalist territory and, disillusioned with the Republic, supported the insurgents, but his views changed. On 12 October, the anniversary of the discovery of America, celebrated as the Day of the Race, a ceremony was held in the great hall of the University of Salamanca. The bishop of the city was there, along with the one-eyed, one-armed General Millán Astray, a highly decorated founder of the Spanish Foreign Legion. Preliminaries over, speeches by professors, officials, writers and priests praised the uprising and condemned the Republic. Singled out for special vituperation was Catalan and Basque nationalism described as cancers on the body of Spain that would be cured by fascism, Spain's health giver. The motto of the Foreign Legions was shouted out— *¡Viva la Muerte!* (Long Live Death!)—while the Falange members gave the Fascist salute.

Unamuno rose to speak. His unexpected words stunned the audience into shocked silence. He condemned the speech referring to Catalans and Basques, reminding the assembly that he was Basque and the good bishop sitting next to him, whether he liked or not, was Catalan. He went on to denounce the absurd cry of "Long Live Death" and then turned his attention to Millán Astray who he said was a war cripple like Cervantes (who had an arm mutilated in the Battle of Lepanto in the sixteenth century), but unlike Cervantes, Millán Astray lacked spiritual greatness and would seek ominous relief in causing mutilation around him. There would soon be many more cripples in Spain.

Angrily Millán Astray then shouted, *¡Mueran los intellectuales!* (Death to intellectuals!), but Unamuno was not finished. He spoke of the university as a high temple profaned by the Fascists who would win the struggle because they had the brute force but who would never convince, lacking reason and right on their side. Falangists menacingly closed in on the seventy-two-year-old rector. Franco's wife, present at the event, moved up and asked Unamuno to give his arm to her. He did, and they left the hall together, surrounded by her bodyguard that kept the menacing crowd at bay. The following day the papers reported the glorious speeches of the participants, all but one. Unamuno was not mentioned. He was dismissed as rector and died a few months later.[26] There was little choice for most intellectuals, as the country fell bit by bit to the Nationalists, except flight into exile.

Born in Sevilla in 1875, a member of the literary movement known as the Generation of 1898, Antonio Machado is recognized as one of the greatest Spanish poets of all time. He remained loyal to the Republic, and in 1939 he was one of the last to leave Barcelona and with his mother crossed the Pyrenees on foot along with thousands of other refugees. Soon after, on 22 February, he died in France, followed by his mother two days later. The outstanding Spanish poet Juan Ramón Jiménez left Spain at the outbreak of the war. He and his wife traveled to America, where he taught literature in the United States, Cuba, and Puerto Rico and was awarded the 1956 Nobel Prize in Literature.

Many other intellectuals left the country such as José Ortega y Gasset whose articles, lectures and essays on philosophical and political issues contributed to a Spanish intellectual renaissance early in the twentieth century and to the fall of the Spanish monarchy in 1931. He was a member from 1931 to 1933 of the Cortes that promulgated the Republican Constitution. After the outbreak of the Spanish civil war in 1936 he lived abroad, returning to Spain in the late 1940s.

At the end of the war the Spanish poet Miguel Hernández was imprisoned by the Nationalists. From his cell he wrote letters to his wife and baby son.

[T]he rats have taken up wandering across my body while I sleep . . . every day I have to pick their dung out of my hair. . . . How little one is worth now! Even the rats ascend to dirty the roof of our thoughts. Now I've got rats, lice, fleas, bedbugs, mange. The corner I use for a home will very soon turn into a zoological park, or more likely a wild animal cage. (6 May 1940)

In the early spring of 1942, suffering from a festering disease, he wrote: "They are curing me by stops and starts through their bright ideas, sloppiness, ignorance, negligence." Miguel Hernández died at 5:30 A.M. on 28 March 1942, aged thirty-one. Scribbled on the wall above his cot were the lines: "Goodbye, brothers, comrades, friends: Let me take my leave of the sun and the fields."[27]

Pablo Casals, cellist, conductor, composer, pianist and humanitarian, one of the most influential musicians of the twentieth century, resided throughout the war in Barcelona, making frequent trips abroad to give concerts and raise funds for food, clothing and medical supplies badly needed by the Republic. He heard one night his own name mentioned by Queipo de Llano in his regular radio broadcasts from Sevilla. The general threatened that if he ever caught Pablo Casals, he would cut off both the cellist's arms at the elbow.[28]

With the fall of Barcelona imminent, Casals crossed the French frontier and made his way to Paris, where he lodged with friends before moving to Prades near the Spanish border where he helped organize aid for the refugees in the French detention centers. Casals remained in Prades throughout World War II under surveillance of the Nazis, refusing to return to a Spain under Franco.

Major Spanish painters were commissioned by the Republican government to present works at the 1937 International Exhibition in Paris. Pablo Ruiz y Picasso, who had lived outside Spain since 1903, displayed his large mural entitled *Guernica*, symbolizing the bombing of that Basque town in April 1937. Picasso expressed his outrage in the painting by employing powerful imagery: a bull, a dying horse, a fallen warrior, a mother and dead child, a woman trapped in a burning building, another rushing into the scene and a figure leaning from a window and holding out a lamp. The complex symbolism makes a powerful impact with its portrayal of the terrors of war. The work is now displayed in Madrid in the Reina Sofia Art Center. Picasso refused to allow the painting to be shown in Spain while Franco was alive, not that the dictator would have wanted it.

Also commissioned to present works at the 1937 Paris exhibition was Catalan painter and sculptor Joan Miró, whose surrealist works are among the most original of modern times; he fled Cataluña for Paris during the war where his posters helped raise money for the Republic. The Republican Basque painter Aurellio Arteta was forced to flee his homeland for exile in Mexico.

The Nationalists also had artists and poets espousing their cause such as Ribera Paco, who depicted Franco surrounded by his victorious troops at the end of the war, and Carlos Saenz de Tejada whose lithographs illustrated the words of the Nationalist song "Cara al Sol" (Face to the Sun). The creative, imaginative art of Republican supporters was never matched in the militaristic, reactionary and stultifying environment of the Nationalist zone.

Some notable intellectuals and writers, once Republican supporters— such as Dr. Marañón (physician and historian), Menéndez Pidal (philologist-historian) and Pérez de Ayala (ex-ambassador and novelist)— but disillusioned with atrocities and by the growing influence of the Communists, went into exile abroad and repudiated the Republic.

FOREIGN ARTISTS AND WRITERS

The civil war also absorbed the sympathies and commitments of foreign writers, poets, intellectuals and artists. Most favored the Republic. Some went to fight for it, such as French novelist, archaeologist and political activist André Malraux, whose writings were major contributions to twentieth-century literature. His experiences with a loyalist air squadron were the basis for one of his novels, *Man's Hope*. Similarly, the writer George Orwell fought with the POUM on the Aragón front to later write about it in his book *Homage to Cataluña*, and the budding English poet John Cornfield, the first British volunteer in the war, died on the battlefield.

Arthur Koestler of the *London News Chronicle*, who had joined the Communist Party in 1931, left it in disillusionment in 1937. Meanwhile, remaining behind after the fall of Málaga, he was arrested and imprisoned in Sevilla under sentence of death as a suspected spy (which he had been for the Russians). He was exchanged for the wife of a Nationalist aviator held by the Republic.

Ernest Hemingway, author of the novel on the civil war *For Whom the Bell Tolls*, admired the military discipline of the Communists and was often taken into their confidence. He helped make two films about the war: *Spain in Flames* and the *Spanish Earth*. For the latter he assisted the Dutch Communist Jordis Iven along with John Dos Passos, Lillian Hellman, Dorothy Parker and the poet Archibald MacLeish.

English poet W.H. Auden, who in 1937 drove an ambulance for the Republic, anti-Fascist Georges Bernanos and the pilot and writer Antoine de Saint-Exupéry came to observe and report, as did novelist Sinclair Lewis.

Some were disillusioned by the experience. The Communist Stephen Spender went to Spain to see events and in search of a former secretary who had joined the International Brigades. He quit the Party after executions carried out in the International Brigades. The English writer Julian Bell, nephew of Virginia Woolf, went as an ambulance driver and was killed in the Battle of Brunete.

Numerically, Franco had little support from the intellectual and artistic communities and writers abroad, especially after the execution of García Lorca. A few writers and artists, however, saw virtue in Franco's crusade such as the American poet Ezra Pound, the English writer Evelyn Waugh (who said if he were a Spaniard, he would fight for Franco against a bad government) and the French poet Paul Claudel.[29]

One American entertainer went to Spain, Paul Robeson. He sang to wounded soldiers such as those in the International Brigade hospital in Benicasim on the Mediterranean, giving a good deal of delight to the men of the Lincoln Battalion, among others. When all was quiet after the battle on the Jarama front, the American and English International Brigades were visited by such diverse celebrities as the scientist J.B.S. Haldane and the actor Errol Flynn.

EDUCATION

In self-governing communes where Libertarian communism was practiced, education had a high priority. A commune might include one or a group of villages, but all aspired to the eradication of illiteracy. Cinema, radio and teaching missions were employed for the purpose.[30]

The attitude of the Republican government was similar. Education was a priority even in difficult circumstances. Saint-Exupéry described a classroom 500 meters behind the Madrid front, situated behind a wall in which a corporal taught bearded soldiers the rudiments of botany.[31] The workers and peasants who had always been shut out of the schoolhouse and labeled uncultured brutes by the upper classes were more than a little anxious to attain some semblance of learning, which their fathers and mothers had never known.

Throughout the war the Republic was involved in education, opening, it was claimed, 1,000 new schools in 1937. The idea of liberation through cultural and self-improvement was a constant theme of the government, and schools were, of course, used as official propaganda centers competing with the Anarchists' educational programs.

The Socialist Federation of Teachers Union, or FETE (*Federación Española de Trabajadores de la Enseñanza*), was heavily engaged in the struggle against illiteracy.[32] The union, like many others, had a militia battalion active on the Madrid front from November 1936 to the end of the war. Female members served in hospitals, helping to educate the wounded, and organized homes and schooling for orphaned children in rear areas.

Theater also played a role even in the front lines where plays were staged to boost morale and educate the soldiers about the social and political implications of the war. In the cultural-educational vanguard women played a major role. María Teresa León, for example, writer, actress and director, organized plays, song festivals and poetry competitions at the front. With a volunteer itinerant theatrical group, she traveled to towns, villages and the forward areas, performing plays for Republican military units and sometimes reading the works of her poet husband, Rafael Alberti.[33]

Republican plays on contemporary topics contrasted sharply with the Nationalist stage that presented primarily religious themes or adulterated works from past centuries. Education in the Nationalist zone was placed firmly in the hands of the Church. Crucifixes were ordered hung in every classroom, and images of the Virgin became mandatory fixtures. Religious instruction was requisite in primary and secondary schools (except in Morocco), and all teachers had to undergo examination of their religious beliefs to make sure they conformed to those of the Church. Many schools were closed for lack of teachers with the right qualifications.

Schoolteachers who sought jobs had to make a sworn declaration to the "glorious National Movement" and to swear they had never belonged to any political party associated with the Popular Front nor any separatist party. If they had ever been in the loyalists' (red) zone, an affidavit describing their activities while there was required. Potential teachers also had to obtain a certificate from the parish priest attesting to their religious, moral, political and social conduct before and during the Nationalist movement along with a similar document from the commander of the local garrison and a statement of good conduct from the mayor of the town. With these testimonials the candidate then appeared before an academic, civil or military board for an interview.[34] Diplomas acquired in the Republican zone were automatically invalid. The school curricula placed the emphasis on religious instruction and the study of the Nationalist movement. Singing was confined to hymns of praise and patriotic songs.

SOLDIER POETS

Among Republicans great value was placed on popular poetry, letters and essays, especially written by soldiers or workers, that embodied a spiritual victory of the Republic over the sterile crusading rhetoric of the Nationalists.

Some of the men of the International Brigades wrote of their experiences in poetry. Alec McDade from Glasgow, assistant company commissar of the British Battalion at the time of his death in the Battle of Brunete, described the battle of the Jarama Valley in the following words:

> There's a valley in Spain called Jarama
> It's a place that we all know too well
> For 'tis here that we wasted our manhood
> And most of our old age as well.[35]

John Leper described the slaughter in the Jarama Valley with the words:

> Death stalked the olive trees
> Picking his men
> His leaden finger beckoned
> Again and again.[36]

Found scribbled in a notebook an anonymous militiaman of the British Battalion wrote:

> Eyes of men running, falling, screaming,
> Eyes of men shouting, sweating, bleeding

The eyes of the fearful, those of the sad,
The eyes of exhaustion, and those of the mad.
Eyes of men thinking, hoping, waiting,
Eyes of men loving, cursing, hating.
The eyes of the wounded, sodden in red,
The eyes of the dying and those of the dead.[37]

NOTES

1. Esenwein and Shubert, 127.
2. Zuehlke, 34.
3. Kurzman, 101.
4. Ibid., 316.
5. Beevor, 137.
6. Thomas, 514.
7. Beevor, 89.
8. Nash, 67.
9. Ibid., 71.

10. Ibid., 151 ff. Medical services financed by foreign donations played an important role in the war. Doctors, nurses and ambulance drivers were as dedicated to the cause as were the soldiers of the brigades. The American medical aid had six hospitals in Spain. Blood transfusions were slow and cumbersome: The donor was placed on a bed next to the patient and a blood line between the two set up. Only a few hospitals performed transfusions, and they were not given at all in front-line casualty clearing stations and field hospitals. Norman Bethune, Canadian medical doctor, arrived in Madrid in 1936 and in a pioneering effort set up a blood donating unit, stored the blood in flasks in refrigerators and sent it around to the hospitals as it was required. Similar units were set up in other cities of Spain, and blood and transfusion equipment was taken to the front lines where it was most needed. Bethune's skill and organization saved hundreds of lives. He was ably assisted by, among others, the Canadian Celia Greenspan, wife of an American journalist. Bethune returned to North America, raised money for hospital work in Spain and died in China attending victims of another civil war.

11. Beevor, 89.
12. Quoted by Nash, 109.
13. Esenwein and Shubert, 129.
14. From Borkenau, 106, who met the girl on the front line.
15. Cunningham, xxxii.
16. Keats, 200.
17. Thomas, 763.

18. Esenwein and Shubert, 183.

19. Opening speech to national council of the women's section of the Falange by Pilar Primo de Rivera. Quoted by Fraser, 309.

20. Jackson, 140.

21. Preston, *Doves of War*, 258 ff.

22. Quoted from Fraser, 309.

23. Ibid., 311.

24. Preston, *Doves of War*, 29.

25. Beevor, 263.

26. For more details, see Thomas, 501 ff.

27. Preston, *Dreams + Nightmares*, 57.

28. Casals, 226.

29. See Beevor, 177, for these and other poets and writers; see also Cunningham.

30. Thomas, 182.

31. Ibid., 865.

32. Ribeiro de Meneses, 113.

33. Nash, 119.

34. Thomas, 762.

35. Cunningham, 43 (first of four stanzas).

36. Spender, *World within World*, 33–34.

37. Quoted by Thomas, 606. The first reasonably objective history of the civil war by Hugh Thomas that appeared in 1961 was banned in Spain.

CHAPTER 9

AFTERMATH

Major weaknesses of the Republic, leading in no small measure to its defeat, were the interminable violent political struggles among the various factions: left and moderate Socialists, Stalinist and anti-Stalinist Communists and Anarchists. Infighting, coupled with lack of discipline in the militia units of the various parties such as the CNT and UGT, made them vulnerable to an organized enemy. The first few weeks of the war were crucial. By the time overall command was imposed on independent militias, it was already too late. Added to this, the farcical performance of the NIC, severely restricting the Republic's ability to acquire modern arms, and Russian aid going generally to Communist units, led to the use of outdated weaponry among other militias.

The Nationalists, on the other hand, who were better led, enjoyed unstinting support from Germany, Italy and Portugal with no demands for participation in political policy. Falangists, Monarchists and CEDA, competing rightist groups, set aside their major differences to concentrate on winning the war. The degree of unity and the steady supply of modern weapons far outdistanced the military capacity of the Republic.

The act of appeasement at Munich, an accord signed by Germany, Italy, France and Great Britain on 29 September 1938, that gave Germany a large part of Czechoslovakia, underscoring Hitler's territorial aggression and the threat to Europe by Fascist dictatorships, sent a message to Washington. Undersecretary of State Sumner Welles pointed out, "Of all our blind isolationist policies the most disastrous was our attitude on the Spanish civil war."[1] Former Secretary of State Henry L. Stimson pleaded against the arms embargo to Spain:

If this loyalist government is overthrown, it is evident now that its defeat will be solely due to the fact that it has been deprived of its rights to buy from us and from other friendly nations the munitions necessary for its defense.[2]

Eleanor Roosevelt, an influential supporter of the Republic, was anxious to see the arms embargo lifted, but she could make little headway with her husband the president who, although sympathetic, knew that the Congress and much of the nation would not sanction such action. He also knew that he could lose many Catholic votes in the next election if he took a position against Franco who was fighting, it was said, for the preservation of Catholic values. One million signatures had already been received by the Congress, gathered by Dennis Cardinal Dougherty in his archdiocese of Philadelphia, in support of the embargo. Ambassador to Great Britain Joseph P. Kennedy also put pressure on the president and the Congress to maintain neutrality toward Spain.[3] His group convinced congressmen, who depended on the Catholic vote, to oppose repeal of the arms embargo even though no more than 20 percent of the nation and 40 percent of Catholics supported the Nationalists.[4]

In a cabinet meeting on 27 January 1939 President Roosevelt said that the embargo had been a grave mistake.[5] In 1945 the undersecretary of the Spanish Foreign Ministry stated that without American petroleum, trucks and credit the Nationalists could not have won the war.[6]

In the summer of 1938 Churchill came around to admitting the embargo had been wrong. In England a public opinion poll showed only nine out of one hundred people supported Franco.[7] All this was now of little comfort to half the population of Spain. The betrayal of all who had fought for the Republic came when Stalin abandoned Popular Front policies and his crusade against the Nazis and signed a pact with Hitler in the summer of 1939. In the long period of his dictatorship, Franco worked diligently to keep the conflict alive in the public mind. For those who might question his heavy-handed totalitarian state, the corruption and bloody repression, he could remind them that he had saved Spain from the barbarous Red Menace and that only he stood in the way of a return to chaos. No public response from the defeated was permitted.

Nevertheless, opposition continued. For some, especially the Young Anarchist Libertarians, mostly living in France, the war was not over. Through clandestine printing presses and illegal distribution of leaflets they assailed the Franco regime's repressive policies. Attempts on Franco's life were kept quiet by the government in the pretext of total popular support. Antigovernment guerrilla activity continued in Cataluña and in the mountains of Asturias and Andalucía for years after the end of the war. A major triumph for the security forces occurred in 1960 with the death of the Libertarian Francisco Sabaté, Franco's enemy number one gunned down in a village in the Pyrenees mountains.

NOTES

1. Sumner Welles, *The Time for Decision* (New York: Harper & Brothers, [1944]), 57, quoted in Landis, xix.

2. Landis, xix; and Henry L. Stimson, letter, *New York Times*, 23 January 1939.

3. Wyden, 472.

4. Beevor, 174.

5. Geiser, 194.

6. Beevor, 115.

7. Thomas, 875.

BIOGRAPHIES OF MAJOR PARTICIPANTS

AZAÑA, MANUEL (1880–1940)

Republican statesman Manuel Azaña was born at Alcalá de Henares, educated in law and found employment in the Registry Office of the Ministry of Justice. He became involved in politics editing the political journal *España*. A candidate to the Cortes for the province of Toledo in 1918 and 1923, he lost on both occasions. In 1925 he founded his own political party, *Acción Republicana*, at the same time writing plays and novels and winning the National Prize for Literature in 1926.

After the abdication of Alfonso XIII in 1931, he became minister of war, purged the army of its overstaffed officer corps and then became prime minister in the new Republican government. Azaña believed that the Catholic Church was responsible for Spain's backwardness and sought to eliminate its special privileges. He promoted agrarian reform and autonomy for Cataluña. Ousted by the center-right coalition in 1933, violent demonstrations and rebellion in Barcelona and Asturias in October 1934 were in part blamed on him, and he was arrested. No evidence was found against him, however, and he was released in December.

In February 1936 he returned to office as head of the Popular Front government and upset the Conservatives by releasing all left-wing political prisoners. He reintroduced agrarian reforms, outlawed the Falange and transferred right-wing military leaders such as Franco and Goded to posts outside Spain.

In May of the same year Azaña became president of the Republic and remained in that post throughout the civil war, but with no real influence over the policies of the successive wartime Republican governments. On

27 February 1939, British Prime Minister Neville Chamberlain recognized the Franco government, and later that day Azaña resigned from office. Worn out, he died in the Grand Hotel du Midi in Montauban, France.

CASADO LÓPEZ, SEGISMUNDO (1893–1968)

Casado was born in Segovia, the son of a military family, and entered the military academy in Valladolid at age fifteen. He later became a Freemason and head of Azaña's presidential guard. When war broke out he remained loyal to the Republic and was instrumental in organizing the mixed brigades of the Popular Front army. He participated in the defense of Madrid and the Battles of Jarama and Brunete as a corps commander. He rose to command the central army in 1939.

Convinced that defeat was inevitable and that Prime Minister Negrín was promoting a Communist coup, along with General Miaja, Julián Besteiro and Cipriano Mera, among others, he formed the National Defense Council in Madrid on 5 March 1939—the junta that overthrew the Negrín government. Casado tried to negotiate a peace settlement with General Franco to no avail; the Nationalist army entered Madrid virtually unopposed on 27 March. Casado fled to Valencia where he boarded an English ship. He lived in Britain for many years and did not return to Spain until just before his death.

COMPANYS, LLUIS JOVER (1883–1940)

While studying labor law at the University of Barcelona, Companys formed the Republican Student Association working closely with the CNT. In 1920 he was arrested for his political activities and was imprisoned in the Castle of La Mola in Minorca. After his release in 1921 he became involved in the Catalan independence movement and edited the weekly journal *La Terra*. Leader of the Catalan Left (*Esquerra Català*), he was elected to the Cortes in 1921 and again in 1931.

He was appointed speaker of the Catalan Parliament. On the death of Maciá y Llusa in December 1933 he later became president of the Catalan Generalitat. He proclaimed an independent Catalan state during the October uprising in 1934, but this separatist revolt failed, and Companys and the entire Catalan government were arrested. Found guilty, Companys was sentenced to thirty years in jail but was released from prison after the Popular Front victory in February 1936.

As president of the Generalitat again from 1936 to 1939, he collaborated with the CNT and the POUM and tried to protect their members from the Communist-dominated PSUC. He attempted to maintain the unity of the coalition of parties in Cataluña but had to contend with threats from the Soviet consul, Antonov-Ovseenko, to suspend arms shipments from Russia if Communist demands were not met. Companys's influence declined after the events in May 1937 in Barcelona.

Although he remained president during the war, he was little more than a figurehead. Seeking exile in France as the civil war approached its conclusion, he was returned to Spain by the Gestapo and shot by a Nationalist firing squad in the moat of the fortress of Mont Juich in Barcelona.

DURRUTI, BUENAVENTURA (1896–1936)

One of the outstanding figures of Spanish anarchism, Durruti was born in León, where he worked as a railroad worker and trade union activist, taking part in the General Strike of 1917. He joined the Anarchist movement and, with Juan García Oliver and Francisco Ascaso (killed in Barcelona storming a military barracks), established the *Solidarios* group in 1919. Two years later, members of the group were involved in the murder of Eduardo Dato, the Spanish prime minister. In 1923 they allegedly assassinated Juan Soldevila Romero, archbishop of Zaragoza (not proved) in revenge for the murder by the police of Salvador Segui, a CNT leader. Durruti and Ascaso fled to France in June of that year and took part in a border raid at Vera del Bidosa on 6 November 1924. They were also involved in an attempt on the life of King Alfonso in Paris and the assault on the Bank of Spain at Gijón.

Threatened with extradition to Spain and constantly on the run, Durruti and Ascaso lived in various Latin American countries but returned to France in 1926. Durruti was arrested, but protests by the Left resulted in his release, and he moved to Belgium, where he lived, condemned to death in four countries, before returning to Spain in 1931. There he plotted to overthrow the Republic. In Barcelona he became involved in organizing strikes, and in January 1932 he was arrested and deported to Spanish Guinea. Durruti returned to Spain but was once again arrested in December 1933 for leading an uprising in Zaragoza. In the elections of 1936 he urged Anarchists to support the Popular Front in order to defeat the extreme right wing. After the victory at the polls he joined with Federica

Montseny and Juan García Oliver to establish communes and workers' committees.

On the outbreak of the civil war, Durruti helped organize the anti-Fascist militias committee in Barcelona that immediately sent him and 3,000 Anarchists to Aragón in a futile attempt to retake the Nationalist-held city of Zaragoza. Failing in this he took his militiamen to Madrid, arriving on 14 November 1936. On 19 November, while talking to some militiamen in the University district behind the lines, he was shot in still unexplained circumstances and died the following day. Durruti's supporters claimed that he had been murdered by the Communists.

FRANCO BAHAMONDE, FRANCISCO (1892–1975)

The authoritarian leader (*caudillo*) General Franco, who governed Spain from 1939 to 1975, was born at El Ferrol in Galicia, son of a naval paymaster. After graduating from the infantry academy of Toledo in 1910, he was posted to Morocco and rose rapidly in the army, earning a reputation for total professional dedication. He was a strict martinet, ruthless, determined, a puritan in habits and brave in battle. When the commander of the Foreign Legion (*Tercio de Extranjeros*), Millán Astray, was wounded, he appointed Franco his successor. Franco commanded the unit from 1923 to 1927, becoming a highly decorated national hero for his role in suppressing Moroccan revolts. The *Tercio de Extranjeros* had a fearsome reputation for brutality. When it attacked a village, little was left but smoking ruins and the bodies of men, women and children.

In October 1923 Franco married Carmen Polo, a member of a wealthy merchant family. His growing reputation in the armed forces was recognized when Alfonso XIII sent a representative to the wedding. At the age of thirty-two he was promoted to general and in 1927 appointed director of the military academy of Zaragoza until its suppression by the Republican government.

Serving as military commander of the Balearic Islands in 1934, he was invited to Madrid by the government as technical adviser to the general staff for the autumn field exercises. He was there when the revolt in Asturias began in October and played a major role in organizing the suppression of the miners—an action that earned him profound hatred in left-wing circles.

When CEDA came to power and Gil Robles took over the War Ministry, Franco was appointed chief of the General Staff, endeavoring to raise the efficiency of the army and to install conservative antileftist officers in dominant positions. With the return of the Left to power in the elections of 1936, Franco joined other Spanish army officers in plotting the overthrow of the Popular Front government. Considered a dangerous conspirator, he was sent to command a garrison in the remote Canary Islands off the southern coast of Morocco. Sometime in early July 1936, presumably before a plane was chartered in England on 11 July to fly to the Canaries and transport him to Morocco, he made his decision to join the insurgents but insisted on the command of the elite army of Africa during the revolt.

Franco was elected head of the Nationalist movement and made chief of state on 1 October 1936 in Burgos, his headquarters, by a consortium of insurgent fellow officers. Giant posters of Franco were displayed all over Nationalist-controlled Spain, along with the slogan, "One State! One Country! One Chief! Franco! Franco! Franco!"

On 19 April 1937 Franco merged conservative groups into one rightist political party with himself as supreme head. On 30 January 1938 a Nationalist decree confirmed Franco in his position, and a Nationalist government was established (as opposed to the legally constituted Republican government). Franco's armies were triumphant, and on 1 April 1939 the civil war officially ended, and he became dictator for life.

No attempt was made by Franco to heal the wounds of the civil war; on the contrary, he exacerbated the hatred by refusing to offer any reconciliation to the defeated. A total reign of silence was imposed upon the vanquished, and everything they stood for was made illegal. Socialists, Communists, Anarchists, Libertarians, Republicans and Freemasons were all lumped under the odious "Red" label, and the regime never let anyone forget that Spain was saved from these demonic evils and from foreign domination by Franco. Hundreds of thousands of political prisoners died as a result of starvation, overwork and executions in Franco's concentration camps and work brigades. The persecution of political opponents continued until 1944. The Franco government had joined the Anti-Comintern Pact in 1938 but remained neutral in World War II. Franco's anti-Communist stance made him popular with the United States, and in 1953 he signed an agreement that enabled the United States to establish four air and naval bases in Spain, a move that greatly improved Spain's impoverished economy. Franco's main foreign policy was to recover Gibraltar and to maintain Spain's colonies in Africa, but he was unsuccessful in both. Britain refused to give up Gibraltar, and in 1956 he was forced to come to terms with the sultan of Morocco. Franco announced in 1969 that on his death he would be replaced by Prince Juan Carlos. Shortly after his death and the establishment of a parliamentary monarchy, almost every vestige of his dictatorship disappeared.

GIL ROBLES, JOSÉ MARÍA (1898–1980)

Born in Salamanca and after a university education in law, Gil Robles became a journalist with the Catholic daily newspaper *El Debate* and was active in right-wing politics, supporting the dictator Primo de Rivera. After the establishment of the Second Republic in 1931, he was elected to the Cortes for Salamanca and was instrumental in establishing the CEDA, a coalition of small right-wing parties opposed to the policies of the Republican government. Although leader of the rightist CEDA that won the election of 1933, he was passed over for prime minister by President Alcalá Zamora in favor of Lerroux to avoid confrontation with leftist parties. Gil Robles was made minister of war in 1935 and named Franco chief of staff of the military.

He espoused the position of "accidentalism" by which he claimed that it was "accidental" whether Spain was to be a monarchy or a republic, but it was essential that law should not conflict with the Church. An excellent speaker and parliamentarian, he admired the methods of Nazi propaganda (such as the use of the radio, dropping leaflets from airplanes and holding intoxicating rallies). Sympathy with Nazism and his preference for monarchy proved provocative. He was shunned by Republicans for his Fascist views and by Nationalists who distrusted him.

Unwilling to struggle with Franco for power, he announced the dissolution of the CEDA in April 1937. He spent the war in exile in Portugal and became more liberal in later days when he returned to Spain. In 1956 the regime prosecuted four young men who had written leaflets opposing the government; Gil Robles defended them at their trial. The accused were condemned, but Gil Robles issued a warning against the worship of the state, stating that it was lawful to criticize the authorities when injustices have been committed in their name. In the spring of 1962 he declared publicly that Spain could enter the European Common Market only on condition of having a democratic regime. He was appointed professor of the University of Oviedo in 1968 and died twelve years later.

GONZÁLEZ, VALENTÍN (EL CAMPESINO) (1909–1983)

Valentín González, son of a miner and a militia leader, gained prominence in the fighting in the Guadarrama mountains north of Madrid at the outbreak of the war and joined the Communist Party, acquiring the name El Campesino (The Peasant). He became commander of one of the mixed brigades and fought in all the major battles around the capital. When 300 Republican soldiers were taken prisoner and later found dead with their legs cut off, El Campesino in retaliation executed an entire captured Moroccan battalion of some 400 men. With the Nationalist victory he fled to Russia but fell out with the Communist authorities and with Stalin himself. Sent to Siberia he escaped in 1948 via Persia to France, disillusioned with communism. El Campesino proclaimed the Third Spanish Republic and began guerrilla warfare against the Franco regime. In 1961 he and a band of thirteen men struck the electric power station of Irabia in the Basque country. A Civil Guard was killed, and the perpetrators escaped back into France. Valentín was arrested by French police and forced to live in Metz away from the Spanish frontier. He returned to Spain in 1978.

IBÁRRURI, DOLORES (LA PASIONARIA) (1895–1989)

The eighth of eleven children, Dolores Ibárruri was born in Gallarta into a poverty-stricken mining family. Although an intelligent student her family could not afford to pay for education, and she became a seamstress. In 1916 she married a miner and bore six children, only two of which survived to adulthood. She later wrote that they had died because of her inability to provide them with adequate medical care and nourishment. The family's financial situation deteriorated when her husband, an active trade unionist, was imprisoned for strike action. After reading the works of Marx, Ibárruri joined the PCE and wrote articles for the miners' newspaper using the pseudonym Pasionaria (passion flower).

In 1920, elected to the Provincial Committee of the Basque Communist Party, she soon becoming an important local political figure and later editor of the left-wing newspaper *Mundo Obero*. In September 1931 she was arrested, charged and imprisoned in Bilbao for hiding a Communist comrade on the run from the Civil Guard. Released, she was arrested again in January 1932 and held in prison until January 1933. Ibárruri was a member of the Spanish delegation of the Communist International that met in the Soviet Union in 1933 and attended meetings of the Comintern, where she supported Popular Front policy.

Elected deputy to the Cortes in February 1936 she became the chief propagandist for the Republic during the war and famous for her passionate oratory, especially during the siege of Madrid when she broadcast appeals for unity over the radio.

Some insight into Dolores Ibárruri's psyche can be garnered from sentiments expressed in her autobiography in which she declared: "Women were freed from brutalizing mine work only to be converted into domestic slaves, deprived of all rights."

[I]n the home, she was stripped of her social identity; she was committed to sacrifice, to privations, to all manner of service by which her husband's and her children's lives were made more bearable. Thus her own needs were negligible; her own personality was nullified; in time she became the "old lady" who "doesn't understand" who was in the way, whose role eventually became that of a servant to her household and a nursemaid to her grandchildren. . . .

When my first child (a girl) was born, I had already suffered a year of such bitterness that only love for my baby kept me alive. I was terrified, not only by the odious present but also by the dismal pain-filled future that loomed before me, as day by day I observed the lives of the miners' wives. . . .

Raw, stark reality struck at me, as at other women, with merciless fists. A few fleeting days of illusion and then . . . afterwards, the icy, wounding, pitiless prose of existence. Out of my own experience I learned the hard truth of the popular saying "Mother, what is marriage? Daughter, marriage is weaving, giving birth, weeping. Weeping, weeping over our hurts and our impotence; weeping for our innocent children, for our dismal lives, without horizons, without hope."

In September 1936 she traveled to France and Belgium to rally support for the Republic and became a member of the committee designated to administer funds sent to Spain by the Comintern. She was also involved in the destruction of the POUM and the dismissal of Largo Caballero and supported the appointment of Juan Negrín as prime minister.

At the end of the war Ibárruri fled to the Soviet Union. Her only son, Ruben Ibárruri, was killed at Stalingrad on 3 December 1942 fighting in the Red Army. Dolores became secretary general of the PCE in May 1944. After the war she remained in Moscow and in 1964 was awarded the Lenin Peace Prize and the following year the Order of Lenin. She returned to Spain after the death of Franco and unswervingly followed the Communist line to the last.

LARGO CABALLERO, FRANCISCO (1869–1946)

A construction worker, Largo Caballero joined the Socialist Party in 1894. In the summer of 1917 he became involved in the organization of a political strike when the strikers demanded the establishment of a provisional Republican government. Members of the strike committee, including Largo Caballero, were arrested in Madrid and sentenced to life imprisonment.

He was released the following year, however, and elected to Parliament when he became head of the UGT, controlling its newspaper, *Claridad*, in which he called for the radicalization of the PSOE. In 1925 he became leader of the party, calling for "the conquest of political power by the working class by whatever means possible" and the "dictatorship of the proletariat organized as a working-class democracy."

Throughout the 1920s two men contested the leadership of the Socialist Party: Largo Caballero had the support of union members, whereas Indalecio Prieto, leader of the moderate wing of the Socialist Party, gained most of his following from the middle class and intellectuals. Largo Caballero's radical views were attacked by Prieto, who wrote that "Largo Caballero is a fool who wants to appear clever. He is a frigid bureaucrat who plays the role of a mad fanatic." Largo Caballero replied that Prieto was "envious, arrogant, and disdainful" and was not a Socialist "either in his ideas or in his action."

After the abdication of Alfonso XIII in April 1931, Largo Caballero joined the new coalition government led by Alcalá Zamora. Serving as minister of labor between 1931 and 1933, he formulated agrarian policies that called for distribution of land to landless laborers, a measure that increased the support for the PSOE in rural communities. His advocacy of a radical Socialist policy helped precipitate the military coup of July 1936.

During the early stages of the civil war, he was critical of the government led by José Giral. Even Largo Caballero's opponents agreed that he was a dynamic leader, and in September 1936 he was chosen to replace Giral as prime minister. He also took over the role of war minister and, concentrating on winning the war, did not pursue his policy of social revolution. In an effort to gain the support of foreign governments, he announced that his administration was "not fighting for Socialism but for democracy and constitutional rule." Largo Caballero introduced changes that upset the Spanish Left including conscription, the reintroduction of rank and insignia into the militia and the abolition of workers' and soldiers' councils. He also established a new police force, the National Republican Guard.

Although he undertook military reforms, he was unable to create a unified war effort among leftist parties. He took Soviet Ambassador Marcel Rosenberg into his cabinet as an honorary minister without portfolio until he grew tired of Rosenberg's interference and had him recalled to Russia. He resisted pressure from the Communists to promote its members to senior posts in the government and refused their demands to suppress the POUM. In May 1937 an extreme left uprising in Barcelona was used by the Communists to provoke a cabinet crisis, and he was forced to resign. After his fall, Largo Caballero was politically isolated by the new government of Juan Negrín. At the end of the civil war Largo Caballero fled to France. After the German invasion he was arrested and sent to Dachau concentration camp, where he survived four years and returned to Paris. He soon died, a broken man.

LISTER, ENRIQUE (1907–1994)

Born in Galicia of a poor family that migrated to Cuba, Lister returned in 1925 and worked in various jobs. In trouble with the Civil Guard he went back to Cuba in 1927 where he became involved with the Communist Party. Persecuted by the police, he again returned to Galicia but continued his Party contacts, joining a Communist cell in Santiago de Compostela. He spent the years 1929 to 1931 in prison for Communist agitation. In 1932 at a regional conference of the Party he was elected delegate to the Communist congress in Sevilla. He went on to spend the years 1932 to 1935 in the USSR as a student in a military academy and working on the construction of the Moscow subway.

Returning to Spain he became an instructor for the MAOC and early in the civil war commanded the prestigious Communist 5th Regiment in the defense of Madrid. Rising to the rank of colonel in the popular army, he headed the 11th Division in the Battles of Guadalajara, Brunete and Teruel and commanded the V Army Corps in the Battle of the Ebro. Behind Republican lines, Lister helped destroy at bayonet point the peasant Anarchist collectives and ordered the detention of their leaders. Near the end of the war Negrín appointed him commander of the Army of the Levant with the rank of general.

Fleeing the Casado uprising in 1939 he emigrated to Russia and served as a general in the Red Army against the Germans in World War II. In 1945 he moved to Paris and worked for the Party in matters of Communist emigration. He subsequently became a military adviser to Fidel Castro in Cuba and was a member of the Central Committee of the PCE until 1970. In 1977 he returned to Spain, wrote several books and died in Madrid.

MERA, CIPRIANO (1896–1975)

Mera was the leading Anarchist commander of the civil war. Born in Madrid, he was forced to forsake school in order to earn a living and gathered mushrooms and wild fruit to sell in the neighborhood. At sixteen he found work in the construction industry and joined the UGT. At twenty he remained illiterate but attended night classes where he learned to read and became interested in social issues. His first contact with Anarchists occurred in 1920. He became part of a revolutionary committee constituted in 1933 with Buenaventura Durruti and for which he was several times jailed. Eventually he became president of the Madrid CNT. Incarcerated in the Model Prison in Madrid for strike action, he was released during the uprising of 1936 and took up arms for the Republic, commanding the 14th Division in the defense of the city. Mera participated in all the major battles on the central front, played a prominent role in the Republican victory at Guadalajara and rose to command the IV Corps of the Army of the Center. By 1939, now a colonel, he was convinced that the Republicans would be defeated and joined with Casado to establish the anti-Negrín National Defense Junta.

After the war, Mera found refuge in North Africa, but the French Vichy government in control of the area extradited him to Spain in March 1942 on the request of the Franco regime, in spite of the protests of a dozen Latin American countries. He was condemned to death on 26 April

1943 but had his sentence commuted to thirty years in prison. While in prison in Madrid he was advised to seek a pardon but refused on the grounds that he would not humiliate himself before the Fascists. In 1946 he was released provisionally, however, and contacted by the Monarchist general Aranda. The upshot of the meeting was that the Monarchists wanted an agreement with the CNT to help overthrow the Franco regime and restore the monarchy. Mera refused, suspecting they were incompetent and untrustworthy. He moved to Paris where he worked as a bricklayer until his death.

MIAJA, GENERAL JOSÉ (1878–1958)

Miaja obtained a university degree in Oviedo before joining the Spanish army. He served in Morocco and by 1936 had reached the rank of general. After the Popular Front victory, he was appointed commander of the 1st Division in Madrid. At the outbreak of the civil war he remained loyal to the Republic and accepted the position of minister of war under Martínez Barrio. He resigned from the post when Giral was appointed prime minister. Miaja was sent to the Córdoba front, where he refused to attack enemy strongholds with his meager forces. He was relieved from his post and sent to command the garrison at Valencia, where he demanded greater authority to deal with insubordinate militiamen. Again he was relieved. A seemingly mediocre officer, fifty-eight years old, indecisive, heavy and out of shape, he seemed the right man to preside over the fall of Madrid as the Caballero government, assuming the city would soon fall, packed up and moved to Valencia.

Miaja was given instructions to set up a *Junta de Defensa* (Defense Council) made up of all the parties of the Popular Front and to defend the capital. He was aided in this task by his chief of staff, Vicente Rojo.

Shortly after learning of his new command, Miaja made haste to the War Ministry, arriving at 2:00 A.M. and mustering all the officers he could find, formed a governing junta, sent out urgent radio appeals for fighters and sent messengers to knock on doors in search of men and women who would defend the city. The response was electric. Thousands of citizens marched off to the surrounding trenches. Madrid held out against all expectations. In April 1938 Miaja was made commander of military forces in central and southern Spain but became increasingly concerned about the ability of the Republican army to win the war. He joined Casado's anti-

Negrín National Defense Junta and became its president in March 1939. At the end of the war Miaja emigrated to Mexico, where he died.

MILLÁN ASTRAY, JOSÉ (1879–1954)

An austere, simple soldier, in Argentina when the civil war broke out, and not having been consulted by Mola about plans for the insurrection, Millán Astray decided for the Nationalist side when he learned of Franco's commitment. Millán Astray was fond of making illusions to the glories of Medieval Spain, comparing the war against Marxism, atheistic Russia and Freemasonry to the chivalrous Christian war against the Muslims during the reconquest of Spain. He coined the battle cry "Long Live Death!"

The son of a lawyer, he was born in La Coruña and entered the Infantry Academy in Toledo in 1894, graduating as a second lieutenant two years later. In November 1896 he volunteered for active service in the Philippines to crush a rebellion against Spanish rule. He became a national hero when he reputedly led thirty men against 2,000 rebels at San Rafael.

After winning three medals for bravery, Millán Astray returned to Spain and attended the *Escuela Superior de Guerra* (Higher School of War) and graduated two years later. In 1910 he joined the staff of the Infantry Academy at Toledo, where he taught military history and tactics. Preferring the excitement of warfare, he transferred to Morocco in 1912, remaining in North Africa until 1917. The following year he argued that Spain needed a mercenary army to serve in the colonies and in 1919 was sent to study the French Foreign Legion in Algeria.

Millán Astray was promoted to lieutenant colonel and in 1920 named head of the new Spanish Foreign Legion (*Tercio de Extranjeros*), appointing Francisco Franco his second in command. Arturo Barea in his autobiography (p. 303) quotes Millán Astray as saying to the new recruits, many of whom were thieves and murderers with little future,

You have risen from the dead—for don't forget that you were dead, that your lives were finished. You have come here to live a new life for which you must pay with death. You have come here to die. It is to die that one joins the Legion.

In 1923 Millán Astray was replaced by Franco as commander of the *Tercio* and sent to France to study the organization of the French army.

The following year he joined the staff of the high commissioner in Morocco. In an ambush by local rebels his wounds led to the amputation of his left arm. Millán Astray returned as commander of the *Tercio* in 1927 and lost his right eye to a bullet. He was promoted to brigadier general and given command of the Ceuta-Tetuán district. In January 1930 he was attached to the Ministry of War and eventually became a member of the Supreme War Council.

Millán Astray held extreme right-wing political opinions. He fully supported the dictatorship of Miguel Primo de Rivera and was dismayed by the abdication of Alfonso XIII and the establishment of a Republican government. In October 1934 he supervised the use of the *Tercio* to repress the left-wing insurrection in Asturias. On the outbreak of the civil war Millán Astray was recruited by General Franco and placed in charge of the Nationalist propaganda operation. He also played an important role in persuading other senior officers that Franco should become commander of the Nationalist army and chief of state. In his speeches he claimed he wanted to establish a Fascist government in Spain. During World War II he was a strong supporter of Nazi Germany and hoped that an Axis victory would lead to a new Spanish empire in Africa. After the war Millán Astray retired and fifteen years later died of a heart attack.

MODESTO, JUAN (1906–1968)

Ex-carpenter from Andalucía, corporal in the Army of Africa, Communist militant and later rival of El Campesino and Lister, among Communist commanders, Juan Modesto was affiliated with the PCE from 1930 and head of MAOC in Madrid in 1933. At the outbreak of war, he helped organize the 5th Regiment and fought in Madrid at the Montana Barracks and in the Guadarrama mountains. In September 1936 he fought at Talavera and Illescas south and west of the capital to try to hold up the Nationalist advance. In October 1936 he took over the 5th Regiment.

In 1937 Modesto commanded the 4th Division of the popular army and participated in the Battle of Jarama. As a lieutenant colonel and commander of the V Corps he fought in the Battles of Brunete, Belchite and Teruel; and promoted to colonel in 1938, he was appointed chief of the army of the Ebro. With the fall of Cataluña, Modesto was elevated to the rank of general by Negrín and made commander of the Army of the Center.

When the war ended he fled to the Soviet Union and fought in World War II in the Red and the Bulgarian armies. He died in Prague.

MOLA VIDAL, GENERAL EMILIO (1887–1937)

Emilio Mola, born in Cuba of a military family, served in Morocco, was popular with his men and in 1927 reached the rank of brigadier general. He became director general of security in 1930 at the time of the fall of the monarchy (under the dictatorship of Berenguer). After the Popular Front victory in February 1936 he was assigned as military governor in Pamplona in Navarra, where he planned the insurrection against the Republic. Diego Martínez Barrio, prime minister on 18 July 1936, contacted Mola and offered him the post of minister of war in the government if he would give up the rebellion. Mola refused and issued his proclamation of revolt on 19 July 1936.

Mola agreed to serve under Franco and was placed in charge of the Army of the North during the first year of civil war but failed to take Madrid as he expected. He coined the term *fifth column* in reference to sympathizers in the capital who would rise up and support his four army columns moving southward to take the city. Mola was killed on 3 June 1937 when his plane crashed during bad weather while flying to Burgos to consult with Franco.

NEGRÍN, JUAN (1889–1956)

Born in the Canary Islands, Negrín was professor of physiology at the University of Madrid from 1923 to 1931. He joined the PSOE in 1929 and was a Socialist member of the Cortes for Las Palmas from 1931 to 1939. As minister of finance he was responsible for the gold being handed over to the Soviet Union in the autumn of 1936. For the loss of the gold Franco would later blame him for much of the economic woes of Spain. Supported by the Communists, he replaced Largo Caballero as prime minister after the events of May 1937 in Barcelona and, under Communist pressure in August 1937, dissolved the Anarchist Council of Aragón. He moved the government from Valencia to Barcelona. After the resignation of Prieto from the Ministry of War, Negrín took the position for himself. In April 1938 he set out thirteen points that, if accepted by Franco, would end the war. Franco was not interested. With the fall of Barcelona imminent, the government moved back to Madrid. While Negrín was away in Elda, Colonel Casado rose against him in Madrid in an effort to sue for peace.

While Negrín showed great tenacity in carrying on the lost war, it was said he was a tool of the Communists. Others have denied this, although he appointed members of the PCE to important military and civilian posts. Communists were also given control of propaganda, finance and foreign affairs. Socialist Luis Araquistain, Republican ambassador to France, described Negrín's government as the "most cynical and despotic in Spanish history." Negrín promoted Communist leaders such as Antonio Cordón, undersecretary for war, and Juan Modesto and Enrique Lister to senior posts.

While President Azaña wished to be rid of Negrín, he no longer had the power, and with Communist support in the government and armed forces, Negrín was able to continue in office until he was ousted by the Casado coup in Madrid. He fled the country for France on 6 March 1939 and after the German invasion in the spring of 1940 went to live in England. He attempted to maintain the Republican government in exile, resigning in 1945 in favor of José Giral. After World War II he returned to France, where he died.

PRIETO Y TUERO, INDALECIO (1883–1962)

Prieto was a moderate Socialist politician and the rival of Largo Caballero. Born in Oviedo, he was the son of a respectable town hall official upon whose death the family was left destitute, living in the slums of Bilbao where Prieto sold newspapers on the street. In 1899 he joined the PSOE. During World War I he emerged as the leader of PSOE in the Basque region and in the summer of 1917 became involved in the organization of a political strike demanding the establishment of a provisional Republican government. He became one of the first Socialists to sit in Parliament in 1918 and was in and out of jail for his views and sometimes on the run from the police. He became the Republic's first finance minister, although he admitted no knowledge of finance, and left the office a year later with three times the deficit as when he took the post. He was always concerned with establishing a progressive movement of Socialists and Republicans but was prevented from becoming prime minister by his archrival Largo

Caballero with whom he had had a bitter falling out when Largo collaborated with Primo de Rivera against the wishes of Prieto.

Probably no one did as much for the Socialist Party as Prieto. During the war he served as minister of the navy and air force under Largo Caballero and national defense minister under Negrín. He clashed frequently with Russian advisers over the course of the war and with the Communists in their arrogant rise to power and control of the SIM. He tried to reduce Communist control in the army and was hated by them for it. They finally forced his resignation from the cabinet. His pessimism, especially after the defeat at Teruel, was contagious. Prieto fled Spain in March 1939 and went to Mexico where he led the Socialist Party in exile until his death from a heart attack.

PRIMO DE RIVERA, JOSÉ ANTONIO (1903–1936)

A lawyer and eldest son of the former dictator Miguel Primo de Rivera, José Antonio, along with Ruiz de Alda, a well-known pilot, founded the Falange in October 1933. In the manifesto published later that year the Falange condemned socialism, Marxism, Republicanism and capitalism and proposed that Spain should become a Fascist state similar to the one established by Mussolini. In that year José Antonio was elected to the Cortes for Cádiz. He also edited the right-wing journal *El Fascio*. After it was shut down by the Republican government, he wrote for the periodical *ABC* and also founded two newspapers, *Fe* (1934) and *Arriba* (1935).

In February 1934 the Falange merged with the JONS of Ramiro Ledesma. In the general election in February 1936, the Falange won only 0.7 percent of the vote, and José Antonio lost his seat; but after the victory of the Popular Front, the party grew rapidly.

The participation of the Falange in intimidation and street fighting led to his arrest. Authorization of the Falange to participate in the military uprising in July 1936, issued from his cell, did not help his case. He was executed in Alicante on 20 November 1936. Although nothing was done to rescue José Antonio from prison, Franco exploited his death by making him a martyr of the Fascist movement.

During the civil war, the Falange was reorganized incorporating all rightist parties under Franco, who made it the official party of his regime and the dominant political movement of the Nationalists.

PRIMO DE RIVERA, PILAR (1907–1991)

The sister of José Antonio, born on 4 November, was close to her brother and helped him launch the Falange. In June 1934 a women's section (*Sección Feminina*) of the Falange was established and Pilar appointed its leader. The women engaged in making uniforms and flags, worked as secretaries and messengers and sometimes provided cover for the Falangist hit-squads including hiding guns under their dresses.

On the outbreak of the civil war Pilar was living in the Republican zone. She sought refuge in the Argentine embassy and with the help of the German ambassador, who provided her with a false passport, managed to escape to Nationalist-controlled territory. She organized the *Auxilio Azul*, a network that found hiding places, false papers and food for Falangists on the run from the authorities. The war increased the support for the Falange, and by 1937 the *Sección Feminina* had nearly 50,000 members. Pilar continued as head of the organization and arranged for its members to serve as nurses at the front.

After the merger of the Falange, the Carlist and other right-wing parties in April 1937 Franco rewarded Pilar by allowing her to remain head of the *Sección Feminina*. In this post she opposed Franco's policy of total annihilation of the enemy and tried to prevent reprisals being taken against the widows of Republican militants.

Probably no other influential woman of the time and place set the clock back further in women's struggle toward equality than Pilar. On 30 May 1939 she addressed 10,000 members of the *Sección Feminina* at Medina del Campo and told the audience that with the end of the war the only mission of women was homemaking, to make family life so agreeable to men that they would have no need of bars and clubs. She stressed that a woman's role in life was to harmonize the wishes of others and to let herself be guided by the stronger will and the wisdom of the man.

A strong supporter of Germany, in the summer of 1941 her organization provided nurses, secretaries and ancillary staff to accompany the Spanish Blue Division fighting in Russia. The Franco government suggested that Pilar should marry Hitler since the marriage would ensure Spain a major position in the new Fascist world order that would follow the defeat of the Allies, but in December 1941 Joseph Goebbels told a representative of the Spanish government that a new Fascist dynasty was not feasible because Hitler had received a bullet wound in the genitals during World War I that incapacitated him.

She was also given responsibility for organizing the *Servicio Social de la Mujer*. This involved all unmarried women between the ages of seventeen and thirty-five doing six months of social service. Pilar supported the scheme to teach women to read but warned her followers not to overdo it, as there is nothing more detestable than an intellectual woman.

When Franco died in 1975 Pilar urged the *Sección Feminina* to support the king Juan Carlos de Borbón, but she opposed the decision of the Cortes to introduce democratic reforms. She became president of the *Sección Feminina* Veterans in November 1977 and held the post until her death.

QUEIPO DE LLANO Y SIERRA, GONZALO (1875–1951)

Born in Tordesillas northwest of Madrid, Queipo de Llano was sent to a seminary but ran away and joined the Spanish army to later become a cadet in the Royal Cavalry Academy in Valladolid. He served in the Cuban and Moroccan wars and gained a reputation for his swashbuckling cavalry charges. In 1928 he was exiled for his opposition to the dictator Primo de Rivera. On 15 December 1930, after an abortive rebellion against the rule of Alfonso XIII in favor of a Republic, he fled to Portugal.

Queipo de Llano supported the Popular Front and in early 1936 became director-general of the Customs Guards. However, he was critical of some of the government's policies including the agrarian reforms. Other measures that irked him included outlawing the Falange and granting autonomy to Cataluña. On the 10 May 1936 Alcalá Zamora was ousted as president and replaced by the left-wing Azaña, which further displeased Queipo de Llano. Soon afterward he began plotting with Mola, Franco and Sanjurjo to overthrow the Popular Front government, resulting in the outbreak of the civil war. With only 200 men, Queipo de Llano successfully took control of Sevilla and soon established a reign of terror in Andalucía. He was particularly known for his vulgar radio broadcasts denigrating the Republican soldiers and civilians.

On 17 January 1937, he launched the attack on Málaga, which fell to the Nationalists in February. Over the next few weeks an estimated 4,000 Republicans were executed. Although he rose to become commander of the southern army, he was never fully trusted by the Nationalists, in part, due to his relationship with Alcalá Zamora through the marriage of their children. He did not get along well with Franco, who at the end of the war sent him as head of the Spanish Mission to Italy. He died at his country estate near Sevilla.

YAGÜE BLANCO, JUAN (1891–1952)

Nationalist field commander, Yagüe gained his reputation and decorations in Morocco commanding the Spanish Foreign Legion and Moroccan indigenous troops. Dubbed the Hyena of Asturias by the Left, he came to public notice when with African troops he helped crush the Asturian uprising in 1934, where his troops killed and raped without restraint. He knew Franco from their days in the military academy and supported José Antonio and the Falange. At the onset of the insurrection he rose in Ceuta and crossed the Straits to support the uprising in Sevilla. He then moved north with his troops and took Mérida and Badajoz (Yagüe was also known as "The Butcher of Badajoz") before moving up the Tajo river valley toward Madrid. Diverted from his plans to attack Madrid, he was ordered to Toledo to rescue Colonel Moscardó trapped in the fortress. As commander of the African army, he met with great success initially but failed to take Madrid as planned. He led Moroccan troops at Teruel and in Aragón but was banished from front-line command in 1938 for disagreeing with Franco. He was later reinstated for the Battle of the Ebro, and his forces took Barcelona on 26 January 1939. On 9 August Franco made him minister of air and later captain general of the VI military region with headquarters in Burgos, where he died.

PRIMARY DOCUMENTS
OF THE WAR

In regard to Fascist organizations in Spain, the Italian embassy official Geissler Celesia reported to Rome on 1 February 1934 that he had spoken with Falangists José Antonio Primo de Rivera and the wealthy Marqués de Eliseda. Celesia found the young gentlemen (*señoritos*) inexperienced and perhaps too pretentious.

Document 1

There is evidence of some intensification of fascist propaganda, with a certain effectiveness despite the dubious means they have adopted. I have spoken with the two young fascist deputies, Primo de Rivera and Eliseda, both young, good orators, full of good intentions, but inexpert and too open to the accusation of being "señoritos," rather than representatives of something new. They complain that Gil Robles gives them no money, that the Grandes de España have provided no funding for their propaganda since the elections. . . . [T]hey assure me that they are holding frequent meetings and have enthusiastic followers, that their propaganda is gaining ground in Catalonia, and that they are making progress among the armed forces. But, in my opinion, they are not sufficiently aware of the need for propaganda and recruitment among the workers and rural sectors and of the need to have young people who are well organized and strongly combative, and, above all, of the need for a well-defined program that can win the support of the masses. Certainly, opposed to that is the problem of not antagonizing the large landowners, whom they ask for economic assistance and who still dream of retaining their lands, privileges, and subjugated peasants. Moreover, many of their new supporters are motivated not by positive convictions but by fear of the worst, and in such conditions their combat value is not equivalent to their numbers, which, for that matter, even their own leaders cannot calculate.

Source: Quoted in Saz, *Mussolini* (Valencia: Edicions Alfons el Magnànim, 1986), 120.
Reprinted in Payne, *Fascism in Spain, 1923–1977*, 97.

As the Falange grew, many new members appeared to have had little
knowledge of its ideology. An American correspondent sympathetic to the
Nationalist cause, writing in 1936, considered them somewhat naive.

Document 2

Actually I found there were very few of them who had even taken the
trouble to inquire into the doctrines of the party. Many of the younger ones had
joined up because the smart blue uniform gave them a decided advantage over
Red youth in the matter of their girl friends. The greatest number had undoubtedly
joined up as being the simplest way to help their country. I have questioned
dozens of them here, there, and everywhere; I found them on duty on the roads,
guarding post-offices, banks, etc., and none of them was clear about anything
except that they were anti-Red. One of them told me quite simply that he "guessed
it was a kind of Communism, only much better expressed."

Source: Quoted from C. Gerahty, *The Road to Madrid* (London: Hutchinson, 1937), 17–18.
Reprinted in Payne, *Fascism in Spain, 1923–1977*, 252.

Alvarez del Vayo reported evidence to the League of Nations concerning foreign military intervention in the civil war in aid of the Nationalists. Such activity was contrary to the dictates of the Non-Intervention
Committee agreed to by the guilty parties.

Document 3

Yesterday Señor Alvarez del Vayo, the Spanish Foreign Minister, sent to the
Secretary General of the League documents containing the latest information in
regard to alleged violations of the non-intervention agreement by Germany, Italy,
and Portugal. It is understood that the documents contained detailed information
of a grave nature.

I understand that so many airplanes have been supplied to the rebels by
Germany and Italy that they now have about three times as many as the Spanish
Government whereas at the beginning of the civil war the Spanish Government
had about four times as many as the rebels. The rebels themselves are unable to
manufacture airplanes, so that all these additional airplanes must have been supplied by other nations. German and Italian airmen who have been taken prisoner
have confessed that they were acting under orders of their Governments.

The documents are understood to contain evidence showing that during the military operations of the rebels in Estremadura the air bases, the supplies, and the movements of the rebel troops were organized on Portuguese territory with the help of the Portuguese military forces. Airplanes and other arms that have fallen into the hands of the Government are of a type that has never existed in the Spanish army and reveal their foreign origin.

The Spanish Delegation asked that the documents should be published and should be distributed to the members of the League. They have not yet been distributed, and it is impossible to obtain from the Secretariat any information as to whether they will be published.

Source: © *The Manchester Guardian*, 28 September 1936.

A top-secret document from the general consul of the USSR in Barcelona to the headquarters of the NKID (People's Commissariat of Foreign Affairs), sent on 14 October 1936, complained about Anarchists and Largo Caballero. The document was the result of a conversation with the unidentified informant, Comrade X, who may have been an Anarchist with Communist sympathies. Strained relations between Communists and Anarchists resulted in clashes and killings; a serious accusation was that the Anarchists were hoarding weapons that should have been sent to the front. Largo Caballero's policies were seen as unrealistic, his attitude toward commissars uncooperative and his proposed move of the government out of Madrid verging on cowardice. (It moved to Valencia).

Document 4 (excerpts)

In his words [Comrade X] the relationship between our people [the Communists] and the anarcho-syndicalists is becoming ever more strained. Every day, delegates and individual comrades appear before the CC [Central Committee of the Party] of the Unified Socialist Party with statements about the excesses of the anarchists. In places it has come to armed clashes. Not long ago in a settlement of Huesca near Barbastro twenty-five members of the UGT were killed by the anarchists in a surprise attack provoked by unknown reasons. In Molins de Rei, workers in a textile factory stopped work, protesting against arbitrary dismissals. Their delegation to Barcelona was driven out of the train, but all the same fifty workers forced their way to Barcelona with complaints for the central government, but now they are afraid to return, anticipating the anarchists' revenge. In Pueblo Nuevo near Barcelona, the anarchists have placed an armed man at the doors of each of the food stores, and if you do not have a food coupon from the CNT, then you cannot buy anything. The entire population of this small town is highly excited. They are shooting up to fifty people a day in Barcelona. . . .

. . . Relations with the Union of Transport Workers are strained. At the beginning of 1934 there was a protracted strike by the transport workers. The government and the "Esquerra" [Republican Leftist Party of Cataluña] smashed the strike. In July of this year, on the pretext of revenge against the scabs, the CNT killed more than eighty men, UGT members, but not one Communist among them. They killed not only actual scabs but also honest revolutionaries. . . .

They have offered our people two posts in the new government—Council of Labour and the Council of Municipal Work—but it is impossible for the Council of Labour to institute control over the factories and mills without clashing sharply with the CNT, and as for municipal services, one must clash with the Union of Transport Workers, which is in the hands of the CNT. Fabregas, the councillor for the economy, is a "highly doubtful sort." Before he joined the Esquerra, he was in the Acción Popular; he left the Esquerra for the CNT and now is playing an obviously provocative role, attempting to "deepen the revolution" by any means. The metallurgical syndicate just began to put forward the slogan "family wages." The first "producer in the family" received 100 percent wages, for example, seventy pesetas a week, the second member of the family 50 percent, the third 25 percent, the fourth, and so on, up to 10 percent. Children less than sixteen years old only 10 percent each. This system of wages is even worse than egalitarianism. It kills both production and the family. . . .

Three days ago, the government seriously clashed with the anarchists: the CNT seized a priest. . . . They agreed to release the priest to France, but for a ransom. The priest pointed out another 101 members of his order who had hidden themselves in different places. They agreed to free all 102 men for three hundred thousand francs. All 102 appeared, but when the money had been handed over, the anarchists shot forty of them. . . . [President Companys] stated he would resign if they continued the summary shooting. The sixty-two priests have been entrusted to [the care of] a judge. . . .

. . . In Madrid there are up to fifty thousand construction workers. Caballero refused to mobilize all of them for building fortifications around Madrid ("and what will they eat") and gave a total of a thousand men for building the fortifications. In Estremadura our Comrade Deputy Cordón is fighting heroically. He could arm five thousand peasants but he has a detachment of only four thousand men total. Caballero under great pressure agreed to give Cordón two hundred rifles, as well. Meanwhile, from Estremadura, Franco could easily advance into the rear, toward Madrid. Caballero implemented an absolutely absurd compensation for the militia—ten pesetas a day, besides food and housing. Farm labourers in Spain earn a total of two pesetas a day and, feeling very good about the militia salary in the rear, do not want to go to the front. With that, egalitarianism was introduced. Only officer specialists receive a higher salary. A proposal made to Caballero to pay soldiers at the rear five pesetas and only soldiers at the front ten pesetas was turned down. Caballero is now disposed to put into effect the institution of political commissars, but in actual fact it is not being done. In fact, the political commissars introduced into the Fifth Regiment have been turned into commanders, for there are none of the latter. Caballero also supports the departure of the government from Madrid. After the capture of Toledo, this question was almost decided, but the anarchists were categorically against it, and our people proposed that the question be withdrawn as inopportune. Caballero stood up for the removal of the government to Cartagena. They proposed sounding out the possibility of basing the government in Barcelona. Two ministers—Prieto and Jiménez de Asua—left for talks with the Barcelona government. The Barcelona government agreed to give refuge to the central government. Caballero is sincere but is a prisoner to syndicalist habits and takes the statutes of the trade unions too literally.

The UGT is now the strongest organization in Catalonia: it has no fewer than half the metallurgical workers and almost all the textile workers, municipal workers, service employees, bank employees. There are abundant links to the peasantry. But the CNT has much better cadres and has many weapons, which were seized in the first days (the anarchists sent to the front fewer than 60 percent of the thirty thousand rifles and three hundred machine guns that they seized).

Source: Vladimir Antonov-Ovseenko, General Consul of the Soviet Union in Barcelona. Printed in Radosh, Habeck and Sevostianov, *Spain Betrayed* (New Haven, CT: Yale University Press, 2001), 75–78. Copyright © 2001 by Yale University.

In an exchange of letters between Stalin and Largo Caballero in 1936, Stalin compared the revolution in Russia with events in Spain and showed concern with Republican unity, anxious to forestall revolutionary movements that might have jeopardized it until the war was won. He emphasized the role of military advisers as just that, concealing the Communist agenda to gradually take over military commands, police and political posts. Stalin was anxious that Spain not appear as a Communist appendage to Russia, alienating his possible allies such as England in a struggle against Germany. He wanted Caballero to report on the adequacy of the Russian ambassador Rosenberg and other advisers. The patronizing advice from Stalin included, among other things, the notion that peasants' and foreigners' property should be respected and partisan forces should be formed behind enemy lines. Small bourgeoisie should be protected, and Azaña and the Republicans should not be left out of events.

Document 5

To Comrade Caballero

Our representative plenipotentiary, Comrade Rosenberg, has transmitted to us the expression of your fraternal feelings. He also told us about your unwavering faith in victory. May we express our fraternal thanks for your sentiments and assure you that we share your faith in the victory of the Spanish people.

We consider and shall always consider it our duty to come, within our possibilities, to the aid of the Spanish government which is leading the struggle of all toilers, of the whole Spanish democracy, against the Fascist-military clique, the agency of international Fascist forces.

The Spanish revolution is following a path in many respects different from that which Russia had followed. This is due to different social, historical and geographical conditions, and to the different international situation which Russia had to face. It is quite possible that in Spain the parliamentary way will prove more appropriate towards the revolutionary development than was the case in Russia.

We still think, however, that our experience, especially that of our civil war, may have a certain importance for Spain if one bears in mind the specificity of the conditions of the Spanish revolutionary struggle. This is why we have agreed, responding to your repeated demands transmitted to us at various times by Comrade Rosenberg, to put at your disposal a number of military instructors. Their task will be to advise and help in military matters those Spanish military leaders to whom they are assigned.

It has been categorically impressed on them that they must always remember that, notwithstanding the full awareness of solidarity which at the present time binds together the Spanish people and the peoples of the USSR, a Soviet comrade, being a foreigner in Spain, can be truly helpful only on condition that he adheres strictly to the role of an adviser, and an adviser only. We think that this is precisely the manner in which you will make use of our military comrades.

As friends, we would ask you to inform us how effectively our military comrades fulfill the task you entrust them with; it is obvious that only if you judge their work positively would it be useful for them to continue.

We would also ask you to let us know, openly and frankly, your opinion about Comrade Rosenberg: is the Spanish government satisfied with him or should he be replaced by another representative?

And here are four pieces of friendly advice for your consideration:

1. One should pay attention to the peasantry, which, in such an agrarian country as Spain, is of great importance. It would be advisable to issue decrees relative to agrarian problems and to taxation which would be favourable to the peasantry. It would also be advisable to attract the peasants to the army or to organize partisan peasant detachments at the rear of the Fascist armies. This would be facilitated by decrees furthering the interests of the peasantry.

2. The petty and middle urban bourgeoisie should be attracted to the government side and be given at least the chance to occupy a neutral position, which would favour the government, by protecting it from attempts at confiscation and securing as far as possible the freedom of trade. Otherwise these strata will follow the Fascists.

3. The leaders of the Republican party should not be repulsed, but on the contrary, should be drawn in, brought nearer and associated with the common exercise of government. It is especially important that the government should secure the support of Azaña and his group and that everything should be done to help them in overcoming their vacillation. This is necessary in order to prevent the enemies of Spain from regarding it as a communist republic and to forestall their intervention, which would constitute the greatest danger to the republic of Spain.

4. It would be advisable to find an opportunity to state in the press that the Spanish government will not condone any action against the property rights and the legitimate interests of those foreigners in Spain who are citizens of states which do not support the rebels.

Fraternal greetings
Friends of Republican Spain
December 21, 1936   Stalin, Molotov, Voroshilov

Source: Guerra y Revolución en España (Moscow: Editorial Progreso, 1971), 2:96–97. Reprinted in Carr, *The Comintern and the Spanish Civil War*, 86–87.

Largo Caballero responded to Stalin's comments in the above letter, agreeing with Stalin's stated views and advice. While Largo Caballero stated that he found Ambassador Rosenberg activity and behavior satisfactory, he was perhaps concealing some resentment against Russia. Not long after sending this letter, he chastised Rosenberg for interfering in government policies and ordered him out of his office with the words, "Out you go, Out! You must learn, Señor Ambassador, that the Spaniards may be poor and need aid from abroad, but we are sufficiently proud not to accept that a foreign ambassador should try and impose his will on the head of the Spanish government." The ambassador was soon recalled to Russia and executed.

Document 6

Dear Comrades,

The letter which you were so good to send me through Comrade Rosenberg gave me a great deal of pleasure. Your fraternal greetings and your fervent faith in the victory of the Spanish people gave me profound satisfaction. I wish, on my part, to respond to your heartfelt greetings and to your fervent faith in our triumph by sending you the expression of my warmest sentiments.

The help you are providing to the Spanish people, and which you your-selves—considering it as your duty—have undertaken to provide, has been and continues to be greatly beneficial. You may rest assured that we rightly appreciate it. From the bottom of my heart, and in the name of Spain, and especially on behalf of the workers, we assure you of our gratitude. We trust that, as in the present, so also in the future your help and advice will continue to be available to us.

You are right in remarking that there are substantial differences between the developments which followed the Russian revolution and those which follow ours. In fact, as you yourselves note, the circumstances in which the two revo-lutions occurred differ: the historical conditions of each people, the geographical position, the economic situation, the social and cultural development and, above all, the degree of political and trade union maturity are not the same. But, in answer to your other remark, one should perhaps state that, whatever may be the future of the parliamentary form, it does not possess among us, or even among the republicans, enthusiastic defenders.

Those comrades who, responding to our call, came to our aid are rendering us great services. Their vast experience is useful to us and contributes notably to the defence of Spain in her fight against Fascism. I can assure you that they are bringing to their task genuine enthusiasm and extraordinary courage. As to Com-rade Rosenberg, I can say in all sincerity that we are satisfied with his behaviour and activity. He is liked by everybody here. He works hard, so hard that this affects his already undermined health.

I am very grateful to you for your friendly advice contained in the latter part of your letter. I regard it as a proof of your friendship and your concern with the successful outcome of our struggle.

The agrarian problem in Spain is, indeed, of exceptional importance. From the first, our government took it upon itself to protect the peasants by improving their living conditions enormously. Towards this end, important decrees were announced. Unfortunately, certain excesses in the countryside could not be avoided, but we earnestly hope that they will not be repeated.

The same should be stated concerning the petty bourgeoisie, which we have respected by constantly proclaiming its right to exist and develop. By defending it against the attacks to which it might have been exposed at the beginning, we are trying to attract it to our side.

I completely agree with what you say about the republican political forces. We have, in all circumstances, associated them with the tasks of the government and with the struggle. They participate largely in all political and administrative bodies, local, provincial and national. What happens, however, is that they themselves do practically nothing to define their own political individuality. As to the property of foreigners established in Spain who are citizens of countries which do not help the rebels, their rights have been respected and interests safe-guarded. That has been stated on several occasions, and we shall continue this policy. I shall certainly re-state this worldwide at the first opportunity which presents itself.

Fraternal greetings,

Valencia, January 12, 1937   Francisco L. Caballero

Source: Guerra y Revolución en España (Moscow: Editorial Progreso, 1971), 2:96–97. Reprinted in Carr, *The Comintern and the Spanish Civil War*, 87–88.

Dolores Ibárruri, La Pasionaria, laughs at her own "death" in 1937.

Document 7

VALENCIA, Thursday.

A deep chuckling laugh was audible all through the offices of the Communist Party here this afternoon when I told Dolores Pasionaria that the London newspapers at that moment were publishing the news of her death, complete with photograph.

The laugh was Pasionaria's. "You don't say?" she said. "Looks like those people really are anxious about having me dead. That is the third time I have been dead in England in this war alone."

I reminded her that when I was here in 1934 I had twice had the job of asking her the same question for the same reason, namely whether she would confirm the London newspapers' account of her death.

She started to laugh again. "Well," she said, "tell them I'm alive and kicking." She paused. "Mind you get that—and kicking!"

"And tell them that when Franco's dead and Mola's dead and Queipo de Llano's dead, I shall start perhaps to think about dying, too.

"And tell them as they don't seem to know it yet, that all those generals have arms a darned sight too short to get me—a darned sight too short."

Still laughing, she rushed out of the room on another job in her eternally busy day as the accepted leader of the honest and decent women of Spain in their struggle against the enslavement and degradation of Fascism.

Source: Daily Worker, 1 January 1937. Reprinted in *Cockburn in Spain,* 140.

German and Italian arms shipments to the Nationalists were stepped up in December 1936 and January 1937, threatening to put the Republic at a severe disadvantage in weapons. Indalecio Prieto, minister of war, asked the Russians for military aid in January 1937 to redress the imbalance.

Document 8

Naval and Air Ministry   Valencia, 26 January 1937
To S-ñr Ambassador of the USSR in Spain
The quantity of airplanes that the government air force has at its disposal, by comparison with that of the enemy, is very insignificant. Today we have a hundred fighters, twenty single-motor attack aircraft, and seventeen bombers. These last are extraordinarily few in the face of the huge numbers that the rebels have, which gives them the capability for offensive action. Of the bombers that we have, fourteen are fighting today on various fronts. This does not allow us to bomb very worthwhile objectives.

Experience confirms the impossibility of acquiring aircraft from other parts of Europe, and also from the United States, where they have established sanctions prohibiting the export of weapons.

It is obvious to us that only Russia can put us on an equal footing with regard to armaments with the fascists, who last week were lavishly supplied with aircraft by Germany and Italy.

In conjunction with this, in the name of the Spanish government, I appeal to the government of the USSR with a request to send us the matériel enumerated below. I take the liberty of emphasizing the urgency of this order in connection with the stage that our civil war has entered.

We need:
—sixty fighters
—one hundred biplane bombers
—one hundred single-motor fighters
All these airplanes ought to be supplied with the appropriate spare parts.
Minister Prieto

Source: 26 January 1937, document 32. Printed in Radosh, Habeck and Sevostianov, *Spain Betrayed* (New Haven, CT: Yale University Press, 2001), 128–129. Copyright © 2001 by Yale University.

Soviet Ambassador Ivan Gaikis (who replaced Rosenberg) wrote to Krestinsky criticizing Antonov-Ovseenko, the Soviet consul in Barcelona. Moscow favored a regular organized army in Spain to fight the war.

Antonov-Ovseenko, a decade before, had published a document in which he favored the use of popular workers' militias in war—a position that was in line with the current thinking of the Anarchists and the POUM. Andreu Nin, leader of the POUM, resurrected this old document that was contrary to Soviet policy. To compensate for his earlier heresy, Antonov-Ovseenko engaged in public attacks on Anarchist policies that the Kremlin found not in keeping with its avowed nonpartisan position. The Barcelona consul was later summoned home and executed.

Document 9

Ambassador of the USSR in Spain   Inc. Sec't Narkom
Copy

                            No 1042 from 27/3/37   Secret

21 March 1937
No 16/s
Valencia
       To the Deputy Narkom of Foreign Affairs Com. Krestinsky

Dear Nikolai Nikolaevich,
       Despite the most authoritative instructions and the instructions of the leadership of the NKID on the line to be taken in Spain that I personally delivered to Com. Antonov-Ovseenko, the General Consul of the USSR in Barcelona again undertook a dispute with the local organ of the anarchists, Solidaridad Obrera, about which you probably already know from TASS dispatches. There is no need to prove the political harm that such polemics cause, especially when undertaken in this period of aggravated interparty struggle in Spain, in which the anarchists, and under their protection the local Trotskyists, naturally are increasing their attacks on the Soviet Union. The interference of the consulate just affords support to our enemies.
       I therefore consider it necessary for you to send direct instructions to Com. Antonov-Ovseenko not to repeat henceforth a mistake of this sort.
With comradely greetings,
Ambassador of the USSR in Spain
Gaikis
Secretary of the Narkom Kozlov

Source: 21 March 1937, Document 38, printed in Radosh, Habeck and Sevostianov, *Spain Betrayed* (New Haven, CT: Yale University Press, 2001), 154. Copyright © 2001 by Yale University.

The destruction of the undefended Basque town of Guernica by Nationalist planes shocked the world. This new kind of warfare targeting civilian populations generated amazement and deep indignation. The British consul, R.C. Stevenson, who arrived on the scene, reported the facts to the British ambassador.

Document 10

Dear Sir Henry,

On landing at Bermeo yesterday I was told about the destruction of Guernica. I went at once to have a look at the place and to my amazement found that the township normally of some five thousand inhabitants, since the September influx of refugees about ten thousand, was almost completely destroyed. Nine houses in ten are beyond reconstruction. Many were still burning and fresh fires were breaking out here and there, the result of incendiary bombs which owing to some fault had not exploded on impact the day before and were doing so, at the time of my visit, under falling beams and masonry. The casualties cannot be ascertained and probably never will, accurately. Some estimates put the figure at one thousand, others at over three thousand. An inhabitant who went through it all, told me that at about 4 p.m. three machines appeared overhead and dropped H.E. and incendiary bombs. They disappeared and ten minutes later a fresh lot of five or six machines came and so on for several hours, until after seven. All told he estimates the number of planes at fifty. After two or three visits panic seized the population. Men, women and children poured out of Guernica and ran up the bare hillsides. There they were mercilessly machine gunned, though with little effect. They spent the night in the open gazing at their burning city. I saw many men and women erring [wandering] through the streets searching in the wreckage of their houses for the bodies of their dear ones.

Source: Letter sent by R.C. Stevenson, British Consul, to the British Ambassador, Sir Henry Chilton, at Hendaye, 28 April 1937. Quoted in Thomas, 986.

The Nationalist response to widespread condemnation of the bombing of Guernica, especially in the foreign press, emphasized Republican atrocities in the war and engaged in a tangle of misinformation, half truths and blatant lies blaming the destruction of the town on Basque leftist militiamen and Communists in order to discredit the Nationalists.

Document 11

With the unanimity which might appear to suggest obedience to orders many English and French newspapers are using a comparatively minor event such as the hypothetical bombardment of a small town as the basis of a campaign designed to present "Nationalist" Spain as anti-humanitarian and opposed to the principles of the laws of nations, thus serving the ends of the Soviet faction which dominates the Spanish "Red" zone. These newspapers clamour against the bombardment of open towns, attempting to lay the blame for such outrages upon the "Nationalists." "National" Spain energetically rejects so injurious a campaign and denounces these manoeuvres before the world.

The newspapers now crying aloud remained silent when in Madrid, under the presidency of the "Red" Government, thousands of innocent beings were murdered. Over 60,000 died at the hands of the "Red" hordes without any motive other than the whims of a militiaman or a servant's dislike, in this way perished old people, women, and children, all of them innocent. In the Madrid prisons murders were committed without check under the supervision of the "Red" Government agents. There fell intellectuals, politicians, many Republicans, Liberals, Democrats, and members of the Right.

At Barcelona also 50,000 or 60,000 horrible murders have been committed, and there have been many thousands more killed in Malaga, Valencia, and other large towns after barbarous tortures. This was not war. It was crime and vengeance. But then the newspapers which are today defending so-called humanitarian principles were silent or spoke timidly or even attempted to justify such barbarous crimes. They were silent too when bishops and thousands of priests, monks, and nuns were cruelly done to death and beautiful artistic treasures were burned in the churches of Spain.

The hospitals at Melilla, Cordova, Burgos, Saragossa, and recently the schools at Valladolid and towns miles from the front have been bombarded by the "Red" aeroplanes. There were numerous victims among the women and children without any word of protest being heard from the self-appointed champions of humanity. The city of Oviedo has been literally destroyed by the "Red Huns" and aeroplanes in the same silence.

And now the Basque Soviet allies have blown up Eibar, a hard-working industrial city before the entry of our troops. They used dynamite and liberally sprayed petrol until most of the buildings were destroyed. But those who today weep for Guernica remained unmoved and suffered no scandal. Irun suffered a similar fate under the eyes of European journalists and witnesses from Hendaye in the same negligent or culpable silence.

Guernica, less than four miles from the fighting line, was an important crossroads filled with troops retiring towards other defences. At Guernica an important factory has been manufacturing arms and munitions for nine months. It would not have been surprising if the "National" planes had marked Guernica as an objective. The laws of war allowed it, the rights of the people notwithstanding. It was a classical military objective with an importance thoroughly justifying a bombardment. Yet it was not bombarded.

It is possible that a few bombs fell upon Guernica during days when our aeroplanes were operating against objectives of military importance. But the destruction of Guernica, the great fire at Guernica, the explosions which during the whole day occurred at Guernica—these were the work of the same men who at Eibar, Irun, Malaga, and countless towns of Northern and Southern Spain demonstrated their ability as incendiarists.

The Spanish and part of the foreign press duly reported the "Red" Militia's threats to destroy Madrid before the "National" troops entered it. The blowing up of great buildings which are today still mined has been systematically prepared by the "Red" Government, which is indirectly served by those now clamouring about Guernica. Let this manoeuvre at the service of "Red" Spain cease and let the world know that Guernica's case, though clumsily exploited, turns against this Government of incendiarists and assassins, who at Russia's orders pursue the systematic destruction of the national wealth of Spain.

Source: Statement issued by the Nationalist Government, 3 May 1937.

Comments follow of an observer of life in the libertarian village of Alcora situated north of Valencia.

Document 12

In Alcora, according to an eyewitness, money was no longer in circulation. Everybody can get what he needs. From whom? From the committee, of course. However, it is impossible to provision five thousand persons through a single center of distribution. Hence, there are stores where, as before, one can satisfy one's requirements, but these are mere centers of distribution. They belong to the entire village, and their former owners no longer make a profit. Payment is made not with money but with coupons. Even the barber shaves in exchange for coupons, which are issued by the committee. The principle whereby each inhabitant shall receive goods according to his needs is only imperfectly realized, for it is postulated that everyone has the same needs. . . .

Every family and every person living alone has received a card. This is punched daily at the place of work; hence no one can avoid working, [for] on the basis of these cards coupons are distributed. But the great flaw in the system is that owing to the lack of any other measure of value, it has once again been necessary to have recourse to money in order to put a value on the labor performed. Everyone—the worker, the businessman, the doctor—receives coupons to the value of five pesetas for each working day. One part of the coupon bears the inscription "bread," of which every coupon will purchase a kilo; another part represents a certain sum of money. However, these coupons cannot be regarded as bank bills, as they can be exchanged only for consumer goods, and this in a limited degree. Even if the amount of these coupons were larger, it would not be possible to acquire means of production and become a capitalist, were it only on the most modest scale, for they can be used solely for the purchase of consumer goods. All the means of production belong to the community.

The community is represented by the committee. . . . All the money of Alcora, about 100,000 pesetas, is in its hands. The committee exchanges the products of the community for other goods that are lacking, but what it cannot secure by exchange it purchases. Money, however, is retained only as a makeshift and will be valid as long as other communities have not followed Alcora's example.

The committee is the paterfamilias. It owns everything; it directs everything; it attends to everything. Every special desire must be submitted to it for consideration; it alone has the final say.

One may object that the members of the committee are in danger of becoming bureaucrats or even dictators. That possibility has not escaped the attention of the villagers. They have seen to it that the committee shall be renewed at short intervals so that each inhabitant will serve on it for a certain length of time.

All this has something touching in its naiveté. It would be a mistake to criticize it too harshly and to see in it more than an attempt on the part of the peasants to establish libertarian communism. Above all, one should not forget that the agricultural laborers and even the small tradesmen of such a community have had until now an extremely low standard of living. . . . Before the Revolution a piece of meat was a luxury, and only a few intellectuals have needs that go beyond the bare necessities of life.

Source: From H.E. Kaminski, *Ceux de Barcelone*, 118–121. Reprinted in *The Spanish Revolution: The Left and the Struggle for Power during the Spanish Civil War*, by Burnett Bolloten, 72–73. Copyright © 1979 by The University of North Carolina Press. Used by permission of the publisher.

Excerpts follow from Emma Goldman's speech to the International Working Men's Association in Paris in 1937, giving reasons why the Anarchists in Spain joined the government in violation of their own principles.

Document 13

I have seen from the moment of my first arrival in Spain in September 1936 that our comrades in Spain are plunging head foremost into the abyss of compromise that will lead them far away from their revolutionary aim. . . . The participation of the CNT-FAI in the government, and concessions to the insatiable monster in Moscow, have certainly not benefited the Spanish revolution, or even the anti-fascist struggle. Yet closer contact with reality in Spain . . . made me understand their tactics better, and helped me to guard against any dogmatic judgment of our comrades.

The revolution in Spain was the result of a military and fascist conspiracy. The first imperative need that presented itself to the CNT-FAI was to drive out the conspiratorial gang. . . . In this process the Spanish workers and peasants soon came to see that their enemies were not only Franco and his Moorish hordes. They soon found themselves besieged by formidable armies and an array of modern arms furnished to Franco by Hitler and Mussolini, with all the imperialist pack playing their sinister under-handed game. . . .

With the most fervent desire to aid the revolution in Spain, our comrades outside of it were neither numerically nor materially strong enough to turn the tide. Thus finding themselves up against a stone wall, the CNT-FAI was forced to descend from its lofty traditional heights to compromise right and left: participation in the government, all sorts of humiliating overtures to Stalin, superhuman tolerance for his henchmen who were openly plotting and conniving against the Spanish revolution.

Of all the unfortunate concessions our people have made, their entry into ministries seemed to me the least offensive. No, I have not changed my attitude toward government as an evil. . . . I still hold that the State is a cold monster, and that it devours everyone within its reach. Did I not know that the Spanish people see in government a mere makeshift, to be kicked overboard at will, that they had never been deluded and corrupted by the parliamentary myth, I should perhaps be more alarmed for the future of the CNT-FAI. But with Franco at the gate of Madrid, I could hardly blame the CNT-FAI for choosing a lesser evil—participation in the government rather than dictatorship, the most deadly evil.

Russia has more than proven the nature of this beast. . . . Since Stalin began his invasion of Spain, the march of his henchmen has been leaving death and ruin behind them. Destruction of numerous collectives, the introduction of the Cheka with its "gentle" methods of treating political opponents, the arrest of thousands of revolutionaries, and the murder in broad daylight of others. All this and more, has Stalin's dictatorship given Spain, when he sold arms to the Spanish people in return for good gold. Innocent of the Jesuitical trick of "our beloved comrade" Stalin, the CNT-FAI could not imagine in their wildest dreams the unscrupulous designs hidden behind the seeming solidarity in the offer of arms from Russia. . . .

They have since learned that Stalin helped to make Spain safe against the fascists so as to make it safer for his own ends.

The critical comrades are not at all wrong when they say that it does not seem worthwhile to sacrifice one ideal in the struggle against fascism, if it only means to make room for Soviet Communism. I am entirely of their view—that there is no difference between them. My own consolation is that with all their concentrated criminal efforts, Soviet Communism has not taken root in Spain. I know whereof I speak. On my recent visit to Spain I had ample opportunity to convince myself that the Communists have failed utterly to win the sympathies of the masses; quite the contrary. They have never been so hated by the workers and peasants as now.

Source: Emma Goldman, Paris, 1937 (spartacus.schoolnet.co.uk/USAgoldman.htm).

Alvah Bessie fought in Spain with the Abraham Lincoln Battalion in 1938 and kept a daily record of events in his notebook. These notes formed the basis of his book *Men in Battle*. The following three documents depict three days in the Battle of the Ebro.

Document 14

August 1–2(?) 2 a.m.: Moved into positions on hill south of "reserve" position. There is to be a mass attack on Gandesa today, supported by aviation and artillery preparation. Co's 1 and 2 have been merged into new Co.1. Lopoff in command, Dick Rusciano ayudante (2nd in command, old style), Archie Brown, political commissar, AB, jefe de plano major. Breakfast at dawn, chocolate, coffee, ham, sardines, bread, marmalade, plums.

Waiting now.

We waited all day in a bottlenecked barranco. The 24th Battalion ahead of us engaged the enemy with some wounded. Mortars and artillery. Heat terrific. Report that the hill we fought three days to take with such losses, has been taken finally. One other hill holding up the advance of two divisions advancing toward Gandesa down three barrancos. . . .

For twelve hours we waited in this natural trap. Aviation overhead, bombing positions near Gandesa. Ours and theirs. Our artillery also active. Nervous tension terrific as mortars and artillery fall in our gully. THIRST.

At 8 a.m. order to advance. Advance started, but at dusk a terrific barrage of artillery and mortars fell all over our barranco, wounding many, killing some. Deafened by sound, terrified, the men moved back and forth in huddled droves like sheep; crouching, frightened faces in the growing darkness. Confusion, panic, cries of wounded. Horrible situation. Heavy fighting broke out ahead in darkness; happy not to be there. Hit by flying stone, rifle smashed in my hand.

Word came to back up hill and assume positions for possible counterattack. Done. All night at intervals, heavy fighting broke out, artillery and mortars, rifle and m.g. Burning buildings in distance.

Food came up at 3 a.m. (August 2), coffee, ham, sardines, tomatoes. Fitful sleep till near dawn; men's nerves strung to humming point—squabbles, arguments and utter confusion during distribution of grub. At dawn, moved off to back of hill where we were yesterday a.m. Mail! from Mom, Jerry Mellquist and Simon Bessie. What now? No word yet from Gandesa. Disorganization a characteristic of our battalion, though the guys behaved, with rare exceptions, pretty well during the barrage. Possibly because there was nothing else to do but lie on your belly on the shaking earth and hope to Christ the shells would not fall close enough to blow you to bits. But when we think how easily we could have been annihilated, it gives you an even worse case of the jitters.

Source: Alvah Bessie, *Alvah Bessie's Spanish Civil War Notebooks*, 80–81. Copyright © 2001, The University Press of Kentucky.

Document 15

August 19: The worst day, so far, of this life. Hell broke loose at 12:30 p.m. . . . artillery and mortars, preparation for a fascist attack. For 7-1/2 hours we were shelled, the shells covering practically every inch of our parapets and the barranco behind our hill. The strain, unbearable, the shells, thousands, falling in groups of 3, 4 at second intervals. . . . Whitney, translator for the company, 1-1/2 years here, scared as a rabbit, nearly hysterical with fear for weeks now, severely wounded two feet from me, together with telephonist who occupied the same shallow refugio . . . the sight of Whitney, his buttocks nearly torn off, holding them, his face dead yellow, covered with rock dust, screaming. Was lying down, hit on head by rock . . . fog of dust and ears ringing for hours. After that, hour after hour of the same, hour in and out, the body utterly exhausted and indifferent to conscious fear, but strained to the snapping point . . . sweat and internal pain, waiting, waiting for the shells and mortars, falling to right and left, above and below, to finish us off. . . . Up on the hill the boys in the trenches were pounded, their built-up rock parapets smashed down . . . many wounded, some killed, many disappeared.

Source: Alvah Bessie, *Alvah Bessie's Spanish Civil War Notebooks*, 90–91. Copyright © 2001, The University Press of Kentucky.

Document 16

September 25: Visited Mac-Paps yesterday p.m. Their experience seems to have been identical with that of other units. Just before going into action, reinforcements (Spanish) in the shape of guys who had deserted, fucked off, been in jails, etc., came up for all battalions. Their presence and bad history made all the men and officers uneasy, and considering this, plus their fatigue, no one had confidence that the brigade could do anything positive in the action. Sure enough, when the going got rough, the lines broke—the new men (few of whom are now to be found in any unit) raised white flags, fucked off to the rear or deserted to the enemy. The Mac-Pap's right and left flanks broke, leaving the center in danger of encirclement. As it is, many were captured by Moorish troops facing us. The Macs have about 150 left; the Lincolns, who went in with 440, have 193 left—70 Internationals were in the Lincolns when they went in—only a few less now. So an inglorious page marks the end of the glorious XVth—a page of retreat, panic, desertion, which has Commissar George Watt feeling low (for his own boy scout reasons) and the men as well, for more valid reasons of pride in the battalion's past achievement—even in the last few actions.

The brigade was relieved by the Campesinos. All day yesterday, though we were about 30 kilometers away on the other side of the Ebro, the sound of artillery and airbombs was heavy. Rain last night and today.

Source: Alvah Bessie, *Alvah Bessie's Spanish Civil War Notebooks*, 116. Copyright © 2001, The University Press of Kentucky.

A personal account follows by Indalecio Prieto on some characteristcs and habits of Juan Negrín.

Document 17

We became very friendly, but later we became political adversaries. The differences that gave rise to our enmity were due to the fact that, while head of the government, he allowed himself to become subservient to the Communists, a subservience that has been fully proved, although he insisted on denying it. . . .

Juan Negrín was a man of very exceptional physical and intellectual vigor and possessed a cordiality and charm that were captivating. His capacity for work was as enormous as his disorganization. He was just as likely to work at his desk for twenty-four hours at a stretch as to leave it without a trace for a week. . . .

At the League of Nations in Geneva, where he appeared in 1937, and where they must have thought that the government of the Republic was made up of ruffians, he sparkled with his winning manners, his culture, and command of foreign languages. But in a normal parliamentary regime, he could never have become a prime minister, nor even a minister, since he lacked oratorical gifts. His method of reading or reciting his speeches—they were written for him—was unsuitable to our Parliament, where very often it was essential to improvise.

He ate and drank as much as four men, but to avoid witnesses to these excesses, he dined two or three times at different places. Many evenings he had his first dinner at my home, then a second in a restaurant, and later a third, if all went well, in some night club. Educated in Germany, he acquired certain habits redolent of Nero's Rome, such as emptying a full stomach, rinsing his mouth, and continuing to gorge himself with food and drink.

At the end of 1936, the official in the finance ministry who audited small accounts questioned the superintendent closely because of the unbelievable sums expended on aspirin. The explanation of the superintendent was in absolute accord with the truth. The new minister would frequently ask for aspirin, open the container, put it to his lips, and swallow all the tablets in one gulp.

Source: Convulsiones, 3:219–221, article entitled, "Un hombre singular." Reprinted in *The Spanish Revolution: The Left and the Struggle for Power during the Spanish Civil War* by Burnett Bolloten, 444–445. Copyright © 1979 by The University of North Carolina Press. Used by permission of the publisher.

Clement Attlee, British Labour leader, criticized his government's decision to recognize General Franco's regime on 27 February 1939. Recognition implemented by Prime Minister Chamberlain was agreed upon with the French government before the House of Commons was notified. Both Labour and Liberal Parties opposed the move and forced a debate.

Document 18

We see in the action a gross betrayal of democracy, the consummation of two and a half years of the hypocritical pretense of nonintervention and a connivance all the time at aggression. And this is only one step further in the downward march of His Majesty's government in which at every stage they do not sell, but give away, the permanent interest of this country. They do not do anything to build up peace or stop war, but merely announce to the whole world that anyone who is out to use force can always be sure that he will have a friend in the British Prime Minister.

Source: Clement Attlee, Statement to the House of Commons, 27 February 1939 (spartacus.schoolnet.co.uk/SPbritain.htm).

During the Nuremberg war crimes trial in 1945, Hermann Göring, head of the German air force, gave Germany's reasons for intervening in the Spanish civil war.

Document 19

When the civil war broke out in Spain Franco sent a call for help to Germany and asked for support, particularly in the air. Franco with his troops was stationed in Africa and he could not get his troops across, as the fleet was in the hands of the communists. The decisive factor was, first of all, to get his troops to Spain. The Führer thought the matter over. I urged him to give support under all circumstances: firstly, to prevent the further spread of communism; secondly, to test my young Luftwaffe in this or that technical respect.

Source: Hermann Göring, statement at the Nuremberg War Crimes Trial, October 1945 (spartacus.schoolnet.co.uk/SPgermany.htm).

GLOSSARY OF SELECTED TERMS

AMA.   Women against Fascism (*Agrupación de Mujeres Antifascistas*).

BOC.   Worker and Peasant Bloc (*Bloc Obrer i Camperol*). Marxist group that fused with the Left Communists (*Izquierda Comunista*) in 1935 to create the POUM.

Carlists.   Supporters of the rival claimant line to the throne of Spain, Don Carlos, adhering to conservative, traditional and ultra-Catholic principles. Their political base was in Navarra.

Catalan League of Industrialists.   (*Lliga Catalá*). A Nationalist party of Cataluña of wealthy bourgeois that represented the Barcelona industrialists dissatisfied with the distant central control and taxation of Madrid.

Cacique.   Political boss usually in rural areas.

Caudillo.   Military leader.

CEDA.   Spanish Confederation of Autonomous Rights (*Confederación Española de Derechas Autónomas*). A political alliance of right-wing Catholic parties brought together under Gil Robles; won the 1933 elections.

CNT.   National Confederation of Labor (*Confederación Nacional de Trabajo*). Founded in 1910. The Anarcho-Syndicalist Trade Union.

Commissar.   Communist Party official assigned to a military unit to teach Party principles and insure Party loyalty.

Communist Left.   (*Izquierda Comunista*). A small anti-Stalinist group of Communists.

Cortes.   Spanish Parliament.

Esquerra.   Catalan Left.

FAI.   Iberian Anarchist Federation (*Federación Anarquista Ibérica*). Militant vanguard of the Anarchist movement.

Falange (or FE/JONS).   Spanish Fascist party (*Falange Española y de las Juntas de Ofensiva Nacional Sindicalista*). The Falange and the Juntas merged in 1934.

Falange Española Tradicionalista y de las JONS.   Traditionalist Spanish Falange and the National Syndicalist Offensive Juntas. Name of the party after the merger of the Carlists with the Falange and JONS in April 1937.

FETE.   Socialist Federation of Teachers Union (*Federación Española de Trabajadores de la Enseñanza*).

FIJL.   Federation of Iberian Libertarian Youth (*Federación Ibérica de Juventudes Libertarias*).

FUE.   Federation of University Students (*Federación Universitaria Escolar*). Students' union controlled by left-wing students; founded in 1927.

Generalísimo.   Top general.

Generalitat.   Autonomous Catalan government.

HISMA.   (*Hispano-Maroquí de Transportes*). The company founded in Morocco on 31 July 1936 to facilitate German aid to the Nationalists.

International Brigades.   Foreign volunteers fighting for the Republic.

JAP.   Youth for Popular Action (*Juventudes de Acción Popular*). CEDA Catholic youth movement.

JCI.   Iberian Communist Youth (*Juventud Comunista Ibérica*). The POUM youth movement.

JONS.   National Syndicalist Juntas on Offense (*Juntas de Ofensiva Nacional-Sindicalista*). Fascist Party merged with the Falange.

JSU.   Unified Socialist Youth (*Juventudes Socialistas Unificadas*). The party formed in the spring of 1936 by the amalgamation of the Socialist and Communist youth movements. Its leader, Santiago Carrillo, was a former Socialist-turned-Communist.

Libertarian Movement.   Youth organization of the CNT.

MAOC.   Peasants and Workers Anti-Fascist Militias (*Milicias Antifascistas Obreras y Campesinas*).

Margaritas.   Carlist women's organization.

Monarchists.   Those who supported a restoration of the monarchy. They had support from Conservative army officers and the Church.

Movimiento.   Franco's single party that united rightist groups in 1937.

Mujers Libres.   Anarchist feminine organization.

Nationalists.   Forces fighting the Republican government.

NKVD.   (Russian) People's Commissariat of Internal Affairs (*Narodnyi Komissariat Vnutrennykh Del*).

OSE.   Spanish Syndical Organization (*Organización Syndical Española*). The Franco government–controlled monolithic trade union.

PCE.   Communist Party of Spain (*Partido Comunista de España*).

Popular Front.   United parties and affiliated groups of the Left.

POUM.   Workers Party of Marxist Unification (*Partido Obrero de Unificación Marxista*). A merger of Communist dissidents and Trotskyites from the BOC and Communist Left united in 1935 to form a militant anti-Stalinist revolutionary party.

PSOE.   Spanish Socialist Workers' Party (*Partido Socialista Obrero Español*). Founded in 1879. The left wing of the party followed Largo Caballero, while the right wing followed Prieto.

PSUC.   Unified Socialist Party of Cataluña (*Partido Socialista Unificat de Catalunya*). Communist-controlled party that appeared in July 1936 as an amalgamation of Catalan Socialist parties.

Radical Party.   (*Partido Republicano Radical*). Party led by Alejandro Lerroux. The party and leader had a reputation for corruption. Its support came from businessmen and landowners. In 1934 its liberal wing broke away to form a new party, the Republican Union (*Unión Republicana*), under Martínez Barrio.

Republican Left.   (*Izquierda Republicana*). Led by Azaña, the party resulted from the fusion of Azaña's Republican Action, Casares Quiroga's Galician Autonomy Party, and the Radical Socialists. Support rested on the lower middle class.

Republican Left of Cataluña.   (*Esquerra Republicana de Catalunya*). Led by Lluis Companys.

Requetés.   Carlist militia, mostly from Navarra.

ROWAK.   *Rohstoff-und-Waren-Einkaufgesellschaft.* Export agency created in 1936 to ship German war material to Nationalist Spain.

SEU.   Spanish Syndicate of University Students (*Sindicato Español Universitario*). Members organized to fight leftists in the streets.

SF.   Feminine Section (*Sección Feminina*) of the Falange.

SIM.   Service of Military Investigation (*Servicio de Investigación Militar*). Communist-dominated secret police counterespionage agency established in the Republican zone.

Sindicado.   State-run corporate trade union after the war.

Social Auxiliary.   (*Auxilio Social*). Feminine unit of the Falange.

UGT.   General Union of Workers (*Unión General de Trabajadores*). Socialist trade union.

UME.   Spanish Military Union (*Unión Militar Española*). Extreme rightist society of army officers.

UMRA.   Military Union of Anti-Fascist Republican Officers (*Unión Militar Republicana Antifascista*). Established to counteract the influence of UME.

POLITICAL ORGANIZATIONS AND LEADERS

Republican and Leftist Organizations

Anarchist/FAI	Ascaso, Francisco
	Ascaso, Joaquín
	Durruti, Buenaventura
	García Oliver, Juan
	López, Juan
	Mera, Cipriano
	Montseny, Federica
	Peiró, Juan
Communist	Carrillo, Santiago
	Díaz, José
	Hernandez, Jesús
	Ibárruri, Dolores
	Togliatti, Palmir
	Uribe, Vicente
POUM	Maurín, Joaquín
	Nin, Andreu
Republican	Aguirre, José Antonio
	Alcalá Zamora, Niceto
	Azaña, Manuel
	Casares Quiroga, Santiago
	Chapaprieta, Joaquín
	Companys, Lluis
	Giral, José
	Lerroux, Alejandro
	Martínez Barrio, Diego
	Maura, Miguel

	Samper, Ricardo
	Valladares, Portela
Socialist	Alvarez de Vayo
	Araquistain, Luís
	Besteiro, Julián
	Carrillo, Wenceslao
	Galarza, Angel
	Iglesias, Pablo
	Largo Caballero
	Negrín, Juan
	Prieto, Indalecio
	Zugazagoitia, Julián

Rightist Organizations

CEDA	Gil Robles, José Maria
	Serrano Súñer, Ramón (later with the Falange)
Falange/JONS	Hedilla, Manuel
	Ledesma, Ramiro
	Primo de Rivera, José Antonio
	Primo de Rivera, Pilar
	Redondo, Onésimo
	Ridruejo, Dionisio
	Ruiz de Alda, Julio
Monarchist	Calvo Sotelo, José
	Fal Conde, Manuel (Carlist)
	The Count of Rodezmo (Carlist)

Note: See also the Glossary of Selected Terms.

ANNOTATED BIBLIOGRAPHY

BOOKS AND ARTICLES

Alvarez del Vayo, Julio. *Give Me Combat*. Foreword by Barbara W. Tuchman. Boston: Little, Brown and Co., 1973. The memoirs of Alvarez del Vayo, his life as a statesman, his encounters with prominent leaders and artists and his constant efforts to seek support for the Spanish Republic during the civil war.

Artiles, Jenaro. *They Had to Die*. México, D.F.: B. Costa-Amic, 1970. The author attempts to convince the reader that Franco was responsible for the deaths of potential rivals such as General Sanjurjo, General Mola and others.

Barea, Arturo. *The Forging of a Rebel*. Ilsa Barea, trans. New York: Walker and Company, 2001. An autobiographical trilogy first published in the late 1940s covers the first four decades of the twentieth century in Spain. No index.

Beevor, Antony. *The Spanish Civil War*. London: Orbis Publishing Ltd., 1982. General history incorporating causes and effects of the civil war with ample photographs, maps and chronological table.

Bessie, Alvah. *Alvah Bessie's Spanish Civil War Notebooks*. Dan Bessie, ed. Lexington: University of Kentucky Press, 2002. A daily record in four notebooks of the civil war by a soldier who fought with the Lincoln Battalion. They formed the basis for Bessie's book *Men in Battle* (1939). The notebooks represent a primary source of information on the war.

Bolloten, Burnett. *The Grand Camouflage*. London: Hollis & Carter, 1961. An account of Communist activity in Spain detailing the Party's duplicitous program to present a popular front against fascism by supporting the Republic's bourgeois government while gaining control behind the scenes of the government, police and military.

————. *The Spanish Civil War*. Chapel Hill: University of North Carolina Press,

1991. A monumental work of over 1,000 pages covering all aspects of politics in Republican Spain.

————. *The Spanish Revolution: The Left and the Struggle for Power during the Spanish Civil War*. Chapel Hill: University of North Carolina Press, 1979. Primarily a treatment of the politics underlying the Spanish civil war. Revised and greatly expanded version of the author's *The Grand Camouflage*.

Borkenau, Franz. *The Spanish Cockpit*. Ann Arbor: University of Michigan Press, 1963. An eyewitness account of the political and social conflicts of the Spanish civil war.

Brenan, Gerald. *The Spanish Labyrinth*. 1943. Cambridge: Cambridge University Press, 1964. An in-depth and impartial study of the causes of the Spanish civil war covering the period between 1874 and 1936.

Brenden, Piers. *The Dark Valley*. New York: Vintage Books, 2000. A panorama of the 1930s with two succinct but informative chapters devoted to the Spanish civil war.

Brome, Vincent. *The International Brigades, Spain, 1936–1939*. London: William Heinemann Ltd., 1965. History of the International Brigades with photographs of leading participants.

Carr, E.H. *The Comintern and the Spanish Civil War*. Tamara Deutscher, ed. London: Macmillan Press, 1984. A concise history in 111 pages of the involvement of the Comintern in the Spanish civil war and letters between Stalin and Largo Caballero and excerpts from confidential reports to the headquarters of the Comintern in Moscow.

Carr, Raymond. *The Spanish Tragedy*. London: Weidenfeld and Nicolson, 1977; London: Phoenix Press, 2000. Disparities in Spanish society and between regions, the conspiracy of the generals, major battles, the political weakness of the Left and international influences are brought into sharp forcus. A list of the main actors included.

Casals, Pablo. *Joys and Sorrows*. New York: Simon and Schuster, 1970. The story of Casals's life and music including the period during the Spanish civil war.

Cockburn in Spain. James Pettifer, ed. London: Lawrence and Wishart, 1986. A primary source of information on the war by a journalist writing dispatches for the *Daily Worker*. His enlistment in a Republican militia in the defense of Madrid allowed him to write from a firsthand, front-line perspective.

Cortada, James W. *Historical Dictionary of the Spanish Civil War 1936–1939*. Westport, CT: Greenwood Press, 1982.

Crow, John A. *Spain: The Root and the Flower*. 3rd ed. Berkeley: University of California Press, 1975. A cultural history of Spain from the beginning to the twentieth century.

Cunningham, Valentine, ed. *Spanish Front. Writers on the Civil War*. New York: Oxford University Press, 1986. A collection of writings on the war from eyewitnesses accounts to poems, essays and letters of mostly well-known people who sympathized with one side or the other.

Eby, Cecil D. *Between the Bullet and the Lie*. New York: Holt, Rinehart and Winston, 1969. Very readable account of the American volunteers who fought in Spain, mostly in the Lincoln Battalion.

Esenwein, George and Adrian Shubert. *Spain at War*. Harlow: Longman Groups Ltd., 1995. The book deals not only with the events of war but with its impact on social problems including gender relations, propaganda and terrorism.

Fraser, Ronald. *Blood of Spain*. New York: Pantheon, 1979. An original study of the civil war based on hundreds of interviews of the survivors and woven into a historical document. Ample maps.

Gallo, Max. *Spain under Franco*. New York: E.P. Dutton & Company, 1974. Translation of the French title *Histoire de l'Espagne Franquiste* (Jean Stewart, trans.). Detailed narrative history of the economic and political balance of forces that allowed Franco to maintain his grip on Spain. Some photographs, mostly of the postwar period.

Geiser, Carl. *Prisoners of the Good Fight*. Westport, CT: Lawrence Hill, 1986. Based on interviews and archival research, the book gives a vivid account of life in Franco's prisoner-of-war camps. Included in an appendix is a list of the names of American volunteeers captured by the Nationalists.

Gibbs, Jack. *The Spanish Civil War*. London: Ernest Benn Limited, 1973. Introduction to the causes and to the war in 123 pages, replete with photograhs of participants, battle maps and cartoons depicting the propaganda of the times.

Gibson, Ian. *The Death of Lorca*. London: W.H. Allen, 1973. Scrupulously documented and comprehensive account of the murder of García Lorca at the beginning of the civil war. Photographs and newspaper articles included.

Gurney, Jason. *Crusade in Spain*. London: Faber and Faber, 1974. A personal account by a London sculptor who fought in the International Brigades for nine months before being invalided home. The book discusses incompetent leadership, inadequate training, useless weapons and squalid quarters. In all, a disallusioning experience.

Howson, Gerald. *Arms for Spain: The Untold Story of the Spanish Civil War*. London: J. Murray, 1998. A detailed description of the sources, types and amount of arms acquired by the Spanish Republic and the Nationalists.

Ibárruri, Dolores. *They Shall Not Pass*. New York: International Publishers, 1966.

Translation of the Spanish title *El Único Camino*. An autobiographical account of La Pasionaria in her early years, her conversion to communism and the civil war. It is replete with condemnation of Anarchists and other leftist parties and well endowed with propaganda glorifying the Communists.

Jackson, Gabriel. *A Concise History of the Spanish Civil War*. London: Thames and Hudson, 1974. A good introduction to the Spanish conflict in a little less than 200 pages, replete with maps of the major battle areas and numerous photograhs of people and propaganda pamphlets. 156 illustrations.

Keats, John. *You Might as Well Live*. New York: Simon and Schuster, 1970; New York: Bantam Books, 1972. The life and times of writer Dorothy Parker.

Kurzman, Dan. *Miracle of November*. New York: G.P. Putnam's Sons, 1980. The battle for Madrid extracted from interviews with people who witnessed the event. Much of the book is written in dialogue.

Landis, Arthur H. *The Abraham Lincoln Brigade*. New York: Citadel Press, 1967. An account of the Lincoln Brigade composed of American volunteers in the Spanish civil war by a veteran of the conflict. Battle maps and photographs are included. Very comprehensive.

Lawrence, R.D. *The Green Trees Beyond*. Don Mills, Ontario: Stoddart Publishing Company, 1994. Autobiography. The author, born in Spain, participated in the Spanish civil war as a soldier and interpreter and describes the experience.

Mangini, Shirley. *Memories of Resistance*. New Haven, CT: Yale University Press, 1995. Subtitled *Women's Voices from the Spanish Civil War*, the text describes the roles, attitudes and commitments of women prior to and during the war, accompanied by about thirty-two photographs.

Mintz, Jerome, R. *The Anarchists of Casas Viejas*. Chicago: University of Chicago Press, 1982. An account of the Anarchist uprising at Casas Viejas in Andalucía and the bloody reprisals of the Civil and Assault Guards. Three sections: peasant struggle with landlords, the uprising, reports of survivors. Some photographs.

Nash, Mary. *Defying Male Civilization: Women in the Spanish Civil War*. Denver: Arden Press, 1995. An examination of the contributions and experiences of anti-Fascist women in the civil war based on research and interviews with women activists of the time.

Nelson, Cary. *Shouts from the Wall*. The Abraham Lincoln Brigade Archives. Waltham, MA: Brandeis University, 1996. A collection of posters and photographs (with comments) brought home from the Spanish civil war by American volunteers.

Orwell, George. *Homage to Catalonia*. 1938. London: Beacon Press, 1955. Orwell's personal experiences on the Aragón front with the POUM and in revolutionary and chaotic Barcelona in late 1936.

Payne, Stanley G. *Fascism in Spain, 1923–1977*. Madison: University of Wisconsin Press, 1999. Description and analysis of the history of Spanish fascism embodied in the Falange.

———. *Franco's Spain*. New York: Thomas Y. Crowell, 1967. In 132 pages, Payne presents a balanced analysis of economic, political, social and cultural developments in Spain under Franco.

———. *A History of Spain and Portugal*, vol. 2. Madison: University of Wisconsin Press, 1973. A general history.

Pérez, López, Francisco. *A Guerrilla Diary of the Spanish Civil War*. Victor Guerrier, ed.; Joseph D. Harris, trans. London: Andre Deutsch Ltd., 1972.

Pierson, Peter. *The History of Spain*. Westport, CT: Greenwood Press, 1999. A general political history of Spain.

Prager, Joel. "Spanish Governmental Performance and Modern Economic Growth: Some Spanish Findings." Paper presented at the Conference on Development and Democracy, University of Calgary, April 1971.

Preston, Paul. *The Coming of the Spanish Civil War*. London: Macmillan Press, 1978. An excellent treatment of the war and its causes in eight chapters and 398 pages.

———. *Comrades, Portraits from the Spanish Civil War*. London: Fontana Press, 2000. Biographies of the major players in the civil war including Millán Astray, Franco, José Antonio Primo de Rivera and his sister Pilar, Salvador de Madariaga, Julián Besteiro, Manuel Azaña, Indalecio Prieto and Dolores Ibárruri.

———. *Doves of War*. London: HarperCollins, 2002. Biographies of four women, two Spanish, two English, who served in the civil war, two on the side of the Nationalists and two for the Republic. Some of the narrative is based on the diaries and letters of the participants.

———. *The Spanish Civil War*. London: Weidenfeld and Nicolson, 1986. Excellent introduction to the civil war in nine chapters, 181 pages, with ample photographs and list of principal participants.

———. *The Spanish Civil War: Dreams + Nightmares*. London: Imperial War Museum, 2001. Photographs and posters depicting the times, along with explanations and introductory text by Preston.

Radosh, R., Mary R. Habeck and Gregory Sevostianov. *Spain Betrayed: The Soviet Union in the Spanish Civil War*. New Haven, CT: Yale University Press, 2001. Eighty-one documents, top-secret letters at the time, involving the civil war from the Russian archives are translated and presented here, making an enormous contribution to an understanding of the Russian role in the conflict.

Ranzato, Gabriele. *The Spanish Civil War*. Janet Sethre Paxia, trans. Gloucestershire: Windrush Press, 1999. A concise treatment of the civil war in six chapters, 126 pages. Over one hundred photographs of people, events and posters and ample maps.

Ribeiro de Meneses, Filipe. *Franco and the Spanish Civil War*. London: Routledge, 2001.

Richardson, Dan R. *Comintern Army*. Lexington: University Press of Kentucky, 1982. The book deals with all aspects of the International Brigades from politics and battle fronts to desertions.

Rolfe, Edwin. *The Lincoln Battalion*. New York: Haskell House, 1939. A personal account of life in the Abraham Lincoln Battalion. Valuable sourcebook.

Rosenstone, Robert A. *Crusade of the Left*. New York: Pegasus, 1969. An account of the Lincoln Battalion and the men who fought in it. Some photographs and a breakdown of the combatants by occupation and state of origin.

Spanish History since 1808. José Alvarez Junco and Adrian Shubert, eds. London: Arnold, 2000. Essays on Spanish history by various authors dealing with social, economic, cultural and political issues, arranged in chronological order.

Spender, Stephen. *Poems for Spain*. John Lehmann, ed. London: Hogarth, 1939. Stephen Spender relives his experiences in the International Brigades.

———. *World within World*. London: Hamish Hamilton, 1951. The autobiography of Stephen Spender.

Stein, Louis. *Beyond Death and Exile*. Cambridge, MA: Harvard University Press, 1979. An account of the Spanish Republicans in France from 1939 to 1955. Based on archival sources and interviews with refugees.

Téllez Solá, Antonio. *Sabaté*. Stuart Christie, trans. London: Davis-Poynter, 1974. The life story of Anarchist Francisco Sabaté, along with the exploits of other guerrilla groups that opposed the Franco regime. Photographs of some of the participants including the Sabaté brothers. No index.

Thomas, Gordon and Max Morgan Witts. *Guernica*. New York: Stein and Day, 1975. The bombing of Guernica based on eyewitness accounts of both villagers on the ground and the German pilots who flew the planes.

Thomas, Hugh. *The Spanish Civil War*. Rev. 3rd ed. New York: Penguin Books, 1965. Comprehensive and detailed account of the war in just over a thousand pages. The classic work on the subject. Ample battle maps.

Trotsky, Leon. *The Spanish Revolution (1931–39)*. Naomi Allen and George Breitman, eds. New York: Pathfinder Press, 1973. Trotsky's political assessment of the civil war particularly related to the causes of the defeat of the Republic. The appendix contains private correspondence between Nin and Trotsky.

Wyden, Peter. *The Passionate War: The Narrative History of the Spanish Civil War*. New York: Simon and Schuster, 1983. An account of personalities and events from interviews, memoirs and documents. Written in novelistic form. Timeline and photographs.

Zuehlke, Mark. *The Gallant Cause*. Vancouver: Whitecap Books, 1996. The story of Canadians in the Spanish civil war, partly based on interviews with veterans, with attention to their personal biographies. Photographs.

WEB SITES

Southworth Spanish Civil War Collection, Mandeville Special Collections Library, University of California at San Diego (http://orpheus.ucsd.edu/speccoll/collects/southw.html). Gives many details of the Spanish Civil War.

Spanish Civil War Factbook by Marcus Wendel (www.skalman.nu/spanish). Has information and links to many details of the Spanish Civil War.

Spartacus Educational (spartacus.schoolnet.co.uk). Has links into the Spanish Civil War in all its aspects.

INDEX

About the Author

JAMES M. ANDERSON is Professor Emeritus, University of Calgary, Canada. He has spent many years in Spain and Portugal, both as a Fulbright Scholar and as the recipient of Canada Council and SSHRC grants, contributing numerous articles and books to the field of Iberian studies. He is author of 12 books, including *The History of Portugal* (Greenwood, 2000) and *Daily Life During the Spanish Inquisition* (Greenwood, 2002).